GREEN ENCHANTMENT

SATVRNE.

The God of Agriculture.

From Whitcombe, *Janva Divorum,* 1678.

Green Enchantment

by
Rosetta E. Clarkson

Author of
Herbs: Their Culture and Uses
Magic Gardens

Foreword by
Tovah Martin

Illustrations from
Early Gardening Books and Herbals

COLLIER BOOKS

Macmillan Publishing Company
New York

Collier Macmillan Canada
Toronto

Maxwell Macmillan International
New York   Oxford   Singapore   Sydney

Collier Books
Macmillan Publishing Company
866 Third Avenue, New York, NY 10022

Collier Macmillan Canada, Inc.
1200 Eglinton Avenue East, Suite 200
Don Mills, Ontario M3C 3N1

Library of Congress Cataloging-in-Publication Data

Clarkson, Rosetta E.
    Green enchantment / by Rosetta E. Clarkson ; foreword by Tovah
Martin.—1st Collier books ed.
        p.   cm.
    Includes bibliographical references and index.
    ISBN 0-02-009461-2
    1. Gardening—History.   2. Gardens—History.   3. Herb gardening.
4. Herbs.   I. Title.
SB451.C5 1991   90-49857   CIP
635'.09—dc20

Macmillan books are available at special discounts for bulk purchases for sales promotions, premiums, fund-raising, or educational use. For details, contact:

Special Sales Director
Macmillan Publishing Company
866 Third Avenue
New York, NY 10022

First Collier Books Edition 1991

10   9   8   7   6   5   4   3   2   1

Printed in the United States of America

THE GARDEN

When God did Man to his own Likeness make,
As much as Clay, though of the purest Kind,
   (By the great Potter's art refin'd)
   Could the Divine Impression take,
   He thought it fit to place him, where
   A kind of Heaven too did appear,
As far as Earth could such a Likeness bear:
   That Man no Happiness might want,
Which Earth to her first Master could afford;
   He did a Garden for him plant,
By the quick Hand of his Omnipotent Word.
As the chief Help and Joy of Human Life,
He gave him the first Gift; first, even before a Wife.

     .   .   .   .

Methinks I see great Dioclesian walk
In the Salonian Garden's noble Shade,
Which by his own Imperial Hands was made:
I see him smile methinks, as he do's talk
With the Ambassadors, who come in vain
   T'entice him to a Throne again:
If I, my Friends, (said he) should to you show
All the Delights which in these Gardens grow,
'Tis likelier much that you should with me stay,
Than 'tis that you should carry me away:
And trust me not, my Friends, if e'ery Day
   I walk not here with more delight
Than ever after the most happy Fight,
In Triumph to the Capitol I rode,
To thank the Gods, and to be thought my self almost a God.

A. Cowley
Chertsea
1666

In his tribute to John Evelyn in *Kalendarium Hortense* which
Evelyn has dedicated to him, England's great poet, Abraham Cowley, inserts, besides occasional verse and couplets, a long poem
"The Garden" in eleven verses, of which the above are the second
and the eleventh.

CONTENTS

ILLUSTRATIONS

FOREWORD

Half a shelf in our family library is devoted to books either penned or published at Salt Acres, Rosetta Clarkson's farm in Milford, Connecticut. Bound copies of *The Herb Journal* (published, edited, and written by Mrs. Clarkson) sit beside several copies of *Magic Gardens*, *Green Enchantment*, and *Herbs: Their Culture and Uses*. The books share the shelf with a series of smaller facsimile editions of rare fifteenth- and sixteenth-century gardening pamphlets bearing the Clarksons' imprint, The Herb Lovers Book Club for Those Who Possess the Priceless Lore of Herbs.

Most of the books are dog-eared now, they have bookmarks stuffed between pages on angelica or scented geraniums, and the dust jackets are ripped and curled. They've seen a lot of wear over the years. I don't know how many times we've reached over to consult one or another of them in the heat of an argument on the publication date of *Paradisi in Sole Paradisus Terrestris* or the alleged healing properties of mandrake.

The rest of the shelf, in fact, the remainder of the bookcase, is filled with other herb books, most of which were published in the 1930s and 40s. Several of the books are duplicates or various printings of works written by my mother-in-law's closest friends and colleagues. Open any volume and you'll find an inscription to Joy Logee, who later became Joy Logee Martin, my mother-in-law.

The bookshelf holds other herbal paraphernalia. The volumes are actually wedged rather snugly between various and sundry notes from Herb Society meetings, symposium brochures, and handwritten recipes seasoned liberally with herbs. One glance at the bookshelf reveals without a doubt that in 1940, herbs were definitely up and coming. During those prewar years, an elite group of ladies were dashing around giving radio shows on herbs, lecturing to garden clubs on herbs, collecting and studying herbs, all the while thoroughly enjoying themselves with a crowd of fellow herb enthusiasts.

It all began quietly enough. In 1933, while the rest of the horticultural world was immersed in sweet peas, climbing roses, and fragrant violets, six Boston women began meeting with a Harvard University professor to study herbs. Those six women would become the nucleus of the Herb Society of America, an exclusive organization devoted to exploring herbs for use and for delight, as their motto stated.

These were six very serious and spunky gardeners, and they were not content merely to meet periodically to enjoy tea and crumpets. By the end of that first year, Helen Noyes Webster, a leading member of the study group, had published this country's first herb book, entitled *Herbs: How to Grow Them*. In 1935, not only was the herb study group invited to exhibit at the Boston Flower Show, but the ladies took home the first of many blue ribbons for their display. The momentum continued at a brisk clip, the Herb Society attracting other horticultural movers and shakers. By 1940, my mother-in-law and Rosetta Clarkson had both joined the frenzy.

Spreading herbal knowledge was undoubtedly a major challenge. In the early 1930s, parsley was the only herb listed in most seed catalogs. At the same time, the average citizen had very little interaction with anything herbal. Herbs were not a big part of the average American diet. And yet the Great Depression had taught us to experiment. The public was definitely open to new ideas, and there was something very intriguing in the notion that a few weeds could spice up a meal or turn hot water into sweet tea. Herbs were a little off the beaten track, but they met with a receptive audience.

The herb movement gained all sorts of followers. The first president of the Herb Society was Dr. Edgar Anderson, the professor who guided the six Boston women in their studies. By and large, however, this was a female phenomenon. In their spare time, between the duties inherent in maintaining an immaculate home, raising a family, and entertaining dinner guests, women somehow wedged in gardening time and study hours. Herbs were usually greeted as an intellectual as well as a physical pursuit, gaining acceptance with both society and spouses.

Herbs broke through barriers, and they were embraced by many women who had not warmed to other horticultural endeavors. We were not inherently a nation of ornamental gardeners, and our no-nonsense approach to horticulture was particularly apparent during the frugal years between the wars. What America needed was a horticultural hobby that would not violate the Puritan utilitarian ethic, but would nevertheless beautify the backyard. People didn't mind getting their hands dirty as long as they could gainfully use the fruits of their labor. Herbs provided the perfect solution.

That is where Rosetta Clarkson came in. She arrived well equipped to lead the crusade. While teaching at New Rochelle High School in New York, she had taken a sabbatical in Britain to write an English thesis. Her topic was Elizabethan literature and, in the course of her study, she discovered a wealth of antique herbals and gardening pamphlets. By the time she returned to the States, she had caught the contagion.

The pages of *Green Enchantment* clearly tell the story of Rosetta Clarkson the Scholar. But, reading between the lines, you can easily catch a glimpse of Rosetta Clarkson the Gardener. Rosetta was the essential earth woman, marching around with wheelbarrow and gardening gloves, fussing over meticulously kept beds of lavender and artemisias. My mother-in-law describes how Rosetta loved to share her rarities and, in exchange, she was always eager to receive herbal novelties from our greenhouses. Rose (as she preferred to be called) was a keen observer of plants, their likes and dislikes, their personalities and preferences in soils, watering, fertilizers, climate, and botanical bedfellows.

Although other writers have recorded herbal history, no one else managed to combine lore with the insights that *Green Enchantment* discloses. What temperatures and soil conditions result in the most aromatic herbs? How should a gardener fertilize herbs? Which herbs are indispensable for a beginner's garden? The answers are as enlightening today as they were half a century ago. And, Rosetta Clarkson revealed all this knowledge so readably. In many ways, *Green Enchantment* was years ahead of its time. Rosetta speaks of companion planting, of phytotoxins (plant-emitted poisons), of soil salinity at a time when scientists had scarcely begun to explore those realms. She was a writer, a scholar, a farmer, and a scientist, all combined into one dynamic voice.

It wasn't long before Rosetta Clarkson acquired something akin to a cult following. By 1936, she began mailing her magazine, *The Herb Journal*, to a circulation of two thousand monthly readers. Visitors came to Salt Acres in droves to meet the new American herbalist, to enjoy her innovatively designed herb garden, and to study in her library filled with vintage herbals, the illus-

trations from which were extracted and meticulously reproduced in *Green Enchantment*.

When *Green Enchantment* was first published in 1940,
it was greeted with all the attendant hullabaloo that a
bestselling novelist might stir up today. To launch the
book, her publisher, Macmillan, put on a huge reception
with displays of Mrs. Clarkson's herbal handiwork. Si-
multaneously, a Fifth Avenue store featured a window
display of Rosetta's potpourri jars, sachets, and tussie-
mussies. After the festivities on Fifth Avenue, Rosetta
and her husband, Ralph, were whisked off to appear on
an important radio broadcast. Herbs had obviously
arrived.

Ralph Clarkson always said that *Green Enchantment*
was the best example of his wife's artistic writing style.
The book provides us with an expert intermingling of
history and cultural advice. In its pages, she continually
draws from ancient wisdom and relates it to modern gardens. For example, Rosetta describes how the herbalist,
John Gerard, took great pride in adapting "the soil to the
plant, the plant to the soil." Then she shares her own
observations on the subject, "the same plant in different
parts of the garden will give widely different fragrances." This is the type of knowledge that enchanted
the ancients and enchanted Rosetta as well.

Green Enchantment was popular with serious gardeners, but Rosetta's next book, *Herbs: Their Culture
and Uses*, published in 1942, had a wider appeal with
the general public at the time. Unfortunately, *Herbs*
would be her last major project. For the next eight years,
Rosetta Clarkson was bedridden with a heart condition
that eventually claimed her life.

The enchantment with greenery never diminished. In
fact, the wartime Victory Gardens only enhanced the

herb trend, and the postwar flower children continued the crusade. Then came a period when Colonial Revival architecture ruled the countryside and herb gardens carried the theme into the surrounding landscape. In a health-conscious society, herbs can function as caffeine and salt substitutes, as well as provide flavor in gourmet and ethnic recipes. They are now widely used by landscape designers who value their subtle colors and intriguing textures in annual and perennial gardens. Without a doubt, green enchantment is still alive and well today. As Rosetta Clarkson illustrates in this volume, herbs are plants that possess a prodigious past as well as an equally formidable future.

Tovah Martin
July 1990

PREFACE

My thought in *Green Enchantment* is to recapture a little of the mystery and lure of gardens, a little of the background that makes the thought of gardens one of peace and happiness to all of us, year in, year out. Always men have been fascinated by green growing things, have built tales and legends all about their plants and have invented plants of even stranger nature than the ones they knew.

In *Magic Gardens* (1939) I told of the dependence on the garden in early days for medicine, for food and flavor, of how each plant was grown for use. The appeal of the garden was a utilitarian appeal for many centuries. But, even then, some strange allurement seized those early gardeners. Many plants took on personalities, became symbolic of good and bad attributes—sincerity, falsehood, love and hate. Yet when that period of enwalled and self-sufficient homes had passed, when life expanded and men were free from compulsory tilling of the soil, the garden still existed and certain of those useful plants were retained just for pleasure. The appeal of the garden became a spiritual appeal.

In poem, picture and in song the garden is a thing of joy and it seems always to have been so. We can thus appreciate today the words John Worlidge wrote in *Systema Horti-culturae* nearly three centuries ago:

"The Original of Gardens was from a Divine Hand: And they also long since delighted in by the wisest of Kings, and in principal esteem ever since by the best of men. . . .

"Neither is there a Noble or pleasant Seat in England but hath its Gardens for pleasure and delight; scarce an Ingenious Citizen that by his confinement to a Shop, being denied the priviledge of having a real Garden, but hath his boxes, pots, or other receptacles for Flowers, Plants, etc. . . .

"So that we may without vanity conclude that a Garden of pleasant Avenues, Walks, Fruits, Flowers, Grots, and other branches sprung from it, well composed, is the only complete and permanent inanimate object of delight the world affords, ever complying with our various and mutable Minds, feeding us and supplying our fancies with dayly Novels."

ROSETTA E. CLARKSON

Salt Acres
Milford, Connecticut

APPRECIATION

I wish to acknowledge my deep thanks to Miss Carol H. Woodward, Editor of the *Journal* of the New York Botanical Garden, who has kindly permitted me to reprint in part, as Chapter XV of this book, the article written by me under a similar title in an issue of that magazine, and to Mr. Paul F. Frese, Editor of the *Flower Grower,* in which some of the material of Chapter IV appeared in a somewhat different form; to Miss Kent K. Lawrence-Wetherill, who so kindly permitted me to reproduce her drawing of Saint Fiacre in Chapter I; to Alfred C. Hottes, who again has permitted the use of photographs of his rare copy of the early German *Herbarius;* to the Massachusetts Horticultural Society, who made available to me the early *Hortus Sanitatis,* and to the Sterling Library of Yale University, which made available the copy of Sir John Maundeville's *Travels.*

CHAPTER I

In a Monastery Garden

"No joy is so great in a life of seclusion as that of gardening. No matter what the soil may be, sandy or heavy clay, on a hill or a slope, it will serve well."
—WALAFRID STRABO, Hortulus, ninth century.

On a bright April day in the year 1530, Brother David was busily spading a plot in the sacristan's garden in Mailros (Melrose) Abbey. Spring had been late in coming to Scotland this year, and the sun felt particularly welcome to younger brothers not yet used to long winters of cold within the dark and cheerless monastery buildings. To be sure, the calefactory (common room) did have a stove, but once the winter's chill got into the body, it just stayed there. So with the exertion of digging and the rays of the sun on his back, Brother David was really warm for the first time in months.

Yet in another sense David had hardly felt the cold. He was warmed inwardly by eager enthusiasm in planning for the season's planting. As he spaded, his mind went back to other springs, other years. Even before he came to the Abbey, which long ago had been dedicated by the good King David to the Virgin Mary, the

1

boy had longed to serve her and her Son. But he had been afraid. He could not sing the divine service. He was unable even to carry a tune. Many were the scowls and frowns in the little village church when of a Sunday he had lifted up his voice in praise to the Lord.

And little could David read or write, but then few children in the town had any school education. Mailros was one of those communities made up of forty or fifty families, all tenants or vassals of the nearby Abbey, which had conferred upon them farms or "feus" for small quitrents. Years before, King David had bestowed much land upon the Abbey, since he felt it was safer in the hands of the Church than it would be under the Crown. Often the monks from this beautiful Cistercian abbey would make friends with some of the tenants, and David's father and mother had been thus favored. The boy, bashful in company, would listen with rapt attention when Brother Robert, who often visited them, would talk of the monastery life, little dreaming of David's longing to be a part of it.

If he only could be a monk, thought the lad, and devote his days and nights to the glory of God, to reading the prayer books, to copying the beautiful illuminated manuscripts. And all the while the Abbey, set like a low-mounted jewel along the curving silver band of the winding Tweed, was waiting to receive David.

Though the boy could not read, write or sing, he could make a seed or seedling grow in any kind of soil. For him plants seemed to spring earlier than for the neighbors. His were the first violets, the first paigles, the first bluebells. If a plant looked sickly or blasted he could coax it back to health. A green finger he had, to be sure, said everyone.

Once Brother Robert, knowing the boy's love for flow-

Saint Fiacre, Patron Saint of Gardens.

An original drawing by Kent Wetherill.

ers and plants, told him about St. Fiacre, patron saint of gardeners. He had been a great prince of Ireland in the sixth century, but had given up all his possessions and left his native country to become a foreign missionary. This once proud prince had settled as a hermit on the outskirts of Meaux in France at the edge of the forest, and there he lived, growing herbs and flowers which he loved, and he built a little monastery at Breuil where he died and where miracles still were wrought.

"Did he grow his flowers for the Virgin? Did he decorate the village church?" asked David eagerly.

"Quite possibly," said Brother Robert absently, but David mulled over his story for days, and a new light shone in his eyes as he thought, "I shall grow my plants for the altar." And after that, while others praised the Lord on Sundays by singing, David was no longer sad. On other days he would bear armfuls of rosemary, lilies, hyssop, into the church and, devoutly kneeling, would offer them to the Virgin. Now he had a new vision. If he could study the needs of the plants and grow more and more beautiful ones, he would serve the Lord as St. Fiacre had done.

One day Brother Robert noticed the boy cutting branches of rosemary more luxuriant than he had ever seen and starting off towards the little village church. He followed after a while and came upon the boy in prayer before the Virgin's shrine. When David arose, the Brother was beside him. "A beautiful gift, my boy," and going out of the church into the warm sunshine, David poured forth his dreams and longings to the friendly monk, who listened sympathetically and encouraged him to talk. When the boy stopped, abashed by his sudden volubility, Brother Robert said quietly, "You shall come to us, David. Our brotherhood believes that there are many ways of preparing for Heaven. I shall teach you to read and to write . . . enough to take Orders. But if I am not mistaken, you will be allowed to serve by the gift God has given you."

So David finally went to the Abbey, was placed under the instructor in the Chamber of Novices, and also under the gardinarius, who set him to work in the kitchen garden as a disciplinary test of the boy's sincerity. But David, who yearned to grow decorative herbs for the church and processions, cheerfully and enthusiastically raised the finest onions, cabbages, and turnips the monastery had known in many a year.

At the end of his trial, David was duly examined, gave a good account of his morals and course of life, and finally was given the sacristan's garden to tend. So all during the winter, his first as a member of the Cistercian Order, he had dreamed and planned for spring. Even in the church at the monastery, although he made full confession, his mind and eyes wandered from the service to the wonderful carvings in stone about the building. Long ago some other monk, perhaps as ignorant as he, had offered to God his one talent of sculpturing and had wrought Nature's loveliness into stone to beautify the holy place when there were no living plants. For untold ages yet to come, this carving would testify to the man's simple piety. Little did the obscure sculptor or David realize that many centuries later a great poet, Sir Walter Scott, would bear witness to the monk's offering:

"Spreading herbs, and flowerets bright
    Glistened with dew of night,
    Nor herb nor floweret glisten'd there
    But was carved in the cloister arches as fair."

The idea of monastic living began and developed quite simply and most commonly in Egypt. In the beginning, from no religious motive but only from a desire to live a contemplative life, individuals lived alone and somewhat apart from any community, self-subsisting and giving to the poor whatever was left over from the season's crops. Persecution and an intense desire not to be interrupted in their contemplations drove the hermits completely away from civilization into the desert oases.

In the fourth century Anthony, famed for his asceticism, holiness and power of exorcism, retired farther and farther away but was followed by disciples who lived in their cells around him. For twenty years Anthony refused their pleadings to be their guide in holy living. Finally he relented, gathered the hermits together and thus began the first monastic establishment. Living alone, or sometimes two and three together, the men occupied huts, with that of their superior the center of the group, the very loosely constructed organization a happy mingling of gardening and religious services, with no regulated community living.

Quite different was the closely knit organization conceived at about the same time by Pachomius, true founder of the first religious Order at Tabennae, an island in the Upper Nile. His, too, was a community made up of detached huts, each housing three monks. The chief meal of the day was at three in the afternoon; fasting was the rule until that hour. The hoods of the men were drawn about their faces so they could see nothing but the food before them. Interested in gardening, grafting and bee culture for purposes of sustenance, they devoted their time to work in the field when not engaged in religious devotions. Almost from the inception of this organization, the Order was a sort of agricultural and industrial community, sending its produce to be sold at Alexandria. The money accruing from the sale was spent on necessary supplies for the monastery, the surplus going to charity.

Early in monastic history, the monks made provision for hostile attacks by erecting about their establishment walls of defense capable of resisting an assault, though for the most part marauders respected monastery property. The general appearance of a medieval monastery became that of a heavily fortified town.

Under the Benedictine Order, begun in 529 by St. Benedict, a life of self-denial but not asceticism was the main feature, the individual devoted to the welfare of the whole. The monks were to live together in a community life as instructed by the teachings of the Gospels, a sort of school for the service of the Lord. Work in the field absorbed more of the routine of the day than the church service. In early days, before the Benedictine discipline relaxed, fruits, vegetables, bread and wine comprised the daily menu, and everything was produced within the monastery walls. The founder claimed that "no person is ever more usefully employed than when working with his hands or following the plough providing food for the use of man. A monastery ought if possible, to be so constituted that all things necessary such as water, a mill and a garden and the various crafts may be contained in it." Food, medicine and flowers for the church were all raised in the monastery gardens. It was the old idea of Satan finding work for idle hands.

One of the earliest Benedictine monasteries about which we now have records was near Lake Constance in Switzerland. St. Gall, who had come from Ireland in the sixth century, built an oratory and dwellings for twelve brethren, and lived there till he died, about 646. We know little about that early church except from a book of miracles of the saint written by Walafrid Strabo,

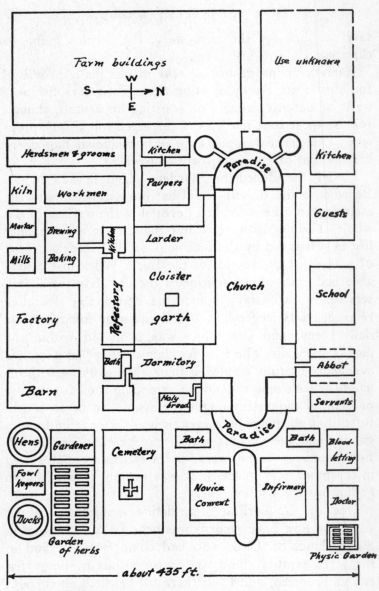

Benedictine Monastery of St. Gall, A.D. 830.

After R. Willis.

abbot of Reichenau, a nearby monastery. At the beginning
of the ninth century, Othmar introduced the Benedictine
rule at St. Gall's and was made the first abbot. Since the
Benedictine rule was the only form of monasticism for
several centuries, and since the layouts of buildings and
grounds were all made from plans purported to be those
of the envisioned monastery at St. Gall, a survey of those
plans is interesting. They are thought to have been made
by Abbot Eginhardus, Prefect of the Royal Gardens of
Charlemagne. The layout resembles that of a fortified
town of thirty-three isolated houses separated by streets,
and all the buildings are made of wood except the church,
which was of stone and was the center of the religious
community within the walls. The church faced on a cloister court surrounded by the chief buildings, all of two
stories, dormitory, common room, refectory, cellarium.

It will be seen how much this arrangement resembles
the Roman villa with its atrium and peristyle corresponding to the courtyard and colonnade, which we renamed
the cloisters. Then there was the same central fountain or
sometimes a tub of flowers and, in place of statues of
emperors and pagan divinities, there were substituted
those of saints. This similarity is explained simply enough
by the fact that the first Benedictine monastery was built
at Monte Cassino in Italy where naturally Italian models
of architecture would be followed. The cloister or portico
all around the court was the most picturesque part of the
monastery. Vines and climbing plants were trained up the
arches. The cloister garth, always on the south side of
the church so the light would not be obstructed, was often
filled with aromatic shrubs and plants. At intervals along
the covered walk were placed benches and here the monks
enjoyed a sunny, warm, protected spot where they could
sit or exercise in winter, or during summer rains when the

fragrance of the plants must have come pleasantly to them.

In one corner of the establishment was the doctor's house and garden while next to it was a twin set of buildings, one the infirmary, the other for novices, each forming a complete monastery with its essential buildings. The so-called infirmary was not only for the sick monks but also for the infirm and superannuated.

In keeping with the Benedictine rule of making the monastery a self-subsisting community, there were buildings and rooms for baking, brewing, repairing clothes, making shoes, stools, knives, trenchers, woodcarvings, for sculpturing statuary, for tanning leather. There were rooms for goldsmiths, coopers, turners, saddlers, fullers. There were granaries, places for drying fruit, barns with threshing floors, mills, factories. And there were sheds for farm animals and a room for the caretaker of each kind of animal. By the time of the ninth century there appears to have been a loosening in the regulations concerning strict diet, so we find quite a space given to animals raised for meat, and for poultry.

The vegetable garden, as shown in the diagram, was oblong, with nine rectangular plots on each side of a central path. Each is carefully labeled, the vegetable-herbs consisting of onions, garlic, leeks, shallots, celery, parsley, chervil, coriander, dill, lettuce, poppy, savory, radishes, parsnips, carrots, cabbage, beets, corncockles. All these plants except carrots were mentioned in the *Capitulare de Villis Imperialibus* written in 812 by the Emperor Charlemagne, a list of plants he wanted put in his royal gardens. St. Gall's was a particular pet of the Emperor's, so it is little wonder that the plants found at the monastery were also on the royal list.

A garden house for men and equipment extended the

width of the vegetable garden. The laborers occupied a narrow strip of the length of this building between the gardinarius' private quarters and the garden, while a tool and seed house cut a strip from the width of his rooms. This was a shed for implements shod with iron, such as spades, hoes, mattocks, and here were kept the vegetable seeds. The gardinarius had a stove in his sleeping quarters, and the living room surrounded a court.

Between the vegetable garden and the novices' convent was the cemetery, a rectangular field inclosed by walls and hedges with the one entrance on the side of the main cloisters, a large cross in the middle of the field being indicated on the diagram. The spaces not devoted to graves were planted with fruit trees and ornamental shrubs, so the whole area resembled a park. The fruit trees listed are apple, pear, plum, service (sorbarius), medlar, fig, quince, peach, and other listings are pine, laurel, chestnut, hazelnut, mulberry and walnut. All of these, too, are in the *Capitulare* of Charlemagne.

The physic garden, placed near the doctor's house, was divided into eight oblong beds down the center with borders of eight more plots. These plots are labeled kidney bean, savory, rose, watercress, cumin, lovage, fennel, tansy, white lily, sage, rue, cornflag, pennyroyal, fenugreek, peppermint, rosemary. Sometimes, as in later years in the monastery at Canterbury, the infirmary was in one of the buildings facing on the cloister court. In that case the physic herbs were grown in the cloister garth.

"Herbs of ill favour filled the vacant square
With thyme and baum and rue, a plant renowned for grace."

These lines from T. D. Fasbrook's *Economy of Monastic Life* applied to the cloister garden which was, of course, the infirmary garden. Perhaps the writer of the lines had been dosed with herb tonic teas too much to appreciate the beauty and fragrance of the living herbs which comforted patients as they lay on sick beds. In some of the large monasteries the care of the physic garden was a full-time task for one of the laborers, the doctor being expected to supervise the work.

But David was interested most of all when the sacristan read from the *Hortulus* in which Walafrid Strabo of the neighboring monastery recorded some of his gardening experiences and his feelings about plants. It was exciting to know how much another monk some 700 years before had loved working in his garden, had observed the little personalities of growth about certain plants. David, also, had observed their habits from his intense absorption in them. Strabo, like David, had been irked by the long winter months and had been impatient to be in the garden, for the sacristan read:

"When last winter had passed and spring renewed the face of the earth, when the days grew longer and milder, when flowers and herbs were stirred by the west wind, when green leaves clothed the trees, then my little plot was overgrown with nettles. What was I to do?"

Joy in the rebirth of spring, dismay at the vast amount of weeds are feelings shared by gardeners of every century. But Strabo dug up the offenders, and soon had his rectangular raised beds made and planted. "Amongst my herbs, sage holds the place of honour; of good scent it is and full of virtue for many ills." Then there were rue, mint, wormwood, fennel, horehound, southernwood. The crop of pumpkins was carefully watched. "Let it [the pumpkin] harden and you can make utensils of the rind, it will serve as a bushel, or pitched inside will be a jar for liquor."

Strabo had his favorite flowers, too. "Yes, roses and lilies, the one for Virginity with no sordid toil, no warmth of love, but the glow of their own sweet scent, which spreads further than the rival roses, but once bruised or crushed turns all to rankness. Therefore roses and lilies for our church, one for the martyr's blood, the other for the symbol in his hand. Pluck them, O maiden, roses for war and lilies for peace."

The sacristan stopped reading and David sighed a long sigh but was silent. So the wise brother left the young monk to think over and treasure up the words of the early abbot, words which would be recalled as he worked among those plants to be brought to flower for the service of the Church.

Even in early monastery days, when the culinary and medicinal values of plants were of chief concern to cook and doctor, some herbs had emerged for the decoration of the church, of candles, of priests on feast days or for processions, an outgrowth of their being placed about and carried to ward off evil vapors. These herbs were often grown and cared for by the sacristan in the cloister garth, which corresponded somewhat to the pleasaunce of a castle. Another spot where the "church herbs" were sometimes planted was the "field of Paradise," an open space at each end of the church. The area was carpeted with thyme or chamomile and dotted here and there with what we now call wild flowers. These lovely spots were enjoyed by the monks, whose instinctive longing for flowers was thus in a little way satisfied. As they walked the cloisters or about the paradise, they filled their souls with beauty of form, of color, of fragrance. Perhaps quite unconscious of the effect, the monks were uplifted and exalted so that only the best and purest of their souls were offered to God.

But while the monasteries were being well organized on the Continent, England was struggling with invaders from the north of Britain and with plunderers from the northwestern coast of Europe. All the fine gardens that the Roman legions had established in the first century had long since died out, and only the hardiest of herbs remained in a wild state. With the natives themselves turning barbarous from constant fighting with even more barbarous men, it is little wonder that interest in gardens was practically forgotten except by the monks.

After Augustine with his little band of monks had landed in Kent in 597, the first task was to find a spot to settle in as quickly as possible. Fortunately the short trip to be made from Europe brought them to the southern part of England where the climate was most favorable to agriculture. Monastic settlements surrounded by walls were made at first with little thought to materials, form or arrangement of buildings. It was long years before the monks even had the time, land or material for a monastery establishment approaching that of St. Gall. For years they spent their time in clearing forests and making waste lands arable. They not only came to grow fruits, grain and vegetables for their own use but taught the natives, who had abandoned peaceful pursuits, how to till their land so as to produce fine agricultural crops, how to care for trees and graft new varieties, how to raise vegetable herbs long forgotten.

The very sight of some hundred monks working on farm and garden from morning till night fascinated would-be invaders, who not only respected the monastic property but seemed to receive a civilizing influence from it. With the passing of years, life became more organized within the monastery walls and, what interests us most, horticulture became highly developed.

Each monastery had at least three gardens, all under one gardinarius, with assistants to manage each garden. There was the physic garden, usually placed beneath the infirmary windows so the patients could be benefited by the aromatic odors. Then there were the kitchen garden, the orchard, and, in the larger establishments, a vineyard.

To the monks certainly goes the credit for conserving the arts of agriculture and horticulture. Books on plants were studied as early as the eighth century and we read of Boniface on the Continent receiving letters from his monastic brothers in England asking him to send more books on medicinal plants and regretting that it was difficult to obtain foreign herbs. Every monk who came from Italy and France to England was more than welcome if he brought a handful of seed of some new plant, or a cutting of an unusual shrub, a seedling of a new tree. Any monk who went on a pilgrimage or missionary venture to the Continent was carefully enjoined to look for plants not grown at his home monastery, or for any information he could pick up about new methods of gardening and farming. Knights Templars and Knights of St. John won much gratitude for the introduction of many treasures from the East and they owned many gardens in England. Hampton Court Gardens are now on the site of the Priory of the Knights of St. John.

Some of the early monks were learned men, often laymen who entered the monastery not from a desire to live a religious life but because they wished to retire and study. Few of the early abbots were ordained, the office being filled by a layman until the end of the seventh century and often into the eleventh century. Later, as some of the missionaries were sent to far-away places where there were none in church authority, the ordination of abbots became customary. However, the interest of the scholarly men continued to be in study, some of our finest early herbal botanies coming from monks who had the advantage of the only libraries in the country and the leisure to observe the plants and write about them.

To the monasteries we owe in a large part the preservation of medical tradition, though it is claimed they added nothing to it. The Benedictines, however, aimed at higher standards away from superstition and much was the daily opportunity for practice. Rich and poor, soldier and farmer, sought medical treatment from the monastery, as well as the brethren within the gates. Whether the monastery was large or small, the infirmary was usually overcrowded. People from the country round knew that at the monastery they would receive better care than anywhere else. Wounded soldiers often dragged themselves to the gates, having faith that their wounds would be healed.

A vast amount of gardening and farming went forward in an establishment that depended on grain, fruit and vegetables. All the garden and farm land, orchards and vineyards were in charge of the hortulanus or gardinarius, who hired his famuli or assistants. Almost from the beginning, the Benedictines hired outside labor, so great was the extent of field work.

Because of the large population, permanent and transient, large acreages were tilled outside the walls, as such lands were bestowed on the establishment. Often the gardinarius himself went outside to direct a corps of farmer-monks. Often the laborers from nearby villages were hired to dig, sow seed, plant vegetables. At Corbie, in Picardy, where there were large gardens, village tenants of church property annually contributed plows and sent men from April to October to plant, weed and harvest.

Since fruit was so important in monastic diet, the orchard played a large part in gardening. To the monks from ancient times we owe our thousands of varieties of fruits, since these adventurers continually made experiments in grafting in order to improve the fruit and to establish new varieties. Wardon pears, for example, were developed through the experiments of the Cistercian monks of Wardon Abbey in Bedfordshire. The fruit went, for the most part, into pies named after this special variety of pear, recipes for Wardon pies being commonly found in the ancient cook books and listed on menus for special feasts. In one medieval record a piece of property was held by the payment of three Wardon pears annually at Christmas.

From early lists we know the English grew several varieties of cherry, pear, peach, apple and plum besides chestnut, mulberry, fig and almond. As time went on, there were quinces and medlars, while gooseberries, strawberries, and raspberries were considered wild fruit. We do not know how many were native and how many had been imported. The almond, for instance, because of the climate of England, must have been brought over as a curiosity, never in sufficient quantities to supply substantial crops for the feasts.

One day when the sacristan was telling about various kinds of trees, David pricked up his ears when he heard his own beloved monastery of Melrose mentioned. Brother Andrew told about the indulgence of boiled almonds granted the monks because Robert Bruce on January 10th, in the twelfth year of his reign, assigned the sum of one hundred pounds for indulgence at the half yearly terms of Pentecost and St. Martin to the abbot and community and monks of Melrose for an added dish of rice boiled with milk, or of almonds or of pears. And it was stipulated that the regular food was not to be cut down because of this. These almonds certainly were imported, for an almond tree would have little chance of growing as far north as Scotland.

Sometimes monasteries in north or central England had or rented lands for orchards in the southern part. Bishop Swinfield, for instance, whose monastery was in Gloucestershire, had an orchard in Kent, although he had a few fruit trees within his own walls. It was common, indeed, to have several acres of orchard near the establishment. These trees not only provided fruit for eating and cooking but also brought an income from sale at the markets of the fruit itself and from cider.

Within the monastery an interesting feature was introduced about the fourteenth century, that of the "mount," an earthwork raised at some point near the outer wall of the monastery so one could look over the landscape for miles around. The mount, with stairs leading to a banqueting hall or summer house, became an important feature in private gardens of large estates.

In early days vineyards were much more common than today in the southern and central part of England, though not as far north as Scotland. John Parkinson in his *Paradisus,* 1629, says,

"I have read that manie Monasteries in this Kingdome having Vineyards, had as much wine made therefrom, as sufficed their convent yeare by yeare: but long since they have been destroyed and the knowledge how to order a Vineyard is also utterly perished with them."

Frenchmen had been brought over to England to try to re-establish vineyards, but either their skill or the vines were not good. Most of the trouble, thought Parkinson, is that "our years in these times do not fal out to be so kindly and hot, to ripen the grapes, to make anie good wine as formerly they have done." These words of the old herbalist are echoed in every age . . . the climate to-day is not like that of the good old times!

Be that as it may, in early days vineyards were important to many a monastic and private establishment. The Venerable Bede in the eighth century says that vines were produced in some places but does not commit himself further. In the ninth century King Alfred considered vineyards so important that he made it a law that any person injuring the vines of another should compensate him. October was "Wyn moneth," the time when grapes were gathered.

According to the Domesday Book, a tax and tenant census of the eleventh century made by William the Conqueror, there were thirty-eight vineyards to be found in England before the Conquest. But the Norman-French, coming from a land where vines grew luxuriantly, naturally brought over some of the best varieties with high hopes of as fine wines as they enjoyed in France. The English monks with these new imports did much toward improving the native vines and established new and better vineyards at that time. William of Malmesbury of the twelfth century said that the vines near the monastery of Gloucester were "more plentiful in crops and more pleasant in flavor than any in England." At Hereford, the terraced vineyards can still be detected, and at Ely the south side of the cloisters was planted with vines, while Vine Street in London is the site of the old vineyards of the monastery at Westminster.

The life of the head gardener in a monastery was a busy one, what with vineyard, orchard, farms outside perhaps miles from the monastery, vegetable and smaller gardens, keeping the elaborate and complicated expense accounts and myriad tasks connected with his office, as some of the records show. The details the gardinarius had to attend to personally or see done were enormous. He had to supply the monastery with herbs and vegetables "in season." One of his assistants visited the kitchen daily to see what was required and to bring the garden produce cleaned and prepared for use. Incidentally, another important office connected with the garden was that of the "mustardarius," who had to furnish all the mustard used in seasoning and at all the places where food was served. In early days it was considered essential to eat mustard with all salted food, fish or flesh, and the amount of that herb grown and prepared was very great.

The expense accounts must have given the gardinarius many a headache. We have from existing records the name of one of these busy men, one Adam Vynour, gardener at Ely, and what a perfect name for a gardener! We find expenses set down for implements, wearing apparel for the laborers, for digging, sowing, weeding, mowing and cutting of herbs. Then there were expenses for such jobs as "extracting the mosse" from the cloister garden, mowing the cloister garden, gathering and threshing the precious crop of mustard seed, cleaning the ditches that divided the various gardens, cleaning out the moat, buying nets and baskets for catching fish in the moat or in the "fish stew" [pond]. Seeds were bought and sold and duly recorded.

The accounts covering the surplus must have been the most intricate of all. Some of the land belonging to the monastery was rented out to tenants who not only took their pay from the actual surplus of the crop but sold part of it. We have accounts of receipts for selling fagots, osiers, timber, hay, beans, herbs, garlic, apples, peas, eggs, hempseed. The accounts for buying, selling and pasturing cattle and the transactions regarding milk also came within the province of the gardener. The pay of laborers was supposed to come out of the surplus sold and in food, but in poor seasons for crops this was not always possible.

Besides the main gardens of the monastery there were several private plots belonging to the abbot, prior, almoner, treasurer. Many abbots loved their gardens so much that they worked in them themselves, experimented and applied themselves diligently to the art and often to the science of horticulture. Brithnold, first abbot of Ely in the twelfth century, was famed for his skill as a gardener and near the monastery planted large areas of gardens, orchards and vineyards, the latter becoming famous. It was said that the abbot of Kinlos about 1500 "was wont to do much with his own hands; he transcribed much and wrote the service books of this abbey; sometimes also he worked even to perspiration in the garden, uprooting and planting trees or in work of that kind." But this abbot, as well as owners of most of the private gardens, had a hired assistant, one of these a man imported from France.

Besides the special gardens, in some monasteries the monks themselves were permitted to have separate little garden plots, often walled, in the common garden. Here they spent their spare time, just as people of all ages have done, working in their garden, experimenting, tending flowers and vegetable herbs, planning, meditating.

Certain rules and regulations were imposed on Sunday contact with herbs, perhaps arising from the desire to discourage the monks from working in their little plots on Sunday, or possibly it was just another superstition. In some monasteries it was forbidden to pluck up pot herbs on Sunday with the hand. If it was necessary to gather them, they were to be dug with a wooden instrument, but in no case were they to come in contact with the hand.

The story is told about a miracle that came to pass near the tomb of St. Etheldreda. A priest's servant girl was rash enough to gather herbs on the Sabbath and, though the instrument was of wood, it stuck to her hand so tightly that it could not be taken away for five years. The story concludes with the statement that by "the merits of St. Etheldreda the girl was cured," but no details are given of the cure.

To these churchmen who loved gardening, we owe some of our first garden books as well as herbals. Besides Walafrid Strabo, Benedictine monk, who wrote the *Hortulus,* there was Alexander Neckham, Augustinian monk, Abbot of Cirencester, author of *De Naturis Rerum,* describing the plants essential for a nobleman's garden. This, however, was not very practical for English consumption, since he described plants more readily grown in southern Europe and Asia as, for instance, the citron and the pomegranate. Neckham set forth the claim that cherries, mulberries and other soft fruits should be eaten only on an empty stomach. Pears were considered indigestible if eaten raw. As with all early monks, he was interested greatly in fruit growing and knew the process of grafting the pear on the thorn. In his *De Laudibus Divinae Sapientiae,* a poem in ten books, he wrote on herbs in the seventh book.

Bishop Grosseteste of Lincoln adapted *De Re Rustica* of Palladius to suit English climatic conditions and this book was read and reread for the next two or three hundred years. Nicholas Ballard translated the section on grafting from Palladius' book, and thus made it available to many gardeners who knew no language but their own. Albertus Magnus, a thirteenth century German Dominican monk, in his *De Vegetabilibus* brought to the attention of the English the Roman custom of forcing fruits and flowers in a hothouse. To Otto Brunfels, a Carthusian monk, we owe the first German herbal. Bartholomaeus Anglicus of the Minorite Order was the first Englishman to write an original treatise on plants, *De Proprietatibus Rerum*, about 1280, and the seventeenth book, devoted to herbs, is indicative of his first-hand knowledge of plants and is not merely a copy of some ancient classic.

The numbers and kinds of gardens in the various monasteries differed with the size and nature of the order. In London the Temple garden, famous for the exchange of red and white roses forever to be symbols of the Lancastrian and Yorkist opposition, was once owned by the Knights Templars during the Middle Ages. The College Garden of Westminster Abbey was formerly the physic garden and joined to the "grete garden" of the monastery. In Brabant Abbey was a large extent of orchards with a chessboard arrangement of garden plots in the cloister garth, besides four other gardens outside the cloisters.

One of the most interesting monastic orders was that of the Carthusian monks. By the tenth century, the discipline of the Benedictine rule had relaxed so much that little groups broke away from it to return to more severe and simple living. The Carthusian Order was a throwback to the early Oriental monastic idea that the hermit way of life was the best preparation for the life beyond this world. Silence and solitude were the main rules according to the plan first adopted in 1084 by St. Bruno and his twelve companions at Chartreuse, near Grenoble in France. Each monk occupied a small detached cottage, isolated from the others, in a tiny garden surrounded by walls, and all connected by a common corridor. The monk left his cottage only to attend church services and general assemblies, held but rarely. Between the cottage and corridor was a passage, so the monk was entirely cut off from all sound and movement. The superior could walk unseen through the main corridor and observe the gardens through tiny open spaces. Food was given the monk through the little hatch into the small passageway, the opening made in such a manner that there could be no view inward or outward.

In the Cluniac Monasteries, silence was also imposed; and since their work was much in the fields, it must have been difficult to keep the rule. An elaborate system of sign language grew up, taught unofficially to the novices as ABC's are taught to children. For example, bread was indicated by making a circle with the two thumbs and forefingers. Eggs called for pecking an imaginary shell with the forefinger. Fish was indicated by imitating the motion of its tail in water, honey by putting out the tongue a little way and licking the lips.

When Brother Andrew came to the history of the Cistercian Order, David simply drank in every word about the organization of which he was a part and which was so dear to him. This Order, he learned, was founded by St. Robert and a group that had broken off from the Benedictines and, in an effort to return to the simplicity of early days of monastic life, had gone to Citeaux, then practically a swamp, and lived in strict observance of the early Benedictine rule. In 1112, St. Bernard with thirty companions developed the Order so that by the end of the twelfth century there were over 500 establishments, some of the great Cistercian houses being Tintern Abbey, Fountains Abbey, Valle Crucis and Mailros. Simplicity was the chief characteristic of the Order, the buildings made without decorations such as stained glass, pinnacles, and turrets. The same attitude decided the location of the monasteries. The monks sought an uninhabited place, often nothing more than swamp land, thickets backed by a forest, if possible. Of these places wholly desolate the Cistercians often made land productive beyond imagination. As we study the locations they chose, we find that though the immediate area was wild and uninhabited, the natural surroundings had great practical possibilities and tended to have an esthetic effect on the monks. The establishment was near the bend of a river, giving not only a beautiful setting, but also furnishing a waterway for produce and water for the mills and factories, and for general use in the buildings. The area was always level, to be made into pasturage and tilled for crops, while the nearby forest was to furnish fuel. As agriculturists, as well as horse and cattle breeders, the Cistercians became the outstanding farmers and scientific gardeners of the country. We have already mentioned that they developed the Wardon pears at Wardon Abbey in Bedfordshire. At that abbey are also records of a great vineyard, a little vineyard, two orchards and a hopyard. By 1296 there was hardly a nobleman's garden that had as many varieties of fruit as could be found on the lands connected with Cistercian abbeys.

For many years after the founding of the Order, the Cistercians refused all sources of income such as tithes, tolls and rents, but depended solely on the land for their living, selling their farm produce, cattle, horses. By the middle of the thirteenth century, the wool exported by them had become an item of commerce to be reckoned with. This agriculture they carried on so extensively that, with their religious duties, almost from the beginning they evolved the system of "conversi" or lay brothers, ignorant men from the lower class whose function it was to do the field work and turn their hands to shop, mill and factory. The conversi also worked in the vineyards and on farms not more than a day's journey from the abbey. They were not taught to read or write and hence could not take part in the services of the abbey, but learned by heart, from following the monks, the simple services which came during hours in the field. At other times the conversi had their own prayers and other religious services in their own quarters at one end of the monastery.

The Abbey of Mailros, meaning "bare moor," situated in the Eildon Hills and near a bend in the Tweed River, was founded in 1136 by David I and dedicated to Virgin Mary, as David was told before. It was the first Cistercian monastery in Scotland and soon increased its numbers from Rievaulx in Yorkshire. Since it was located on a direct road from England, it was often attacked during that long, bitter fight between England and the then almost savage Scotland, though monasteries in southern parts of England were usually safe from invasion. In 1322 it was destroyed by Edward II and rebuilt for the most part by gifts from Robert Bruce, whose heart lies buried beneath the high altar. Again the Abbey was nearly burned down in 1385 by Richard II. Little did Brother Andrew or David know, in the spring of 1530, that in another fifteen years nothing would be left of their beloved abbey but ruins, or that long years later a great novelist living in nearby Abbotsford would write *The Monastery,* which was to tell the story of Melrose and its destruction in that great struggle between Protestant and Catholic.

Within the walls of Melrose Abbey were many separate gardens, that of the abbot, of the prior, of the sacristan. So, thought David, his superiors were cleansing their hearts continually in their worship of God, both by prayers in the church and by work in the garden—for who could live among growing plants and still think small, petty thoughts? The sacristan searched monastic history for all he could find out about early sacristans' gardens, which David absorbed eagerly because he wanted to make those of Brother Andrew to be most beautiful of all. Here, as in the sacristan garden of all monasteries, were grown all the living decorations in connection with the church. There were rose garlands for the great festival of Corpus Christi, and for St. Barnabas' Day, wreaths to be worn by the priests in processions on all feast days, to adorn candles and banners. As far back as the ninth century the sacristan's flowers at Winchester were grown in that piece of ground called the paradise.

At Norwich the sacristan had at least two gardens. One was termed the "green garden," which might have been the paradise; another was St. Mary's garden, dedicated to the Virgin, and containing plants sacred to her. This last was the one item that Brother Andrew had held as a climax of his talks with David. The sacristan himself had long wanted a St. Mary's garden, but had never had the time to take care of one, nor had he ever before had a gardener so brimful of enthusiasm as David. As he expected, the young man looked eagerly to the sacristan. "Could we have a St. Mary's garden?" breathed David, and when Brother Andrew had but nodded, this gardener monk simply trod on air. For the rest of the winter, plans were afoot for the innovation; making diagrams, searching into garden history, lore and church tradition for the appropriate plants.

Little did David dream in his enthusiasm, that within a few years, in 1533, the General Chapter at Citeaux would inquire into the state of the Order in Scotland. With papal sanction, a commission was sent to reform

the Cistercian houses. The investigator, Abbot of Char-
lieu on the Loire, found the most serious offense was that
of possessing private gardens, and left orders for this
practice to be discontinued. The orders proved to be as
effective as King Canute's commands to the waves to
cease rolling in to shore, for it is instinctive for people to
yearn for a garden of their own. The next year the commission wrote, instead of making the long trip from
France to Melrose. Promises had been made and not
kept. The abbot and others still had their gardens, and
since the superior of a great house like Melrose dis-
obeyed the orders of the commission, it was very bad for
the morale of the smaller abbeys. The abbot was threat-
ened with excommunication if he did not give up the personal rights to his garden and see that all houses depend-
ent on him obeyed the orders. A special dispensation was
made that gardens could be worked by individuals, but no
individual ownership could be claimed, and free access to
all gardens was to be allowed.

But all unsuspecting of the storm brewing, David joy-
fully planned his St. Mary's garden and devised ways for
making the other garden of the sacristan more of a picture of beauty, even though it had its useful purpose.
When spring came he petted and coaxed the plants and
bushes to grow for him as they had never done for any
other gardener. When Corpus Christi Day came, such
luxuriant branches, such beautiful garlands and wreaths
came from that garden for the church and for the great
procession that even the abbot, the almoner, the treasurer, all with gardens of their own, came to admire
"David's garden," as it came to be called, and often, I
fear, with a little bit of envy, much more than was proper
for men of holy living.

But the garden that everyone loved was the St. Mary's

garden. It had such a special significance for Mailros since the abbey itself had been dedicated to her. In it there were as many plants with white flowers as could be obtained, for the white was symbolic of her purity and holiness. There was rosemary, over which the Virgin threw her blue cloak, and ever afterwards the flowers were a beautiful blue in her honor. We see that blue rosemary now and then today. Roses and lilies, above all flowers, were especially grown for the Virgin; the lily for its pure whiteness; the roses white and red connected with her from earliest times, St. Dominic recognizing that significance and forever perpetuating it when he instituted the devotion of the rosary.

Many flowers bear the words "Our Lady" in the name, as Our Lady's Bedstraw, which filled the Holy Manger, with thyme, sweet woodruff and groundsel. The cuckoo flower, found in meadows, is Our Lady's Smock and there are Our Lady's Thistle, Our Lady's Garters (ribbon grass), Our Lady's Slipper (a variety of orchid), Our Lady's Tresses, Our Lady's Candlestick (a variety of prunella), Our Lady's Fingers (Anthyllis vulneraria), Our Lady's Bunch of Keys (cowslip), Our Lady's Thimble (harebell), Our Lady's Tears (lily-of-the-valley). The number of plants named in honor of the Virgin is endless, and each new one David came upon delighted him. Many were the letters sent to the Continent and then the long wait for more plants and more information. Every visitor to Mailros was pressed to add more Mary plants, every brother who went abroad was begged to bring back plants. A German monk who came to the abbey told of Our Lady's Milkwort, a German name for lungwort, and costmary, he said, was called Our Lady's Balsam by his countrymen. A French monk from Citeaux was so delighted with the garden that he promised to go through all the history he could find in the home monastery. His present contribution to information was that in France dead nettle was called Our Lady's Hands, spearmint was Our Lady's Mint, and that the foxglove was Our Lady's Gloves.

And in the Mary garden there was the snowdrop, "Fair Maid of February," supposed to open always on Candlemas Day. The monks believed it bloomed then in memory of the Virgin's having presented the child Jesus to the temple. Her image was removed from the altar on the day of purification in February, and snowdrops, as an emblem of purity, strewn over the vacant place. Besides all these there were hollyhocks, marigold, flowers of the Cruciferae family, violets for humility, daisies for innocence.

Thus did the monk David work and labor and worship, offering his one talent to God.

CHAPTER II

The Golden Age of Herbalists

Caxton had brought printing to England in 1476–77 and opened a new world to thousands who had never seen a written page, much less a printed one. Until then, a book resulted only from laborious hours of copying by hand from some manuscript preserved, perhaps in monastery or library, and which was itself a copy. Moreover, these were written in Latin, Greek or sometimes in Arabic or Persian, occasionally in Anglo-Saxon. The average man never came in contact with such treasures. He couldn't have read them if he had. He wouldn't know what they were.

But now printing had made it possible to turn out many duplicates at once, perhaps 200 at a time. This made books available for private purchase and people were seized with the desire to learn to read. Many of the old manuscripts were translated into English before printing. Others were printed in the original Latin or, if copied from earlier books printed in another language on the Continent, they often were kept in that language. The same book was printed by various publishers if it was found to be popular.

A Page from the Ninth Century Manuscript of the Fifth Century Apuleius.

Codex Casinensis 97.

Into this exciting time was born one William Turner, son of a tanner in Morpeth, Northumberland, far from London as travel was in those days. If his birth year was 1510, as some think, his life spanned all the Tudor monarchs, ending in the tenth year of the reign of Queen Elizabeth, the greatest Tudor of them all.

There were herbalists before his time. All through the centuries men had written manuscripts about plants, their descriptions and their virtues. These manuscripts were copied, largely by the monks, and scattered copies existed here and there, some of them forming the basis of the earliest printed works—Dioscorides, Apuleius, Macer, Albertus Magnus, *De Proprietatibus Rerum,* and others whose authors were unknown and from which came the herbal of Bancke and of Askham, and the *Grete Herbal.*

On the Continent the Renaissance and Reformation were on in full force. There was a reawakening of desire for knowledge of what the ancients knew, and word of this awakening spread to England. Students at universities were given new subjects to study, new schools were established, new books began to be written for publication, new alignments forced in politics and religion as Henry VIII turned the church world upside down, Protestant and Catholic following each other in supremacy in kaleidoscopic fashion.

Turner, a student at Cambridge, was won to the Protestant banner. Qualified to take orders for the Church in 1537, his conflicts with the authorities caused him to spend many years on the Continent, where his old love for plants engaged him as he wandered about Holland, Switzerland, Germany and Italy, where he received a degree in medicine at one of the universities and also studied botany. He wrote two little religious works which were promptly banned in England. Then in 1538 he wrote a

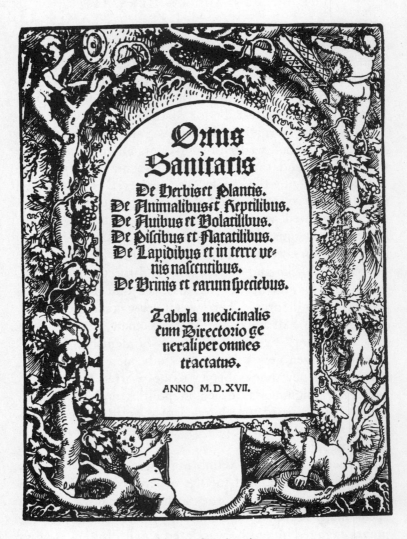

Ortus Sanitatis.

Title page of one of the earliest of titled herbals, derived from the German *Herbarius* of 1485 and printed in 1517, *Garden of Health*.

small book in Latin about plants, *Libellus de re herbaria novus.*

When Edward VI came to the throne in 1547, Turner returned to England, although not until Elizabeth's reign could he remain there undisturbed. In 1550 he became chaplain and physician to the Duke of Somerset and established himself at Kew, where now the Royal Botanic Gardens form a fitting memorial for the man who is called the "Father of Botany" in England.

He had in mind an herbal and, in fact, had written one in Latin which was never published. On the advice of other physicians, he made field trips all over England and thoroughly acquainted himself with the native herbs, supplementing the wide knowledge he had gained abroad. He chose then to write down what he knew, not in Latin, but in English and produced an herbal in three volumes comparable to any written by the ancients and standing alone as the only great printed herbal having any claim to being an original text. Indeed, it is the only original work written by an Englishman and dealing with botany which appeared during Turner's lifetime and for many years thereafter. The complete herbal was published in 1568 although parts had appeared previously, the first part being printed in London in 1551; but Turner was a tired man, as he concluded in a letter to Lord Burleigh . . . "Your old and seikly client" and he died that year. His son, Peter, diligently compared the printed copy with his father's manuscript and prepared a list of errors, which was bound in some of the copies. The complete herbal in any form is very rare but only one copy with the list of errors has been found in this generation and that was sold in London in 1939 to an unnamed purchaser. (Miss Rohde stated in 1922 that such a copy existed in the Linnean Society's library.)

British botany dates from Turner, the churchman, the-ologian, physician, herbalist and botanist. With him the "Golden Age" of herbalists began and we can vision the lusty joy he took in his observation and writings. Of "birch" he tells so many uses, but none better, he says, than for "betinge" of stubborn boys that either lie or will not learn. He tells how the boys in his native section of England scraped the root of wild hyacinth for a "slime" with which to glue their arrows; of how spots can be taken out of cloth by a lye from gentian roots; that parsley thrown into fish ponds will heal ailing fishes.

In one particular Turner reminds one of the later Cul-peper who so outraged the College of Physicians when he published in 1649 a translation of their Dispensatory in English. To those who condemned Turner for writing his Herbal in English, he pointed out that Dioscorides wrote in his native language with no disastrous results and he, Turner, writing in his native language to his countrymen is combating ignorance and dishonesty among those who dealt with herbs. Incidentally, he inquires, how many surgeons and apothecaries could understand Latin anyhow!

A decade before Turner's death, William Bullein, who styled himself "Doctor of Phisicke," wrote *The Government of Health*. To him the herbs that he prescribed were more than simples to heal broken bones or heads. Though his calling kept him from devoting much time to his garden, he studied his plants to learn their characteristics, their habits, their likes and dislikes, just as we strive really to know our friends. All through his book, we come upon little gardening quirks that he was so pleased to have discovered that he wanted others to know, too. Besides the garden proper, the orchard pleased him and he tells us much about the kinds of fruit prospering in

ALYTEL
HERBALL OF THE
PROPERTIES OF HER

bes newely amended and corrected, ·
with certayne addicions at the ende
of the boke, declaryng what herbes
hath influence of certaine Sterres
and conftellations , wherby may be
chofen the beaft and moft luckye
tymes & dayes of their mini=
ftracion, accordynge to the
Moone being in the fig=
nes of heauen, the
which is dayly
appoynted
in the
Almanacke, made and gathered
in the yere of our lorde god
M.D.L. the.xii. day of Fe=
bruary by Anthonye
Afkham Phi=
fycpon.

The first book printed in England which could be considered as
an herbal was this little volume. It was first printed by Banckes
and in 1550 by William Powell for Anthony Askham, who added
nothing, but became the first Englishman to have his name as
author on the title page of an herbal.

England in the sixteenth century. How proudly he would
have held his own in talks with William Lawson, Ralph
Austen or John Evelyn, the experts on fruit-growing in
the century which followed. We know little about Bullein
except how the appeal of the garden humanized this
otherwise bookish man. In 1562 he published another
book in such demand that in 1579 a second edition was
required. The very title sounds as pompous as I have
imagined Bullein to be, but a title altogether delightful
in its heaping up of words:

"Bulleins Bulwarke of Defence against all Sicknesse,
Soareness and Woundes that doe dayley assaulte mankinde: Which Bulwarke is kept with Hilarius the Gardener, and Health the Phisicion, with the Chirurgian, to
helpe the Wounded Souldiours. Gathered and practised
from the most worthy learned, both olde and new: to the
great comfort of Mankinde."

Yet how simply, how lovingly he speaks of the pansy,
our little Johnny-jump-up of today: "Pray God give thee
but one handfull of heavenly hearts ease which passeth all
the pleasant flowers that grow in this world." The learned
doctor, the educated scholar bows in humility, awed before the miracle of Nature.

In Thomas Hyll we find a gardener-herbalist who practiced medicine but, unlike William Bullein, was "rudely
taught" and writes, he says, for the "simple and unlettered." Would that we knew more about this young man
to whom credit goes for writing the first real book on
gardening printed in English. Perhaps Hyll was not as
unlettered as he chose to state, because in this book and
in the later *Gardeners Labyrinth* he leans heavily upon
the classical writers, although he turns their information
into his own phraseology.

We know that he was well connected at court. One of his friends was Henry Dethicke whose father, Sir Gilbert, was principal King of Arms for Elizabeth. To Henry, Hyll, at his death, left the loving task of editing the unfinished *Gardeners Labyrinth* and Dethicke wrote as a preface a dedicatory letter to Cecil, Lord Burleigh, Lord High Treasurer of England. Finally, George Baker, "chirurgian" to Queen Elizabeth, credits Hyll with help on his *Newe Jewell of Health,* 1576, saying "Thomas Hyll dyd also take paynes in this worke, but before it coulde be brought to perfection, God tooke him to his mercie."

The London of Hyll's time was really a pleasant, friendly small town with neighbors exchanging seeds and plants over their fences, begging a cutting of this or a root of that. Nearly everyone had a garden and on his own acreage, however small it was, Thomas Hyll thoroughly enjoyed trying anything at least once to produce a fine and useful garden. As other gardeners the world over from time immemorial have liked to share their findings, so did Hyll, and he imparted all in a "simple treatyse," not to "scholars, poticaries and also surgeons" but to the "gentle reader," simple-hearted and single-minded in wanting to improve his garden.

We have no copy of the previous book that Hyll speaks of in his preface to this first existing edition of 1563, a tiny volume known as *A Most Briefe and pleasaunt treatyse* but laden with the comprehensive and delightfully naïve title of:

"A Most Briefe and pleasaunt treatyse teachynge howe to drese, sowe and set a Garden, and what propertyes also these few herbes heare spoken of have to our comodytie: with the remedyes that may be used against such beasts, Wormes, flies and such lyke, that commonly noy gardēs, gathered out of the principallest Authors in this Art by Thomas Hyll Londyner."

I have always felt the importance of noisome insects in Hyll's books bespoke his own disgust and annoyance with them. Perhaps cut worms laid low his seedlings of woad, as they do mine. What would he have done if he had had to combat the Japanese beetles chewing their way through his hollyhocks and roses!

Besides the descriptive title and on the same page is the drawing of a lovely garden, traditionally rectangular, doubly inclosed by hedge and fence. Within, the garden proper is neatly divided into rectangular beds with an open knot design in the center. There was a second edition of the *Pleasaunt Treatyse,* but in 1568 and in further editions it appeared enlarged under the title of *Proffitable Arte of Gardening.* In 1577 there was published another book, *Gardeners Labyrinth* by Hyll, to which I have referred above. This laid down "New and Rare inventions and secrets of Gardening not heretofore known" and "Likewise here is set forth divers knots for the beautifying of any Garden for Delight. Lastly, here is set down the Physical benefit of each Herbe, with the commodities of the Waters distilled out of them, for the use and benefit of all." This last is typical of Hyll—"for the use and benefit of all"—and it was not information set down by the gentleman gardener, the dilettante, but "Collected from the best approved Authors, besides forty years experience in the Art of Gardning." For some reason this book, published in two parts after Hyll's death, was signed "Didymus Mountain," a play on his name, a prank somewhat like that played by Parkinson some sixty years later in the title "Paradisus in Sole" or "Park in Sun." Because of the signature "Didymus Moun-

tain," or "D.M." as in some editions, the proof of Hyll's
authorship rests on the contemporary statement by Ed-
mund Southerne that Hyll was the author. However, Hyll
could not have had "forty years experience." On a picture
published in 1568 is the statement that Hyll was then 28.

Thomas Hyll was a true dirt gardener and in his last
years the paragraphs that he wrote disclose that he still
was enchanted with green growing things. For an example, let me set down here the opening lines of Chapter
XXVIII of *The Gardeners Labyrinth:*

"The life of man in this world is but a thraldom, when
the Sences are not pleased; and what rarer object can
there be on earth, (the motions of the Celestial bodies
excepted) then a beautifull and Odoriferous Garden plat
Artificially composed, where he may read and contemplate on the wonderfull works of the great Creator, in
Plants and Flowers; for if he observeth with a judicial
eye, and a serious judgement their variety of Colours,
Sents, Beauty, Shapes, Interlacing, Enamiling, Mixture,
Turnings, Windings, Embosments, Operations and Vertues, it is most admirable to behold, and meditate upon
the same. But now to my Garden of Flowers and sweet
Hearbs, and first for the Rose."

One feels that Hyll must have been a lovable man, a
simple man to whom you could take a drooping plant and
he would nurse it back to health but tell you, however,
how to avoid such near catastrophe in the future.

And then came John Gerard, citizen of Chestershire
and surgeon of London. Those are the descriptive words
of the scroll around his portrait in his *Herbal,* published
in 1597. He had some fondness for his boyhood home. In
speaking of the raspberry in the herbal he says: "I have
found it among the bushes of a cawsey, neere unto a village called Wisterson, where I went to schoole, two miles

from the Nantwich in Cheshire." As a grown man, years away from schooldays, he still remembered handfuls of berries he gathered on some boyish trip in which, no doubt, many another plant caught his interest and instilled in him that love of growing things that later made his herbal a warm friendly book about living plants with personalities, about scores of men, famous and humble, with whom he consulted or from whom he proudly accepted seeds and plants, about late sixteenth century London.

Some people to whom the names of scientific botanists mean nothing have heard of Gerard's *Herbal;* to others this old book has been the source of many a pleasant hour. For this we can almost forgive Gerard's fall from grace in the way he obtained the nucleus of the herbal. The publisher, John Norton, had engaged one Dr. Priest to translate the Dutch Rembert Dodoens' *Pemptades,* just as Henry Lyte had translated the French edition of Dodoens' *Cruydt-Boeck* in 1578. Dr. Priest died, however, and in some manner Gerard got hold of the translation, made adjustments and comments to suit himself, but ran into difficulties trying to attach to the correct flowers the 1800 woodcuts, many of which had originally furnished the illustrations for Tabernaemontanus' *Eicones* of 1590. So Norton hired the French botanist L'Obel to make the necessary corrections but, eager to get the book done, Gerard stopped him before all the corrections were made and in 1597 the *Herbal* appeared, full of errors, and with an amusing evidence of haste.

In the letter "to the courteous and well-willing Readers," Gerard says "Doctor Priest, one of our London Colledge, hath (or I heard) translated the last edition of Dodonaeus, which meant to published the same; but being prevented by death his translation likewise perished." But a few pages removed from this amazing statement, among the prefatory and laudatory comments customary in early days, one Stephen Bredwell, Phisition (later in the book identified as "a learned and diligent searcher of simples in the west of England"), says, "Dr. Priest for his translation of so much of Dodonaeus, hath hereby left a tombe for his honorable sepulture. Master Gerard . . . hath many waies accommodated the whole worke unto our English nation." Gerard, in the fifteen years that followed, must have stared frequently at these words but I question if any sense of guilt disturbed him. Anyone could have dug up all that dull material about routine description of the plants, their names in various countries, the "temperature" according to the belief in humours, the virtues. That did not particularly interest him and, if it hadn't come from Dodoens by way of Priest, there were a dozen other places to get it.

What did fascinate Gerard was the breathing, living plant, every little peculiarity he himself noticed. He was quite matter of fact about plants not found in England or not grown in his gardens but, when he came to his own plants, he warmed to his subject and it was that which made his herbal without rival for a generation.

Gerard must have led a busy life. He was a practicing physician in Holborn, was appointed October 6, 1587, as superintendent of the garden of the College of Physicians, then in Knight Rider Street, besides caring for and studying the thousand plants in his own plots to which he added constantly. But for twenty years he was supervisor of the gardens of Lord Burleigh at Theobald's, just north of London. It is surprising how often Burleigh seems to have come into contact with the herbalists, with Turner, Hyll and Gerard, the latter dedicating his herbal to this Lord High Treasurer of England in a letter which hints

THE SECOND PART
OF THE
Gardeners-Labyrinth,

Vttering fuch skilfull Experience, and
worthy fecrets, about the particular fowing and
removing of the moſt Kitchin Herbs, with the witty ordering of other dainty Herbs, deleĉtable Flowers, pleaſant
Fruits, and fine Roots, as the like hath not heretofore
been uttered of any. Befides, the Phyfick benefits of
each Herb annexed, with the commodity of waters diſtil-
le d out of them, right profitable to be known.

LONDON,

Printed by *June Bell,* and are to be ſold at tho Eaſt-end
of *Chriſt-Church,* 1 6 5 1.

Hyll's inclusion as an herbalist rests on the contents of the second
part of the *Gardeners Labyrinth* which is largely the "Physick
benefits of each Herb annexed."

more than once of the magic spell that plants cast over him.

Gerard regrets "that which sometimes was the studie of great Philosophers and mightie Princes is now neglected" except by a few "among whom I may justly affirme and publish your Honor to be one . . . for under your Lordship I have served, and that way imployed my principall studie, and almost all my time now by the space of twenty years. . . . I have laboured with the soile to make it fit for the plants and with the plants to make them delight in the soile; that so they might live and prosper under our climate as in their native countries: what my successe hath beene and what my furniture is, I leave to the report of them that have seene your Lordships Gardens, and the little plot of my speciall care and husbandrie." That little plot was his own garden on Fetter Lane in the fine London suburb of Holborn.

In 1596 Gerard published a 24-page list of the plants in his garden, the first known catalogue of the plants in a private garden. In some copies of the *Herbal* this catalogue may be found bound in with the other material. Gerard records in the *Herbal* the name of whoever has added to his pleasure by contributing another plant to his garden—Mr. Garret, apothecary; Mr. Wade, one of the clerks of "her Maiesties Counsell." Many a name, otherwise lost to posterity, remains known to us because he had brought Gerard a much longed for plant, fruit, or flower. And what a picture he gives of sixteenth century London in his accurate notes and definite locations of where plants are to be found:

"White Saxifrage is in a fielde on the left hand of the way as you go from the place of execution called Saint Thomas Waterings, unto Dedford by London."

The title page of Henry Lyte's translation of Dodoens' *Cruydt-Boeck*, much as Priest translated Dodoens' *Pemptades* which Gerard seized upon and put out as his herbal in 1597. The above translation is dated 1578.

More than two centuries before, Chaucer had written of the same spot in the prologue to the Canterbury Tales:

"And forth we riden [from Southwark] a litel moe
    than pas
Unto the watering of seint Thomas."

Now this quiet spot has become part of the bustling, noisy, smoky suburbs of twentieth century London.

Wild burnet was found "betweene Paddington and Lysson greene neere unto London upon the high way." Today all Americans think of Paddington in connection with the great railroad station, the gateway to the west country.

Sometimes we stand quite in awe of Gerard's ability to grow difficult plants and between the lines we can read a pride not too secret either! He speaks of cumin, "My selfe did sowe it in the midst of Maie, which sprung up in sixe daies after; and the seede was ripe in the end of July." Wild clary was to be found in "the fields of Holbourne neere unto Graies Inne in the highway by the end of a brick wall," but there was a second kind of clary with purple leaves and Gerard says, "The other is a stranger in England: it groweth in my garden." A simple enough statement but it signifies the complete character of Gerard, to whom the whole of life was lived each day that he had adjusted a plant to its environment and he could say at the end, "It groweth in my garden."

Gerard died in 1612 when one John Parkinson was beginning to achieve wide fame as a gardener and herbalist. In 1629 his great gardening book *Paradisi in Sole Paradisus Terrestris* appeared. It began to be recognized that Gerard's book, only partially corrected before publication, was a bit shaky, and the publishers who had succeeded Norton decided to give it as firm a foundation as possible. So in 1632 they commissioned Thomas Johnson to revise and enlarge the herbal within a year. Johnson was an herbalist but he was also a learned botanist, an outstanding figure. We pass over the terrific amount of work that assignment entailed, to say that in 1633 the new edition appeared with 2766 illustrations and far more accurate botanical material but certainly with no added charm.

In the Preface to the *Paradisus,* Parkinson had explained that the contents of that book would be the garden of pleasant flowers, the "kitchin garden" and the orchard but, if the book were well received, another part would be forthcoming, a garden of simples, which part would be "quiet no longer at home, then that it can bring his Master newes of faire weather for the Journey." But it was eleven years before the "newes of faire weather" came, years beset with trouble. Not until 1640 was the herbal called *Theatrum Botanicum* published and the author was then 73 years old, an age when most people would think of taking life a little easier. Parkinson gives some insight into the struggle in his letter to the reader:

"The disastrous times but much more wretched and perverse men have so farre prevailed against my intended purpose, and promise in exhibiting the Worke to the publicke view of all; that their extreme covetousnesse had well nigh deprived my Country of the fruition . . ."

But "by the revolution of time it hath changed the note [that is, from a Physicall Garden of Simples to a Theater of Plants] yet not the Nature."

Throughout, the impression is somehow given of an aging man who had long ago entered exuberantly upon an enterprise of limited scope with all his heart and soul.

But, as time marched on and obstacles we know not of fell in his way, he plodded on in a work he was determined to finish for a Cause, he felt, to correct mistakes of previous herbals . . . "not to teach Doctors but to helpe their memories, and withal to shew them my judgement, that they mistake not one thing for another or one mans plant for another." On the title page we read "Collected by the many yeares trauaile, industry, and experience in this subject." In that phrase, we sense the painstaking care expended on the book that Parkinson hoped would be his masterpiece . . . "Goe forth now therefore thou issue artificiall of mine, and supply the defect of a Naturall, to beare up thy Father's name and memory to succeeding ages." But that was not to be; the childless man was to be remembered by his joyous garden book, the *Paradisus*, universally acclaimed in all the centuries to this day as the loveliest of all the garden books.

The *Theatrum* was dedicated to Charles I, as the *Paradisus* had been to Henrietta Maria, his Queen. Parkinson explained:

"Having by long paines and endeavors, composed this Manlike worke of Herbes and Plants, most gracious Soveraign (as I formerly did a Feminine of Flowers and presented it to the Queenes most excellent Majesty) I could doe noe lesse than submissively lay it at your Majesty's feet."

Parkinson's definite purpose in the herbal is not to write of a fragrant, colorful, ornamental flower garden, but to tell of the medicinal virtues of plants, and he seems let down a little by the assignment.

"From a Paradise of pleasant Flowers, I am fallen (Adam like) to a world of profitable Herbes and Plants . . . namely those Plants that are frequently used to helpe the diseases of our bodies."

The task Parkinson set for himself was stupendous and he produced an enormous herbal, discussing far more plants than mentioned in Gerard, some 3800 in all. He leaned heavily upon the works of the ancients, Dioscorides, Cratevas, Theophrastus, Galen, Tabernaemontanus, and many another herbalist and upon the French botanists, L'Obel and Caspar Bauhin, whose help he acknowledged on the title page. Besides the works of these authors, his information was "encreased by the accesse of many hundreds of new, rare and Strange Plants from all parts of the world." Many of these he grew in his own gardens at Long Acre, some brought back from his own travels and some presented by friends returned from abroad. In addition, he had the practical advantage of actual use of the medicinal herbs, since he was a practicing physician and an apothecary in London.

As we read the herbal, we become more and more aware of what those seventeenth century gardens must have been. What a variety of plants, little seen in our own gardens, were commonly grown in tiny cottage plot, city grounds or country estate. Parkinson notes of some plants that he has given a complete description in the *Paradisus* to which interested readers should turn. He speaks of plants from America, from the Orient and some from Russia, the latter brought by the botanist John Tradescant from a voyage around North Cape to Russia. Parkinson himself was proud to have discovered several native plants such as the Welsh poppy and a variety of lady's slipper. He writes of the common garden sage, of "Balme" and hyssop, but of rosemary he says: "Our ordinary garden Rosemary is so well knowne, I think to all manner of persons being continually in their hands, that I shall scarce need to describe it." In writing of basil, he says: "There are divers sorts of Basill, the most whereof are very great strangers to our Nation, and but entertained by a few that are curious and industrious." Parkinson indeed was one of these.

When Parkinson died in 1650 he was 83 years old. Gerard had died at 67, Turner at 58. These are the three great English herbalists, the authors of those great tomes of heroic size, each containing thousands of illustrations. But there followed two other and much younger men who, too, became of note. Both wrote herbals but they were relatively tiny things and illustrations played no part in them. They were exponents of conflicting theories concerning herbs. One was Nicholas Culpeper and the other William Cole or Coles.

Culpeper must have had a particularly strong personality to have been so loved and so hated. His father was a clergyman in Surrey. He went to Cambridge, was later an apothecary's apprentice, was a fighting Roundhead, an astrologer, an herbalist in Red Lion Street, Spitalsfield, where he died at 38 in the year 1654. His open-handedness to worthy and unworthy alike, his youth, good looks, a disposition gay though melancholy, his independence, all combined to make a most attractive, cynical young man, beloved by the poor. There at Spitalsfield in London he had his garden of English medicinal herbs and scorned the many precious foreign plants such as Gerard and Parkinson had collected. These were not within the reach of the poor. He studied the stars and the herbs and wrote down in plain English the relation between them. He believed that certain parts of the body were governed by different planets, that the planet in the ascendant when the patient was ill determined the herb to be given. Like the doctor in Chaucer's time,

"To speke of phisik and of surgerye;
For he was grounded in astronomye."

The belief in astrologo-physical methods of treating patients had been current from early times and a great many people still put a good deal of faith in it. William Coles, who wholly scorned Culpeper, said: "Although I admit not of Master Culpeper's Astrologicall way of Planets Dominion over Plants yet I conceive that the Sunne and Moon have general influences upon them, the one for Heat, the other for Moisture . . ."

Charging a small fee with little to-do of manner annoyed the learned College of Physicians, whom Culpeper describes as a "company of proud, insulting, domineering doctors, whose Wits were born about 500 years before themselves." But the act which put Culpeper absolutely beyond the pale was his publication in 1649 of "A Physicall Directory or a translation of the London Dispensatory Made by the College of Physicians in London . . . with many hundred additions." Culpeper had not only translated this book into English so that it could be read by anyone but he had had the effrontery to comment on the book, on the formulas and on the College of Physicians itself. Until then the pharmacopœia had been for the elect. It was an exclusive tome consulted by those learned doctors who could read Latin, or thought they could, and not to be pawed over by the vulgar. And then came this upstart of 33 with no authorization, making it possible for his poor clientele and the common people everywhere to delve into its mysteries. The dignified College never ceased to attack Culpeper, even after his death. In 1652 they released a broadside with a long title beginning "A farm in Spittlefields where all the knick-knacks of astrology are exposed to open sale."

The sale of knick-knacks and of books was, however, enormous, and by that time, too, had appeared Culpeper's herbal with the title:

"The English Physician or an Astrological Discourse of the Vulgar Herbs of this Nation being a Compleat Method of Physick whereby a man may preserve his Body in health; or cure himself being sick, for three pence charge, with such things one-ly as grow in England, they being most fit for English Bodies."

He pointed out that few authors had written on the astrological relation of the herbs and those few "were so full of nonsense and contradictions as an Eg full of meat." He listed 369 English medicinal herbs, their properties, and the planet by which each was governed, and gave a description so that anyone might recognize it unless, like the elder, it was too well known to deserve any space, "sith every Boy that plaies with a potgun will not mistake another Tree instead."

Culpeper warned readers to beware of false copies and the warning proved necessary. After his death in 1654 numerous pirated editions were printed by envious publishers, usually including a spurious letter to Mrs. Culpeper as a preface. Mrs. Culpeper promptly wrote a "Vindication and Testimony" which was inserted as a preface in all genuine copies but it had little effect and reprints of the pirated editions appeared even as late as the nineteenth century. Close to 250 separate editions of Culpeper have been traced.

William Coles, like Culpeper, was raised in the atmosphere of the church but attended Oxford University, then went to London and settled in Putney, then a little village, where he died in 1662 at the age of 36, "the most famous Simpler or Herbarist of his time," as Anthony à Wood describes him in the annals of the university. His fame is now somewhat obscured by the rarity of his books, *The Art of Simpling* and *Adam in Eden*. As Mr. Albert E. Lownes has pointed out, Coles was one of the first writers, perhaps the first, to write in the plain, direct, colloquial English soon to be recommended by the Royal Society.

The facts of Coles' life do not indicate difficulties or Causes except one young man's quarrel with another over two bases of administering simples. Culpeper believed the answer was in the stars, Coles that it was in the plants themselves. Both were old, old beliefs, Coles having a little the better of the argument in that some plants, whose value appears through the Doctrine of Signatures, are still used for the diseases that he mentions. Even "Weeds and poysonous Plants" were not created in vain, he points out, for they would not be without their use "if they were good for nothing else but to exercise the Industry of Man to weed them out, who had he nothing to struggle with, the fire of his Spirit would be halfe extinguished in the Flesh."

The first issue (1656) of *The Art of Simpling* carries stinging attacks against Culpeper, "a man now dead, and therefore I shall speak of him as modestly as I can, for were he alive, I should be more plain with him." A sample of this modest speech occurs where he speaks of Culpeper as

"a man very ignorant in the forme of Simples. Many Books indeed he hath tumbled over, and transcribed as much out of them, as he thought would serve his turne (though many times he were therein mistaken) but added very little of his owne."

This issue was dedicated to Elias Ashmole but Ashmole was a leading astrologer and Coles' attacks upon astrologers were scathing. What happened, no record discloses. However, within the year the offending passages were removed from the book and the dedication to Ashmole omitted. The issue with 1657 upon the title page bears but little trace of the controversy and even indicates that Coles had accepted for his own the views of the astrologers. Years later when Anthony à Wood asked Ashmole about Coles, Ashmole's reply dated July 3, 1682, indicated that Coles, like others who had dedicated books to him, was a stranger of whom he had never heard after.

The Art of Simpling, a tiny volume, is the most readable of all the herbals. It contains no description of plants, no illustrations, but a series of thirty-three delightful essays: "Of Simpling, its Antiquity, Dignity, Pleasure, and usefulness in Physick, etc."; "Of the differences of Roots"; "Plants for making Cloth, Cordage, etc."; "Of Plants used in, and against Witchcraft." Throughout the book Coles, the gardener, shines through. How much he really loved the garden is revealed in Chapter XXXII, "Of the Speculative and pleasant use of a Garden," which I reproduce here in its entirety from my copy dated 1657:

"To leave off the properties of Simples, we come now to the conveniences of a Garden, which are manifold in respect of Speculation, by which I mean meer walking, or at most, but gathering such things as please them, which I count no labour, for that I intend to oppose as the practicall use. That there is no place more pleasant, may appear from God himselfe, who after he had made Man, planted the Garden of Eden, and put him therein, that he might contemplate the many wonderful Ornaments wherewith Omnipotency had bedecked his Mother Earth. It was not so much for Adams recreation, who at that time was not acquainted with wearinesse, as it was for his Instruction, but to us it will serve for both. There is not a Plant which growes but carries along with it the legible Characters of a Deity, according to the verse:

Presentemque refert quoelibet herba Deum.

As for recreation, if a man be wearied with over-much study (for study is a wearinesse to the Flesh as Solomon by experience can tell you) there is no better place in the world to recreate himselfe then a Garden, there being no sence but may be delighted therein. If his sight be obfuscated and dull, as it may easily be, with continuall poring, there is no better way to relieve it, then to view the pleasant greennesse of Herbes, which is the way that Painters use, when they have almost spent their sight by their most earnest contemplation of brighter objects: neither doe they onely feed the Eyes, but comfort the wearied Braine with fragrant smells, which yeild a certaine kinde of nourishment, as will appear by the following stories. My Lord Bacon in his Naturall History reporteth, that he knew a Gentleman that would fast sometimes foure or five dayes without any manner of sustenance: In which time he would have lying by him a wispe of Herbes, to which he would smell now and then, having in it, Garlick, Onyons and othes Esculents of strong scent. Doctor Hackwill in his Apology for the worlds not decaying, tells a story of a German Gentlewoman, who lived fourteen yeares without receiving any nourishment downe her throat, but onely walked frequently in a spacious Garden full of Odoriferous Herbes and Flowers. And that this is possible is further apparent by the story of Democritus, who when he lay a dying, heard his Nursekeeper complaine, that she should be kept from being at a Feast and Solemnity (which she much desired to see) because there would be a Corps in the house; whereupon he caused Loaves of new bread to be sent for, and opened them, and so kept himselfe alive with the odour of them till the Feast was past. The Eares also (which are called the Daughters of Musick, because they delight therein) have their recreation by the pleasant noise of the warbling notes, which the chaunting birds accent forth from amongst the murmuring Leaves. As for the Taste, they serve it so exceedingly, that whether it be affected with sweet, sower or bitter things, they even prostitute themselves. And for the feeling likewise, they entertaine it with as great variety as can be imagined, there being some Plants as soft as silke, and some as prickly as an Hedgehogge; so that there is no outward sense which can want satisfaction in this Cornucopia. And if the outward senses be so delighted, the inward will be so too, it being as it were, the School of Memory and Fancy. Hereupon it was that the antient Poets did so much extoll the Gardens of Alcinous and the Hesperides. The grove of Mars was not unknowne to Juvenal, neither were there any Poets which had not recesses into those sacred places: The first institutor of them at Athens was, Epicureus, in which he had a School where he taught, one that knew as much what belonged to pleasure as any Man: Seneca the P[h]ilosopher was likewise a great admirer of them, and is said to have expended vast summes of Money this way. A house though otherwise beautifull, yet if it hath no Garden belonging to it, is more like a Prison then a House."

In 1657 Coles published *Adam in Eden, or Nature's Paradise,* a far larger and more detailed treatise of some 629 pages of plant description, signatures and virtues, and lists following those pages, creating a thorough index not only of Latin and English names of plants, but also of their uses from "Abortions, remedied" to "Yellowes, in horses cured." Whatever the Ashmole experience had taught him, we find that this book is dedicated to the "Truly Noble and Perfect Lover of Learning, Sir William Paston, Knight and Baronet" and the reason is not concealed. In case any "Malevolent Spirits" should "cast forth their venemous detractions and aspersions upon it," the luster of Paston's name would frighten them away. There were other laudatory reasons given for the dedication but that one seems to be dominant.

In his letter to the reader, Coles said: "I hope I shall not need any motives to encourage the green Herbarist to this study. If Pleasures may invite him, what fairer objects are there for the sight then these painted Braveries?

What Odours can ravish the sense of smelling more than
those of flowers?" Not only to the green herbarist, then,
has the garden appealed but to learned doctor and clergyman, those whom we think of as buried in books, to whom
the out-of-doors would have no more than an academic
appeal. All these were lured out of the study into the sunshine, into the garden.

Dr. Salmon's huge *Herbal* of 1710 was the swan song
of the great herbalists. He was an astrologer, alchemist
and botanist, a prolific writer and a book collector. In this
herbal he gives not only the full account of the plants but
also the preparations made from them and how these
preparations are distinguished. But the herbals had
served their purpose. Caspar Bauhin's "Pinax theatri
botanici" had given the world a natural system of classification of plants and introduced the binomial method of
nomenclature often ascribed to Linnaeus. A science of
botany was on its way. The College of Physicians was
taking medicine from the hands of herbalists. The household "Receipt Books," forerunners of our cook books,
had appeared, garden books had multiplied, the "Golden
Age" of herbalists was over. But a little bit of sentiment
touches us as we turn the pages of the old volumes. They
still are treasures.

CHAPTER III

Beginnings of the Flower Garden

"*For out of olde feldes, as men seith,*
Cometh al this newe corn fro yeer to yere;
And out of olde bokes, in good feith,
Cometh al this newe science that men lere."

—CHAUCER (1340–1400).

In medieval England, the garden of the mistress of a castle was limited by walls, while the little plot of the cottage housewife was compassed within the few feet permitted by the huddling of buildings together. Of course, the farm lands of the lord and the areas allotted to tenants were beyond protection and often were trampled down by the soldiers of quarrelsome barons in search of a fight. The problem of the gardener then, before the sixteenth century, was to grow as many purely useful herbs as possible within a small space. It was a utilitarian garden.

As the foreign herbals or translations of them began to drift into England, perhaps a knight and his lady, if they could read or someone in their service could, would be inspired to take a really good look at the plants pictured in the book. Many were in their own gardens; others, un-

59

known to them, were grown beyond the seas. How they must have longed for more garden space wherein they might coddle a stranger-plant till it grew to like English soil.

But this dream of many a dweller of castle and cottage was not materialized until 1485, when Henry VII ascended the throne after the defeat of Richard III. He determined that never again would barons be allowed to become so powerful that a king could be overthrown. It was forbidden to fortify castles, and in time the castle moat was filled in, the grounds were no longer a thoroughfare for armed retainers, and the little gardens began to spread out. Many of the poorly built cottages of the tenants were torn down, and when rebuilt spread out comfortably beyond the cramped areas of the towns. With this feeling of safety and expansion, more attention was given to gardens and getting the most from farm land. Gardeners from France, from Italy, from Holland, were invited to England to consult about these bigger and better gardens. With all this renaissance of gardening, Englishmen who had never put pen to paper suddenly grew articulate. They translated foreign books on gardening or wrote about their own farms, orchards and gardens, and advised others how it all should be done. And the "others" clamored for those writings.

For instance, there was Thomas Tusser, living long enough on his land in East Anglia to put his farming ideas into practice and then into print, so that his *Five Hundreth Points of Good Husbandry,* written in 1573, was in such demand that 13 editions were made within the next 25 years. Even as late as the nineteenth century several new editions appeared. Thomas Fuller, of *Worthies of England* fame, said of Tusser that "He was successively a musician, schoolmaster, serving man, husbandman, grazier, poet, more skilful in all than thriving in any profession. . . . Whether he bought or sold, he lost. . . . Yet hath he laid down excellent rules in his book of husbandry and housewifery, so that the observer thereof must be rich, in his own defence." Warton wrote of him, "Without a tincture of careless imprudence or vicious extravagance, this desultory character seems to have thrived in no vocation." Yet at Tusser's death, his brother owed him about $1500, so he could not have been very poor, and he left several good sized bequests.

As a boy, Thomas was given singing lessons in a music school and was soon placed as a chorister in the collegiate chapel of the Castle of Wallingford, and having a fine voice was pressed into service in several choirs, finally being admitted into St. Paul's, London, under John Redford. From St. Paul's he went to Eton, then to Cambridge, first at King's College, then to Trinity, but a long sickness cut his university life short, and during the latter part of the reign of Henry VIII he was employed about the court, his patron being William Lord Paget, in whose family Tusser appears to have been a retainer, but, disgusted with the life at court, he became a farmer in a hamlet now named Cattiwade, in Suffolk. Here he wrote *A hundreth good pointes of husbandrie,* 1557, a small quarto of only 13 leaves containing the dedication to Lord Paget and the "Pointes" in 109 quatrains, for the 12 months, a sort of prelude to his much larger book to come. His wife died shortly afterwards when he had moved to Ipswich, and he went to West Dereham and then to Norwich, where he probably sang in the cathedral. He married one Amy Moon, much younger than he, and again took up farming at Fairsted near Rivenhall, his birthplace in Essex, as a tithe farmer, but soon gave it up and returned to London. The plague in 1574 drove him to Cambridge, but not until his *Five hundreth points of good husbandry united to as many of good huswifery* was published in 1573, following no less than four editions of the earlier work.

What a portrait of himself and of a sixteenth century existence this enlarged book paints, all in rhyming couplets. We feel that he was kindly but exacting, with an eye to the last farthing, keeping a strict watch over household management. In the *Points of Huswifery* he discusses many details, all the "doings" of the day from Breakfast Doings to After Supper Matters, Baking, Washing, Table Lessons, Admonitions to the Huswife. But in the husbandry section he is more at home and speaks with evident liking. His books were the ancestors of all our Farmer's Almanacs, both being divided under the headings of the twelve months, the first beginning in August, but the larger book starts with September.

The farmer learns what tools he should have, when to plow, plant and harvest, how to care for the cattle, the farm land, the hedges, the trees, fences, ditches, how to raise hops.

Tusser writes so simply and directly that we can see the farm hands working on the land, the harvest festival that capped the season's work, the Christmas festivities in progress, the dairy maids making butter and cheese, the wife and maids making bed and table linen, preserving and storing food for the winter. We see them concocting medicines for the household and tenants.

> "Good huswives provide, ere an' sickness do come,
> Of sundry good things, in her house to have some."

This providing, the housewife has been busy doing since early spring with Thomas' help. Although by his alert mind he organized the other activities of farm and home, the carrying forward of the garden engaged his heart. He loved the fragrant activity about it, lacking in such dull work as sowing and harvesting great fields of grain. The garden was different, a smaller soul-satisfying area. If he had lived in our day of brilliant, alluring seed catalogues, his "must" list each year would have been long enough to bankrupt him. As it was, there were few new varieties except what he might get by exchange with other garden lovers.

> "Good huswives in summer will save their owne seeds
> Against the next year, or occasion needs:
> One seed for another, to make an exchange,
> With fellowly neighbourhood, seemeth not strange."

But Tusser had seven "must" lists that he considered necessary for a household, an amazing variety, names of herbs but rarely seen now as skirrets, samphire; and others commonly used today such as beets, cabbages, carrots, beans. He was discriminating to the top degree, not crudely jumbling his plants into just vegetables and flowers. Of his culinary herbs he lists 42 under Seeds and Herbs for the Kitchen, including primrose, marigold, tansy, violets. Then he lists 22 herbs and roots for salads and sauces, such as artichokes, sage, asparagus, and again violets. Eleven of our common vegetables appear under "Herbs and Roots, to Boil or to Butter." The 21 strewing herbs he listed were, of course, important for the floors of his farmhouse, and how fragrant they must have been when freshly strewn with lavender, lavender cotton, pennyroyal, roses, mints, violets, savory! There were 17 herbs to be distilled in summer and 25 to be used for medicine. But 40 herbs were listed as "Herbes, Branches, and floures for windows and pots." What a picture this garden of Tusser's recalls, a beautiful old-fashioned garden such as we may have seen on our grandmother's farm of long ago. There was a medley of flowers, some bearing names long forgotten but loved and cherished in the old days, as they are now under other names . . . daffydowndillies, flower de luce, Queen's gillyflowers, sweetbrier, lark's foot, heartsease, paggles, sops in wine, sweet Williams, sweet Johns, holyoaks.

In this book of Tusser's we have the first complete picture of an English farm and country garden told by the gardener himself. Can't you see him, tired but satisfied with his day's work? "Come," he calls, as he turns toward the door, and out dances his young wife, Amy Moon, takes his arm, and down they stroll in the long English twilight through the fragrant garden, as millions of happy couples will do in the ages that are to follow.

The English had long been interested in having trees in the garden. In the early pleasaunces, however small, there were trees and if not room for more than one, that one was in a prominent spot, the center usually, where later the fountain was to be. Fascinated by the cultivation of trees, nothing much was known about it until Leonard Mascall in 1572 made a book compiled from two sources, one of which was a French book written by "one of the Abbey of Saint Vincent in France" and the other a Dutch source he does not name. Although this compilation did not attain the popularity of Tusser's, there were several editions, as there were of nearly every early gardening book. Mascall's book told "how to plant and graffe all sortes of trees, how to set stones, and some Pepines to make wyld trees to graffe on, as also remedies and medicines," a title with allure enough to attract almost any gardener.

There not being any English books about grafting at the time, Mascall, who was an educated man, had looked abroad for this material and thus published his translations. He also compiled a book of husbandry and fishing for the farmer and the angler. Into the moat which surrounded Plumpton Place, his home in Sussex, he is supposed to have placed the first carp to be seen in England. But Mascall's claim to fame will always be based on his translation and publishing in English of the early book on tree grafting, an art to be pursued with gusto by nearly every gardener within the next two hundred years.

These early English gardeners became interested in every kind of gardening brought to their attention. Hop raising attracted them when the Huguenot refugees showed how profitable a crop could be. Tusser devotes many a stanza to the care of hops.

> "The hop for his profit, I thus do exalt,
> It strengtheneth drink, and it favoureth malt
> And being well brewed, long kept it will last,
> And drawing abide, if ye draw not too fast."

Reynolde Scot in 1574 wrote a treatise on hops which bore a most formidable title but, simmered down, purported to give instructions for maintaining a hop garden and "rules for reformation of all abuses commonly practised therein, very necessarie and expedient for all men to have which in any wise have to doe with Hops." Among the delightful parts of the title are the maxims:

"Proverbs 11 Whoso laboureth after goodnesse findeth his disire. Sapien 7. Wisedome is nymbler than all nymble things. She goeth through and attayneth to all things."

Richard Gardiner of Shrewsbury, a merchant and a churchman, published a garden book in 1603, still remembered. It was believed to be the second edition of a work first published in 1597, the year of Gerald's *Herbal,* but the early edition has not been found and there were no later ones. The title of the book reveals his interest in helping others:

"Profitable Instructions for the Manuring, Sowing and Planting Kitchin Gardens. Very profitable for the commonwealth and greatly for the helpe and comfort of poore people."

There are a great many "firsts" in the gardening books of Tudor and Elizabethan times. To Gardiner goes the distinction, in his little 30-page booklet, of producing the first book solely on vegetables and the first seed catalogue we know. But though about vegetables only, the book has no sign of the potato in it, the one vegetable usually considered cheap and filling, but then known only as a prized rarity and not commonly grown for many years. By 1664 its usefulness was recognized and in an eight-line-titled book devoted to that vegetable alone, John Forster then told how "England's happiness may be increased by planting of these Roots, Ten thousand men in England and Wales, who know not how to Live or what to do to get a Maintenance for their Families, may of One Acre of Ground make Thirty Pounds per Annum."

But back at the earlier date, the panacea of starvation ills to Gardiner was carrots, which, he deplored, were imported from Holland. To a man who loved the soil, it seemed incredible that the English did not get out into their gardens and raise their own vegetables. Gardiner's severest chiding, however, was of the cheating seedsellers whom he called "Caterpillars," avowing that they yearly rob from the poor by selling them "olde and dead seedes." He held that though no laws on earth would punish these dishonest men, "the Almighty God doth beholde their monstrous deceipt and except those doe repent with

speed, both God and man will abhorre them as outragi-
ous theeves."

From devout preface to two concluding prayers we are
confronted by the militant churchman and Christian.
From seed time to harvest, his instructions are interrupted here and there by religious exhortations and re-
bukes. Gardiner concludes his tirade on seedsellers with
the wish not only that they would sell good seeds but
would be reasonable in the price. He himself sold seeds
and in the book he gives a price list which was certainly
modest in its demands. He had turnip seed at 12d a
pound, bean seed 2d a quart, and carrot seeds 2d "the
waxe pound without deceit."

Gardiner's invectives against cheaters, his railings at
the English for importing vegetables they could easily
grow, his prayers and preachings, all came from a true
earnestness to help "his loving neighbours and friends
within the towne of Shrewsburie in the countie of Salop."
At the beginning of the book, some lines of doggerel
verse by his friend, Edward Thorne, indicate that he did
really help, although we have no information as to
whether his book had any effect in teaching them to live
more by their own labor on the land. Thorne's lines include

> "The poore which late were like to pine,
> and could not buy them breade:
> In greatest time of penury
> were by his laboure fed."

but, of course, these lines were written before the book
appeared.

Hugh Plat, Cambridge graduate and lawyer, though
he seems never to have practiced, was a man of means
who lived between 1552 and 1608, at a period when the

eyes of gardeners were opened to the broader possibilities of gardening by what seemed to them limitless space and endless varieties of plants. The garden became a gardener's paradise, and so it was thought of as a Garden of Eden where grew all that was lovely and fragrant and wonderful. There man would find the complete life. In his beautiful gardener's paradise at Bishops Hall, Bethnal Green and at Kirby Castle, Hugh Plat experimented, studied and turned his active brain upon inventions little dreamed of before his time. The results of his life in and about his garden, however, were in the main not presented to the public until the year he died, when his *Floraes Paradise* was published, to be called in later editions *Garden of Eden*. Still other gardeners caught the spirit of this practically unhampered freedom for the scope of one's ideas, and we find in 1629 the *Paradisus* of Parkinson and in 1657 Coles' *Adam in Eden*.

What a versatile mind was Plat's, typical of the Elizabethan age, individualistic, alert to seize upon an idea and make it his own. In his *Jewel-house of Art and Nature,* published in 1594, we find all sorts of devices . . . "To helpe a chimney that is on fire presentlie"; "An excellent cement for broken Glasses"; "A readie way for children to learn their A B C"; "to keepe Inke from freezing and moulding." In 1602 came the *Delights for Ladies,* the first printed collection by itself of still-room recipes, written for the purpose of publication, concerned with the "Arte of Preserving Cookerie and Husewiferie," "sweete powders," ointments.

For his work Plat, in the last year of his life, was knighted by James I. In the British Museum today are many of his unpublished works on alchemy, "Secrets of Physicke and Surgery," etc., but we are most concerned here with the gardener. Plat was outstanding in that he did not consider the soil just something firm with which to prop up plants, but studied the needs of individual plants and disclosed information about what they most wanted. By this careful attention to soil he came to be regarded as an authority on the subject. But he was not a lone wolf nor did he set himself up unguided as a know-it-all. He knew or had correspondence with the important gardeners of his time and was always careful to give the source for information: Mr. Pointer of Twickenham, Mr. Tavener, Pigot the gardener, and many others.

Plat believed in carrying the garden to the house, by window boxes which we think of as modern, by training plants up over doorways, and by setting some in pots in the house. He suggested that many flowers might be forced by means of indoor heat.

Although we hear of vineyards in very early days in England, by the seventeenth century the making of wines had long since been left to France and Germany. Plat was convinced that it could be done again in England if gardeners would only give more attention to the soil. Parkinson, however, laid the blame on the unfavorable climate of England and to the art of cultivation being lost with the dissolution of monasteries, where the main vineyards had flourished.

Plat also was interested in orchards and discussed the soil, fertilizer, grafting and location of the apricot, a specially prized fruit introduced in Tudor times. "Mix cow-dung and hors-dung well rotted in fine earth and claret wine lees of each a like quantity." Applied to the roots of the trees this combination seemed to make the trees bear well, and "This of Mr. Andr. Hill." A true gardener at heart was Sir Hugh Plat, one who believed in the soil of England to make gardens, orchards and vineyards alike grow and flourish as they had done in the original Garden of Eden.

Gervase Markham, scion of a once wealthy family, was a soldier of fortune in the Low Countries, later a captain under the Earl of Essex in Ireland, acquainted with Latin and a linguist of several modern languages, a noted horseman, breeder, and importer of the first

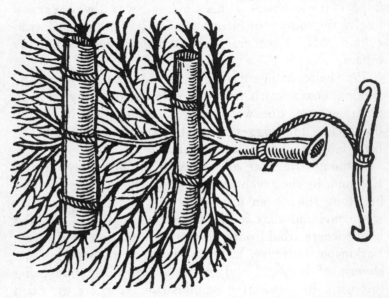

Markham's Horse-Drawn Harrow.

From *Farewell to Husbandry*, 1660.

Arabian horse to England. He had a wide practical knowledge of forestry and agriculture, was well versed in the details of ordering a household, but above all had something more than a boundless enthusiasm for writing.

Widespread as were his interests in life, as a writer he was equally versatile and prolific. We are amazed at such works as "Marie Magdalene's Tears," a long poem on the Passion and Resurrection of Christ; "Herod and Antipates," a tragedy written in collaboration with William Sampson; "A Discourse of Horsemanshippe"; "The Souldier's Accidence." Markham's booksellers, however, were more amazed at the great number of books he could produce in a short time. Rumor hath it that different titles given to books on the same subject and new titles to former books that had not been sold, answered the natural question. Finally, in 1617, the booksellers drew from Markham a statement that he would produce no more books on certain subjects. Sifting out his gardening books from the number, we rejoice in the *English Husbandman* done in two parts, the first in 1613, the second in 1614, and both brought together in 1635.

In the first part of *English Husbandman,* Markham comprehensively undertakes to discuss the "true Nature of every Soyle within this Kingdom" and the necessary farm implements. Besides that, he includes "the Art of Planting Grafting and Gardening," vineyards, hop gardens, preservation of all sorts of fruit, and gives the "Draught of all sorts of Knots, Mazes, and other Ornaments." The great value of the book is the picture we get of a formally laid out estate of Stuart times.

By that period the form of architecture was well established, the central hall flanked by small rooms, those on the south giving on the garden. The garden had not outgrown the medieval pleasaunce with trees as a chief feature, and a fountain and "banqueting house" where the owners could spend many hours out of doors in rain or shine. The garden of pleasure was laid out in shrub mazes and knots, the paths between being of gravel or sand, which were better for walking in "the evening dews and damps," besides being a pleasing contrast to the prevailing garden green.

In 1638 in *A Way to Get Wealth*, Markham gives "Sixe Principall Vocations or Callings, in which every good Husband or Housewife may law-fully imploy themselves." The first is the care of cattle, fowl and horses; the second is the knowledge and practice of all the recreations meet for a Gentleman. The third section is the "Office of a Housewife in Physicke" etc., originally appearing as the *English Housewife* in 1615, while the fourth section is the "Enrichment of the Weald in Kent," and the fifth is Markham's "Farewell to Husbandry" or "the inrichment of barren grounds making them equall with the most fruitfull." That last title might well have been a welcome note to the bookseller. However, an addition all by itself, tacked on after the last table of contents, has its appeal. It is given here:

ADDITION

An excellent way to take Moals, and to preserve good Ground, from such annoyance.

Put Garlick, Onions, or Leeks, into the mouths of the holes, and they will come out quickly as amazed.

Markham's one extensive work of editing was that of Richard Surflet's *The Countrie Farme*, a translation in 1600 by Surflet of the *Maison Rustique*, which in 1573 was "compyled in the French Tongue by Charles Stevens and John Liebault, Doctors of Physicke." Markham's edition was published in 1616 and was dedicated to Lord Willoughbie with the comment that, "It first belonged to your Noble and Heroical Father as the gift of a learned and well experienced Gentleman, who in the translation, tooke a long and well meriting labour; it must needs then, now be yours both by order and inheritance." Markham says that when it came to the father's

hands it was all French except the language, so that
people were uncertain about trying out in England directions for French soil, but he fixed everything. "Now it is
put into other garments, and how homely soever the
stuffe be; yet . . . it will become any Husbandman of this
Kingdome."

This large and pleasant treatise, and truly it breathes
of the garden, is divided into seven parts; the first part
deals with the location of the house, the state and "dutie"
of the farmer, his wife, people, cattle, fowl, etc. The
second part, "Of Gardens," has the most charm for
us, though the other parts on fruit and nut trees, distilling, meadows, tilling, vineyards, woods to be made
into parks for wild beasts, are instructive. There is a
complete and exhaustive chapter on tobacco.

Right at the beginning of the garden section, the author
describes the layout of the seventeenth century country
farm garden. First,

"the Kitchin Garden: which hath been devised and appointed to joine to one side of the Garden of pleasure,
and yet separated from it by the intercourse of a great
Alley of the breadth of three fathomes, having either a
Well or a Conduit from some Fountaine in the middest
there of"

and all surrounded by a "Quickset hedge" in which there
are three doors, one to the house, one to the well, the
other to the orchard. And there you have a typical garden
on the best authority.

The author then discusses the sowing of the culinary
herbs, the "physicke hearbes," the garden of pleasure
or flower garden, not only to serve the "chiefe Lord,
whose the inheritance is, to solace himselfe therein, as also
in respect of their service, for to set Bee-hives in." Then

we see the lovely garden, with "delightfull borders of Lavender, Rosemarie, Boxe"; we "heare the ravishing musicke of an infinite number of pretie small Birdes, . . . and to smell so sweet a Nose-gay so neere at hand." Then comes a description of the herbs for flowers or nosegays, the March violets, gillyflowers, daisies, lily-of-the-valley, "Narcyssus," hyacinth, tulip, peony, daffodils, "Canterburie-bells," and many others. Then the sweet smelling herbs, such as basil, mint, thyme, marjoram, savory, sage, rosemary, caraway, dill, melilot, balm.

After this, we are told how to lay out knots, how to set and care for trees, how to raise bees, and the "remeding of strange accidents that may happen unto hearbes." And there follows such a collection of insects, frogs, snails, adders, besides hail, frost, blasting, birds, little beasts, scorpions, it fairly makes you shudder. But Markham had recognized a good opportunity to edit, and we can forgive him most of his failings generously, for having given us this one book.

"Butcher, baker, candlestick maker!" Though they could not have written upon law, science, philosophy, politics, yet they were all drawn together in a common interest of gardens and were articulate about them. We have heard from an East Anglican farmer, a Shropshire merchant, a well-to-do lawyer, a horse breeder experienced in the ways of the world. Now comes a simple-hearted Yorkshire gardener, William Lawson, who must needs tell his own countrymen how their gardens can be improved, "all being the experience of 48 yeares labour." As he says in his "Preface to all well minded,"

"Where upon have I of my meere and sole experience, without respect to any former written treatise gathered these rules & set them downe in writing, not daring to hide the least talent given me of my Lord and Master in Heaven."

Nothing was taken from the ancient and time-honored classic authorities upon whom botanists, herbalists and many gardening writers before him had leaned so heavily. This north country gardener had studied the soil of that locality, tried growing various plants and trees, and learned which ones thrived and why others did not, how to care for the bees, what kind of boundaries were best for the garden, what the country housewife needed to grow in her garden. No ancient writing could tell what a north country English garden needed. Although other writers had told of husbandry in glowing terms, "how ancient, how profitable, how pleasant . . . how loved, how much practiced in the best places . . . I only aime at the common good. . . . I shew a plaine and sure way of planting which I have found good by 48 yeares (and moe) experience in the North part of England." Lawson also assures us that "The stationer hath (as being most desirous with mee, to further the common good)" taken great pains with the cuts that nothing might be wanting in any way "to satisfie the curious desire of those that would make use of this Booke."

Through all Lawson's insistence that the book is merely to give unadorned instructions on the best method of cultivation, he does show us "how pleasant and how loved" the art of husbandry can be. A Yorkshire orchard, far north of London though it was, would be bright in spring with blossoms of apples, pears, cherries, plums, but "we meddle not with Apricoekes [newly introduced to England] nor Peaches nor scarcely with Quinces which will not like in our cold parts unlesse they be helped with some reflex of Sunne." Some of "our great Aborists," he says, "plant them by a wall, and with tackes" fasten them to it.

Lawson advises the form of orchard to be square, the old traditional form, and his stationer made a cut (reproduced in *Magic Gardens*) that has made Lawson's ideas live for centuries. Of the six squares, three are for trees, two with garden ornaments, the third a real

Fruit Tree.

Lawson thought it necessary to designate the proper terms "boall," "arme," "boughes," "braunches." From *A New Orchard and Garden,* 1638 edition.

orchard as we know it with trees 20 feet apart; one square is for a garden knot, and strange to say, the two squares for the kitchen garden are farthest away from the house. A fountain stands in the middle alley, beehives near the kitchen garden, mounts and still-houses at each corner.

"But all your labor on the orchard is lost unless you

fence well," and here Lawson adds a homely touch. Each owner should make the fence himself, "for neighbours fencing is none at all, or very carlesse," and in fact he didn't trust them much. "Take heed of a doore or window, (yea of a wall) of any other mans into your orchard; yea, though it be nayld up or the wall be high, for perhaps they will prove theeves." Lawson believed with Robert Frost's New Englander who said "Good fences make good neighbors," only the stronger and higher, the better.

Having given what he considers all possible necessary details about cultivation of trees, Lawson then enumerates the great profit accruing from the orchard, which he takes in the ancient sense of space for growing plants as well as trees, and concludes,

"Hee that will not bee moved with such unspeakable profits is well worthy to want, when other abound in plenty of good things."

Lawson leaves the "unspeakable pleasure" of the orchard for the last, and here we see why the old gardener loved it all:

"The very workes of, and in an Orchard and Garden, are better than the ease and rest of and from other labours."

He compares it, as others did, to a Paradise where God had placed man. "What was Paradise?" he cries, "but a Garden and Orchard of trees and hearbes full of pleasure? and nothing there but delights."

In the *Country House-wives Garden,* published in 1617, Lawson gives simple, definite instructions to women, the first gardening book in all the world written for women gardeners, and perhaps he felt that the simpler

THE
COVNTRY HOVSE-WIVES
GARDEN,

Containing Rules for Hearbs and Seeds
of Common ufe, with their times and feafous
when to fet and fow them.

Together,

With the Husbandry of Bees, publi-
fhed with fecrets very neceffary for every *Houfe-
wife*: As alfo diverfe new Knots for Gardens.

The Contents fee at large in the laft Page.

Genef. 2. 29.
*I have given unto you every Herbe, and every tree, that fhall bee to you for
meate.*

LONDON,
Printed by *Anne Griffin* for *Iohn Harrison,* at the Golden
Vnicorne in Pater-nofter-row. 1637.

The title page of the first gardening book written for women;
the author, William Lawson.

it was made, the better. But in *A New Orchard and Garden*, 1618, Lawson's enthusiasm cannot be held back and readers over 300 years later are still grateful for the picture of that Yorkshire orchard and garden painted in fragrant words by a gardener who had loved those "48 yeares of labour."

In the previous chapter we saw John Parkinson, the herbalist, collecting botanical specimens from near and far to be recorded in his *Theatrum Botanicum*, by which he hoped to be remembered down through the ages, but it was as a gardener surrounded by friendly flowers, not medicinal simples, that he was destined to be known through his *Paradisi in Sole Paradisus Terrestris*, his own Paradise or Park-in-Sun, this "Speaking Garden," as he called it. He dedicated the book to Henrietta Maria whom he knew to be really "delighted with all the faire Flowers of a garden," and whose particular favorite was the white flowered lavender.

Parkinson tells in his letter "To the courteous Reader" that his purpose in writing the book is to enlarge on other writings, giving many flowers not known before and describing them fully; to discuss the "Herbes and Rootes" that are edible; to tell of fruit trees "fit for this our Land and Countrey." Fully three-quarters of the book is about the Garden of Pleasure, with hundreds of woodcuts of the flowers. After eight introductory chapters discussing soil, location, knots, the nature and needs of "outlandish" or foreign flowers, and of English flowers, he devotes one very interesting chapter to the impossibility of making a double from a single flower, changing its color, or making it bloom out of season. His last sentence will find sympathy with gardeners everywhere whose visitors expect their gardens to be in full bloom the whole year round:

"There is no power or art in man, to cause flowers to show their beauty divers moneths before their naturall time, nor to abide in their beauty longer than the appointed naturall time for every one of them."

As we read the *Paradisus,* the spring and early summer-like quality of it strikes us, for the emphasis is on the lilies, crocus, daffodils, cowslips, primroses, iris, hyacinth, violets, tulips. What a spring garden we have there! After the initial book on the ordering of a garden, he begins thus:

"The Crowne Imperiall for his stately beautifulness, deserveth the first place in this our Garden of delight, to be here entreated of before all other Lillies."

From there on, page after page is like the gradual blossoming of spring. Before us unfold innumerable varieties of the spring flowers, the yellow Beares eares "that seeme to be a Nosegay alone," the Lilly Convally "of very strong sweete sent and comfortable for the memory and senses," the "checkered Daffodill or Ginnie Hen flower."

We learn much about the life and hard times of the plants in his garden, and vicissitudes of others in the gardens of his friends. The woolly Iacinth [hyacinth] "hath been sent divers times out of Turkie into England where it continued a long time as well in my garden as in others, but some hard frosty winters caused it to perish with me, and divers others, yet I have had it againe from a friend and doth abide fresh and greene every yeare in my garden. This flowred in the Garden of Mr. Richard Barnafley at Lambeth onely once in the moneth of May in the yeere 1606 after hee had there preserved it a long time: but neither he, nor any one else in England that

I know but those that saw it at that time ever saw it beare flower, either before or since." And such was the interest that Parkinson took in unusual varieties.

Many are the people who sent him flowers, Guillaume Boel, a Freezelander born, Mr. Humfrey Packington of Worcestershire, Esquire at Harvington, . . . many he had simply "of a friend."

Pansies, or "hartsease," came under the classification of violets, the viola tricolor, "Some give it foolish names as Love in idleness, Cull mee to you, and Three faces in a hood." Perhaps the botanist in Parkinson rebelled against such unbotany. Would he have liked better our name Johnny-jump-up? Indian cresses or yellow Larkes heeles (nasturtiums to us) "which is of so great beauty and sweetnesse withall that my Garden of delight cannot bee unfurnished without it . . . being placed in the middle of some Carnations or Gilloflowers (for they are in flower at the same time) make a delicate Tussimussie, as they call it, or Nosegay, both for sight and sent."

Of the honeysuckle Parkinson says, "The Honisuckle that groweth wilde in every hedge, although it be very sweete, yet doe I not bring it to my garden but let it rest in his owne place, to serve their senses that travell by it, or have no garden." That is so typical of Parkinson, the desire that there may be flowers in woods and fields, as well as in the garden, to please passers-by, particularly those who have no gardens. His would have been a powerful voice upraised today to protect our wildflowers from people who have no love for the flowers they kill.

As Leonard Mascall had in 1572 by his translation of the French and Dutch books given an incentive to growing fruit trees, so Ralph Austen, dissenting somewhat from what had been published nearly a century before, in 1653 wrote his *Treatise of Fruit-Trees,* then in 1658 his

Observations upon some part of Sir Francis Bacon's Naturall History as it concernes Fruit trees, Fruits and Flowers and in 1676 *A Dialogue . . . betweene the Husbandman and Fruit-trees in his Nurseries, Orchards and Gardens.*

The English had given little attention to growing vegetables and seemed quite satisfied to import them, but in that early time fruit had always interested them. Mascall in his translation had, of course, discussed cultivation of trees on the Continent, but Austen gives definite instruction for grafting, setting, pruning and ordering them on English soil, which may be "improved in a short time, by small cost and little labour." In his earliest book he puts forth the claim that his learning had come through 20 years of experience and experiment of much that has been wrong "both in ye Theory and Practise of ye Art of Planting Fruit-trees." In the next book he tells that he has made improvements on the experiments made in the fifth, sixth, and seventh centuries, while in the *Dialogue* we catch the spiritual interest of Austen in orchards. The Husbandman says, "Methinks yee swagger and are very brace this May-morning; in your beautifull blossoms, and greene leaves, whence had yee all this gallantrie?" and the Fruit trees answer, "It pleased our Creator to bestow it upon us; but it is for thee . . . and all men to acknowledge it; and to serve him and praise him with more chearefullnesse: This is our language and lesson to all Men."

While Austen thus encouraged fruit growing, William Hughes was urging again the restoration of vineyards, which he thought could be grown in England to great profit. In his *Compleat Vineyard,* 1665, he gives not only the method of cultivation "according to the German and French way but also long experimented in England," but he doesn't stop with the cultivation; he goes into the methods of wine-making, a further incentive to gardeners in growing vines.

There were other gardeners at this time who felt the need of telling others of their experience, Stephen Blake, for example, who published *The Compleat Gardeners Practice* in 1664. He divided his book into three parts, the "Garden of Pleasure," the "Physical Garden," and the "Kitchin Garden," and prefaced them all on the title page with this modest couplet:

"Search the World, and there's not to be found
A Book so good as this for Garden Ground."

What self-portraits these early gardening writers unwittingly painted in their writings! Leonard Meager's main complaint about other gardening books was their lack of "sure and particular Rules whereby a learner might benefit himself." He was going to make everything simple, "plainly without any deceitful Dress and unnecessary Flourishes," whereby his book might become "very useful for all sorts of Practitioners, yea though of very weak capacities."

The facts known about Meager are very scanty but his *The English Gardner* was highly popular, running into a dozen editions between 1670 and 1721. It was a "sure Guide to young Planters and Gardeners," dedicated to "the Worshipful Philip Hollman of Warkworth in the County of Northampton, Esq; Grace, Mercy and Peace be Multiplied." We learn that Meager "had the advantage and opportunity in your Worship's service" to study and practice gardening and had been a practitioner in the art "above Thirty Years," Hollman having been "rather as an Indulgent Father than a Master to me." And so the book is "intaken in thankfulness" and the "Tract is performed with so much Sincerity and Exactness" that he hopes his master will have no cause to be ashamed of it.

Book I of Meager's volume tells all about the cultivation of fruit trees in a direct, unadorned style, not a reference to any classic authorities, no bits of philosophy. At the end he presents an amazing list of varieties of fruit trees common to us, but in innumerable varieties, of cherries, plums, apricots, nectarines, peaches, apples, pears, figs, and he includes grapes. There are no less than five pages, listing somewhat over 100 varieties of pears, for instance, and 80 varieties of apples. All these fruits were from a catalogue which Meager said he had "of my very Loving friend Captain Gaule . . . who can furnish any that desireth with any of the sorts. . . ." Indeed, England had come a long way by industry in the cultivation and grafting of fruit.

Then follows the "Ordering of the Kitchin Garden," with first a discussion of vegetable herbs and then a catalogue of "Ordinary Herbs and Roots, by the View whereof any Gardener may readily call to mind what Sorts of Herbs he is to provide for the Furnishing of his Garden," far too many to be remembered, pages of sweet herbs, physick herbs, chopping herbs, sallet-herbs, and roots, nine sorts of "Pease," and many herbs to be pickled for winter salads.

The Garden of Pleasure, he says, should be in a spot where it forms a lovely picture to be seen from the house and where it is protected from cold winds, and you will have "in a manner a perpetual Spring, something or other continually in its Beauty, either Flowers, or ever Greens, except in extream Frost and Snow." In this section Meager tells how to form knots, while in the back of the book he adds a multitude of diagrams for garden forms. Our imagination conjures up a lovely garden, simply to read his list: candytufts, hollyhocks, marigolds, gillyflowers, crown imperials, hyacinths, primroses, violets, daisies, "Flower-de-luces."

Meager thus gives us simply and directly, as he promised, his own methods and the results of his experiments which he commends "to everyone that desires to practise the nearest way to the Art of Gardning." John Worlidge, however, in the same decade, was beginning to feel the impact of new ideas, of the grand manner of the eighteenth century, so that a pleasure garden laid out under his directions would have made Hyll, Tusser and Markham rub their eyes and wonder whether they were "seeing things." Worlidge felt there was a need for his book with the changing times.

"Any one would esteem it a grand deficiency in the improvement of this Art if none should have written of it since Mr. Parkinson, Sir Hugh Plat, Meager, and several others, because these had written before on the same subject."

I wonder whether those who had enjoyed the old formal simplicity of Elizabethan and Stuart times would have called the changes "improvements"!

Worlidge called his book, published in 1677, by the title *Systema Horti-culturae* and the title page sets forth the contents. Book I "Treateth of the . . . Arbours, Springs, Fountains, Water-works, Grottos, Statues and other Magnificent Or-naments of Gardens"; Book II "Treateth of all sorts of Trees and Flowers usually propagated in the Gardens of the best Florists"; Book III "Treateth of the Kitchin Garden . . . together with Instructions for the making of hot beds." The book is "Illus-

Systema
Horti-Culturæ
Or
The Art of
Gardening
By J.W.
Gent.

The frontispiece of the first English gardening book in the grand manner by John Worlidge, 1677.

trated with Scultures, representing the form of Gardens, according to the newest Models."

The design of Worlidge in setting forth these matters was not simply for the benefit of "such that have fair estates and pleasant Seats in the Country to adorn and beautifie them: But to encourage the honest and plain Country man in the improvement of his Ville." To achieve this "I have wav'd as near as I could all hard words and intricate expressions."

With the early herbalists, Worlidge believed in the salutary effect of breathing refreshing odors. The main entrance to the garden, he says, should be out "the best Room in your House or very near it, your Walks being places of divertisement after a sedentary repast. The Aromatick Odours they yield, pleasant refreshment after a gross dyet and such innocent exercises, the best digestive to weak Stomachs." Instead of taking a soda mint after a heavy dinner, how much more pleasant to stroll about the herb garden! Such a garden would be surrounded by a brick wall "best for growing fruit," and walks would be of paved stone that you may walk "securely underfoot in all weathers without prejudice to your self or walks."

Good solid arbors with windows and doors "usually term'd a Pleasure-house or Banqueting house may be made at some remote Angle of your Garden: For the more remote it is from your house, the more private will you be from the frequent disturbances of your Family and Acquaintance." Worlidge tells that this house may be erected on "a Mount," a feature nearly always found in early gardens. Thus far our Elizabethan gardeners would have been one with Worlidge; but they would have been shocked to find in the long section of the book on fountains fed by secret pipes underground "that when any Ladies unawares or casually walk or stand over them by the turning of a stopcock you may force the water upright under their coats to their sudden surprize." Surprize indeed!

Other fountains had figures that ejected water from their mouths. Some made "Musical Artificial sounds" until the cistern feeding the fountain was full. Then there were grottos or caves in the earth constructed so as to furnish a cool retreat on a hot day. Finally, there were statuary and figures of animals, glass dials, white painted flower pots and an aviary. Worlidge does not discuss the aviary since he is in favor of "an Aviary at large," that is, the whole garden should encourage the birds that they "may with their charming Notes, raize up our dull Spirits, that are too intent upon the cares of this world, and mind us of the Providence, the great God of the Universe hath over us, as well as these Creatures."

In Book II besides trees, Worlidge discusses many roses, among which he mentions that the "Damask Rose with some of its Leaves marked with a faint blush is usually termed the York and Lancaster Rose. I suppose because it was the first variegated Rose that was here known after the Uniting of the two Houses or Roses."

So we leave Worlidge to his ornamental garden and turn to one of another mind, and we read a note in his diary:

"12th November was the battle of Brentford, surprisingly fought. . . . I came in with my horse and arms just at the retreat . . . and on the 10th [of December] returned to Wotton, nobody knowing of my having been in his Majesty's army."

Such was John Evelyn's military contribution to the great Civil War in England. During all the troublous years

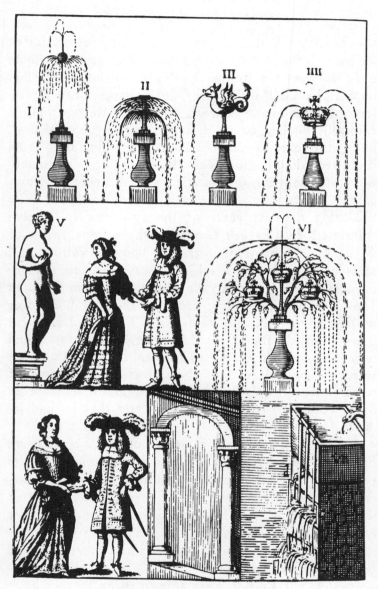

"All Sorts of Fountains."

From Worlidge, *Systema Horti-Culturae,* 1677.

that followed, during the Protectorate, the restoration of
Charles II, the bloodless revolution which placed William
and Mary on the throne, Evelyn remained quietly and
unobtrusively a Royalist. During the Protectorate he followed his gardening interests. After the Restoration, he
faithfully discharged the duties of many a political post,
hating the corruption of the Court, remaining aloof from
it all, recording in his famous diary nothing of personalities either political or domestic, as did his contemporary,
Samuel Pepys.

During the last years of the Protectorate, Evelyn
translated *The French Gardiner,* the original work of
N. de Bonnefons. This instructed "how to cultivate all
sorts of Fruit-trees," a subject always dear to Evelyn;
in most of his gardening the emphasis was on trees. In
1664 he published *Sylva,* probably the first book ever
written on conservation of forests. Trees had been cut
down wantonly for firewood for the glass factories and
iron furnaces, and there had been no organized attempt
to plant new ones to take their place. Evelyn, lover of
trees, was seriously concerned, and in the preface to
Sylva addressed to the King, he states that he had induced landowners to plant many millions of trees.

At the back of *Sylva* was printed the "Kalendarium
Hortense," a calendar of what to do each month of the
year, first in the orchard and olitory garden, and sec-
ondly in the parterre and flower garden. At the end of
the calendar is a twelve-page catalogue of such excellent
fruit trees and berry bushes "as may direct Gentlemen
to the Choice of that which is good and Store sufficient
for a moderate Plantation."

In 1693 the English were able to enjoy another book
of Evelyn's, his translation of *Directions for Cultivating
and Right Ordering of Fruit Gardens and Kitchen-*

Gardens, a work in six volumes originally written in French by De La Quintinye, head gardener of Louis XIV's fruit and kitchen gardens. This book was called *The Compleat Gard'ner,* which indeed it was. Before this, a project dear to Evelyn's heart had been to surround smoky, dirty London with fragrant hedges and herbs. This he set forth in a slender volume, *Fumifugium,* in 1661.

Toward the end of his life, which he spent at his ancestral place, Wotton House down in Sussex, Evelyn continued to interest himself in the gardens of his estate, and in 1699 wrote *Acetaria: A Discourse of Sallets,* known to twentieth century gourmets probably more than any other of his books, except his *Diary.* But to gardeners, his *Sylva* will remain the book by which he is remembered. With his death in 1706, we are well into the reign of Queen Anne, the last of the Stuarts. An epoch had passed, a time that had seen the decline of the herbalists, the establishment of the flower garden as a garden of pleasure, the rise of the first gardening writers in our language. In eight years more, a new era altogether was to begin with the first of the four Georges of the House of Hanover, and gardens ceased to be gardens, but became parks and extensive lawns and parterres with no flowers at all. The "good old days" were over, never again to be known in England.

CHAPTER IV

Herbs of Beauty

But the beauty of the herbs would not be denied and in the humble cottage and country gardens, when the great estates went berserk with fountains and grottos, with parks and lawns, and parterres of brick dust and coal, gardens of lovely flowers were still preserved so that today we might know a flower garden, a flower garden that holds the "floriest" of the medicinal herbs which down the long centuries of time have ministered to man—hollyhock, bleeding heart, cornflower, iris, peony, rose, violet, crocus, primrose, pyrethrum, larkspur and so many, many more, every one even now found in any list of crude drugs, and in some form or other in every drug store, but which we know as flowers.

Why those early gardeners chose some herbs of beauty for the garden of pleasure and left others just as lovely in the herb plots, cannot with certainty be answered. We might ask a similar question today. Why have we neglected certain flowers and raised others to an unbelievable eminence? There are waves of popularity in flower growing, fads and fashions year by year among those who have no real depth of feeling. No doubt our dependence on commercial growers has a part. Some flowers lend themselves to huge size, striking color; others fit more readily into landscaping, into greenhouse culture, into early blooming, into use for house decoration. But as we study the old gardens and seek to find somewhere, somehow, a neglected plant or a few seeds, we are adding bit by bit to our delightful store of beauty.

Space permits but a scant discussion here of these little-known herbs of beauty and only of those that can be easily obtained today. So I have chosen those, not only beautiful as flowers, decorative in any garden plot, but such as have lived in such an aura of lore and legend for untold centuries that they will become real personalities in your garden, clumps that you will point to with pride and joy. I give you woad, lady's bedstraw, wild senna, rue, santolina, angelica, bergamot, borage, hyssop, winter savory, purple basil, and some of their varieties.

Both woad (*Isatis tinctoria*) and bedstraw (*Galium verum*) are tall plants, both have yellow flowers, both bloom for months to give bright clumps of sunshine day in, day out. Woad is three to four feet tall, the stalks ending in racemed panicles of small, bright yellow flowerlets. The long leaves resemble arrow heads which clasp the stem. A fairly fertile soil is best for luxuriant growth where the herb is grown only for its beauty. But for a thousand years and more, woad has been grown for use, the bluish green leaves steeped to produce a blue dye. Julius Caesar found that the natives of Britain before they went into battle painted themselves with this dye and he called them Picts (our word "picture" from a similar word in Latin meaning "to paint"). Some authorities believe "Britain" derives from an old Welsh word that means "Painted men." Gerard tells in his *Herbal*, 1597, how Pliny describes the custom in Britain of men and women dyeing themselves all over with woad and going naked to feasts and sacrifices.

Bedstraw is totally unlike woad in appearance, the thin wiry stems for a year or two tending to sprawl, unless they are clumped and staked, but after a time they will rise upright, the yellow-green threadlike leaves giving a delicate filet lacelike background to the bright butter-yellow flowers that are unbelievably brilliant. Practically any visitor coming upon this blazing clump will demand it. It blooms from early summer until autumn and is steeped in legend. There are both red and white varieties known.

The plant is sometimes called "Our Lady's Bedstraw" in the belief that it lined the Holy Manger in Bethlehem. It was used for stuffing mattresses even through the Elizabethan Age. Dr. Fernie says the name is a corruption of "Beadstraw" and tells how Irish peasant girls use the round seeds for beads in the absence of a rosary. The plant has had a number of names, once being called "Maid's Hair," as girls used it for dyeing their hair, the flowers giving a bright color which also was used to color cheese and was used as rennet, country people calling the plant by the name "cheese rennet." The roots will give a red dye, long used for wool dyeing. The best soil is a loose, rough, well-drained spot, but bedstraw will grow anywhere.

An early American herb is listed here, wild senna (*Cassia marilandica*). Long a favorite with herb growers, it is just being discovered by many gardeners. In a single season it will grow into a five-foot bush with a multitude of delicate branches bearing light green leaves like the locust, there being a dozen pairs of opposite, bluntly oblong leaflets with all the characteristics of a sensitive plant. It is amusing to watch these leaflets before a storm or when the plant goes to sleep for the night. They will twist completely over, upside down, and fold down together.

The flowers of the wild senna are bright yellow flowerlets in loosely formed clusters toward the end of the stem and will last through August and September in northern climates. The flowerlets have a brown center and resemble a pea blossom, the seed pods hanging down like a long string bean, but brown. The bushes are gorgeous in clumps or rows and will grow in any soil.

Rue (*Ruta graveolens*) is one of the most ancient herbs of beauty, all but unknown to modern gardeners. Yet there are few plants to compare with it for versatility and charm. It is really an evergreen sub-shrub and is one of the first perennials to turn freshly green in the spring, the stalk then being a chalky blue. Only in the coldest weather do the leaves get bronzy. When mature it will reach a height of three feet, if it isn't clipped. It has a lacy foliage, blue-green in color, the whole form bushy with a much branching light blue-green stem in summer. At the very top, clusters are formed of golden yellow flowerlets. It is delightful in blooming clumps or scattered plants or in a long border. It may be clipped to give a formal hedge a foot or two high but, of course, it will not then flower. Poor dry soil anywhere seems to satisfy all its desires and drought or rain doesn't affect it. It is one of the great historic herbs of literature and is often called "Herb o' Grace." There is a variegated variety.

Santolina Chamaecyparissus, also called lavender cotton, is one of a number of forms of santolina, all of which are delightful wherever a low growing, decorative clump is desired. All are woody, pungent smelling perennials, the lavender cotton being gray and closely like coral in appearance but very finely cut. The *Santolina viridis* is much the same but a rich green. There is a shaggy, grayish green variety called *S. pinnata*. The flowers are globular, about the size of marbles, and most plentiful on the *S. viridis,* being bright yellow. On the lavender cotton they are more lemony in color and almost drip with the pungent oil. The santolinas grow in a season or two into large clumps and can be easily divided, or layered branches cut off to form other clumps.

Another native American herb, bergamot, offers all kinds of color possibilities from the rich red of the "bee balm," or Oswego tea (*Monarda didyma*), which may be brilliant, through the rose colored, salmon pink, or white varieties or the lilac colored wild bergamot (*Monarda fistulosa*). Oswego tea combined with the blue flowers of chicory or the orange buttons of tansy gives a high spot of brilliant color contrast. At the back of a cool moist pool, a mass of Oswego tea is most striking. This old-fashioned brilliant red variety was a great favorite with the Indians in early days. The plants thrive in any soil and in full sun or shady spots.

One of the few great herbs of literature from far northern countries is the angelica (*Angelica archangelica*). And what a handsome, tropical looking plant it is, towering to a height of six or seven feet or more with most luxuriant foliage, flowering in June of its second or third year, with a lovely pompon of greenish white at the top with lesser umbels at the ends of smaller stems at intervals along the stalk, which is hollow and jointed, not unlike sugar cane. The stalk is often candied and is sold as French rhubarb. Morning sun and rich moist soil are best. New plants will grow from the fresh seed planted as soon as it is ripe but there is little growth the first year. In dry years it will come to maturity but will not grow tall. In beauty, fragrance and usefulness, few plants have been so famed. It has been the favorite of kings and poets.

Two of the most ancient herbs, mentioned in even the earliest of printed herbals and spoken of in ancient manuscripts, are treasures for the flower garden. They are borage (*Borago officinalis*) and hyssop (*Hyssopus officinalis*). They are widely different and each has peculiarities. Borage, for instance, is an infinitely more glorious plant when it is self sown. That is, the reseeded plants that come up year after year surpass the lovely little plants that come from your first sowing. It is best grown on a height so that you can look up to it to see the hanging racemes of star shaped flowers which first are pink and change to a lively blue color. The result is that in full bloom you have an unforgettable group of stars, some pink, some blue, some partly pink and partly blue. At the center of each star is a tiny brown pyramid. The exquisite flowers are often candied by brushing with white of egg and then dusting with sugar. The plant is sometimes over two feet tall with rough, hairy gray-green leaves which irritate tender skin if handled roughly. Poor loose soil is preferred and a sunny spot is best. The leaves have a cucumber taste and the tender upper leaves are much used in iced drinks.

Hyssop is a woody perennial, evergreen, bushy, easily grown from seed, and quickly forms a delightful hedge which can be clipped to formal shape but it is most attractive in blossom and will swarm with bees. I like it in clumps, or single bushes here and there, or a row along the bottom of a fence. The blue variety is most common but in any commercial package of seeds there will be a few pink, which can be sorted out and the seeds from these plants will give you a huge store for the next year.

The white variety is quite rare but can be obtained as plants and, by the same process, a large quantity of seed will be obtained.

Hyssop loves the sun and light soil but it will do well in part shade. It will bloom from July to October, and in Elizabethan days was largely used to form the ribbon designs in knot gardens. It can be easily transplanted and placed where you want it. The clippings from the hyssop hedge were always saved in olden times and used to strew on floors or to brew up for a medicinal tea. It was grown as a protection to ward off the Evil Eye.

The savories and basils have certain varieties which are grand for garden purposes. Winter savory (*Satureia montana*) and the dwarf variety are both delightful perennials, the dwarf being a tiny low plant but otherwise similar to the somewhat larger bush. They are woody, slow growing. The little leaves mass together to form a solid green border or edge; and when the tiny lilac-white flowers come, they are so numerous that it seems as if the plant had been sprinkled with a delicately tinted snow, and they last for weeks and weeks. Because of the slow growth, most gardeners would prefer to buy a few plants and either layer the branches or make slips. It roots easily and quickly, and the tiny plants can be set out and quickly become established.

Like hyssop, the winter savory was much used in knots and the clippings used for strewing or for drying and burning to give a fragrant odor. The foliage is used in cooking and has the same flavor as the much harder to raise summer savory, but the latter is less woody. Winter savory will grow in any soil with reasonable drainage, and does best with a little sun during the day and not too crowded in with other plants. It fills in around bare stalks of taller plants and the little dwarf variety, not over six inches tall, fits into rock gardens beautifully.

When we come to the basils, there are several to delight both eye and nose. The sweet basil (*Ocimum basilicum*) is grown for cookery, to impart that slightly peppery, clove-like taste to tomato and cheese dishes. But the same plant (var. *purpureum*) has gorgeous bushy foliage of reddish purple with delicate pinkish blooms. This is known as the purple sweet basil and is also used for culinary purposes, although a most decorative plant for the flower border. Still more attractive are the bush basils, dwarf varieties of both green and purple foliage. They are little cone shaped "trees," the purple particularly attractive, for it is but eight inches high, the green growing somewhat taller. The purple has lovely rosy blossoms, the green having white flowers. Both are grand pot plants for gifts.

Basil seeds, sown in ordinary well-drained soil, will germinate and show characteristic colors in a few days. The bush varieties can be left alone but the sweet basils, both purple and green, will bush most desirably if the center is pinched out as soon as the plants begin to branch. You will love the clove-like fragrance which perfumes the air whenever anything brushes the plants and you will like sprays of the purple basil for table decoration, or of either the green or the purple as a garnish for the meat platter. Many flower perfumes owe their fragrance to the oil of basil. In earliest days the plant in many sections grew to symbolize love. A pot of it on the window sill was supposed to drive away flies. In ancient paintings, just as a wattle fence indicated the presence of a garden, so the basil plant indicated poverty.

There are so many garden plants of ancient lineage.

In the next chapter we talk of those whose beauty lies not altogether in their blossoms, but in their lovely foliage, often a delight to the eye and always joyous with the fragrance they have gathered since men first knew of gardening. These are the mints and creeping thymes, plants whose lineage is lost in the dim light of earliest days.

CHAPTER V

Some Creeping Thymes and Fragrant Mints

Thymes and mints offer a long study of contrasts and similarities, and some of both are "musts" for a fragrant garden. Hardly a variety of either but pleases the nose, as brushing by them or bruising them under your feet releases their odors.

Sir Francis Bacon's much quoted statement from his essay "On Gardens" can still bear repeating:

"Those Plants which Perfume the Air most delightfully, being trodden upon and crushed are Three: that is Burnet, Wilde-Time and Water-mints, therefore you are to set whole Allies of them to have the Pleasure, when you walke or Tread."

In listing varieties of each for your garden, no matter how large, it will be a difficult problem of selection, since each one has some special appeal. Both herbs have distinct functions in producing the garden picture. Thymes are all low-growing, even the most erect variety scarcely reaching a foot high, while some of the mints rise to a height of three feet. One variety grows even higher while, on the other hand, English pennyroyal has half-prostrate habits. Thymes like the full sun unprotected and resent crowding. Mints favor cool damp spots and are not annoyed by being crowded; they simply creep underground to find a vacant spot for an outlet. They, too, will grow in the sun.

These herbs are more than just aromatic plants for the garden; they are the combined fragrances of sweet lore and legend from ancient times. It used to be the custom for maidens to wear a nosegay of sprigs of thyme, mint and lavender to bring them sweethearts. Perhaps from your garden will go forth many a little cluster of these herbs, borne in high hopes by feminine visitors.

The name, thyme, is connected with the Greek word meaning to fumigate, for the herb was early recognized as having antiseptic qualities. The dried thyme was commonly burned to mask the odor of burning flesh, as sacrificial animals were offered to the gods. The Roman Pliny claimed that, when burned, thyme "puts to flight all venomous creatures." In Virgil's "Georgics," thyme is mentioned as a fumigator. There was also a Greek word similar to the word for thyme, meaning courage, and some trace the name of the herb to that word. At any rate, courage from renewed strength was given to tired warriors who bathed in thyme-scented waters. The whole region about Mt. Hymettus, near Athens, was sweet with the thyme which has ever been loved by bees, and honey from Hymettus is world and legend famous. Thyme became the symbol of activity, bravery, energy; and ladies embroidered the thyme-loving bee hovering over a sprig of the herb, on the scarves they gave to their knights. Romans administered thyme as a certain remedy for melancholy spirits.

Mounds of thyme are much liked by the fairies who choose the aromatic flower heads for their hours of recreation. So, if you want the little folk in your garden, offer them the inducement of a fragrant playground.

The more than fifty varieties of thyme can be classified as erect, prostrate and low mounds. The first do not spread but self-sow; the second do not creep but self-layer; the third not only self-sow but also creep. Most gardeners are aware of the possibilities of the erect varieties for prim little clumps which know their boundaries and keep within them. But they must have some protection in really severe winter weather. But those other restless varieties eager for adventuring beyond and around them, have an appeal and fragrant use in our gardens. From June until October some of the thymes will be in bloom, clouds of inconspicuous blossoms varying from white, lilac, mauve and light pink to rose, rose-purple, reddish purple and red. The foliage of most varieties is small, close set, some hairy, some smooth and the color ranges from gray-green and blue-green to bright and dark shades or pure green. Some varieties have distinct odors that cannot be mistaken, such as caraway or lemon, while others are so elusive that everyone disagrees with his neighbor, and you will hear such descriptions as peppermint, orange, tangerine, fresh varnish, soap, wet cat, spice, anise.

Natives of the Mediterranean regions and Central Asia, where they wandered all over the sunny hillsides, the thymes seem to expect light, well-drained, limestone soil. They like the fullest of sun and the broadest of space, impatient of restriction by other plants. In Richard Surflet's translation in 1600 of the French *Maison Rustique,* we read that "Thyme . . . craveth a place upon the Sunne neere unto the sea and leane, . . . as also that it may grow the fairer and fuller leafe, it will be good to water the ground oft with water wherein hath been steeped for the space of one whole day drie thyme somewhat bruised." Perhaps the author thought that the plant itself, as well as people, would be invigorated by an infusion of this herb.

In the calcareous light soil, thyme will grow especially fragrant but, as with other herbs, enrichment of the earth will make the foliage luxuriant but will lessen the aroma. If you are preparing a spot for the thymes, make a plot, raised to prevent excess moisture. Provide for good drainage by digging out some of the earth, filling in with broken stones and ashes, sifting sand among the spaces and then adding poor gritty soil on top. Here the thymes will root easily, while in compact clay soil they will die out. A pleasant feature about the thymes is that you may divide the clumps at any time of year so long as you take quite a bit of soil with the clump.

In warm climates the gardener has no worries about winter care; but in New England and other parts with long hard winters, some of the sun-loving herbs which like to snuggle down in warm soil are apt to winter kill. In localities that freeze, therefore, protect these plants by salt hay, leaves or straw, pressing down the earth if they begin to heave out of the ground. A little blanket over the top to prevent melting snow from lodging on the plants will help. You will be rewarded by finding the plants among the first to sally forth to meet the sun in the spring.

In choosing the creeping thymes, we must decide upon the same questions as those in choosing a carpet for our home, the color, suitability for the spot to be covered and whether we prefer long or short nap ... whether we want to step lightly over the carpet or let our feet sink in deeply. And with these questions in mind, so we shall choose the thymes laid before us for inspection and approval.

First, the place to be covered is important. The very flat varieties are lovely set between flagstones in a path or bordering each side. They are beautiful to carpet a bank along the garden where you are going to sit, as on a wattle seat surrounding the trees in your garden. If you have none, do build one up as the gardeners of the Middle Ages did, around the base of a tree and held by wattles, a low fence of woven osiers or, to get acquainted with the idea, you can use hemp rope.

Perhaps you may prefer the longer nap for covering garden banks and seats of earth, and will choose the thymes that form high spreading mats. These make a very decorative carpet for any barren bank or lawn where no grass will grow. You know from experience, no doubt, that thymes are "naturals" for rock gardens.

Another lovely use of thymes is for covering the ground where bulbs are planted. When the rains come, the foliage of the thyme will help to keep the flowers of the lower stalks from being mud spattered. But since the thymes grow so thickly, keep the carpet thinned so that the bulbs will grow up through them. What a lovely background contrast for the bright blossoms of jonquils, daffodils, hyacinths and tulips!

Any spaces along the top of a red brick or gray wall, filled with earth, will be another grand spot for the low creepers, and the red or gray of the wall offers a fine background for the shades of green. To surround a sundial by thyme seems obvious but in early days people were not so sophisticated as to object to a pun, and the result was something of beauty to remember.

As we clean our carpets, so we have to take care of our carpeting thymes lest any weeds, such as white clover and chickweed, grow up through and mar the smoothness. The roots of these weeds seem to wind themselves around the roots of thyme and in uprooting them you are apt to make holes in the carpet, just as moths do. But, fortunately, the thyme will reweave, if you dig out the intruders before they get too firm a grip. If allowed to grow, your entire carpet will be destroyed.

The source plant of many varieties of creeping thymes is laden with many names. Botanically it is known as *Thymus serpyllum* but commonly called shepherd's thyme, hillwort, Pella Mountain, brotherwort. According to location, it takes on different forms of growth and is most confusing. In its natural state on dry, stony, open hillsides, it is prostrate and forms thick mats; but when restricted by other plants, its slender stalks reach upward sometimes to as much as 12 inches, seemingly to make up for the inability to spread out. No one unacquainted with its habits would dream the two growths could be the same plant. If given enough space, this "mother of thyme" will carpet a large area by simply placing clumps a few feet apart. They will touch in a few weeks. It is said that it can be mowed with a lawn mower when well established but the very thought is chilling to my heart. How could a closely cropped carpet of mother of thyme be so lovely as the uncut stems thick with tiny green leaves and a cloud of purplish flowers! The idea leaves me as cold as that of topiary work on trees or hedges trimmed into forms.

The other flat creeping thymes are the red variety, *Thymus serpyllum coccineus,* and the white variety, *albus.* The first has very dark green, tiny smooth leaves almost hidden under masses of small, purplish red flowers, while the other variety has light green leaves covered with a snow of white flowers. Both spread out into lovely mats and the flowers, beginning in June, last a long time. These two varieties, quite hardy in nature, are particularly good for crevices in walks, or between flagstones, or just for carpeting the paths.

The woolly thyme, *T. serpyllum lanuginosus,* has tiny, hairy leaves, not so aromatic as most varieties, but the most delicate and lovely variety of all. It does best on a hummock or on a slope over stones and is hardy if protected from ice and melting snow. It simply demands rocks or stones for a foundation to lift the stems and leaves from the earth. In hot weather it may die out in spots but quickly revives. The flowers, of a bright purplish pink, are but few and appear in June in little groups scattered over the top.

Two other creepers, also hardy, but not flat mats, are the *T. serpyllum pulchellus* with thick, soft, hairy, light green foliage and purplish rose flowers and the *T. serpyllum splendens,* a rapidly spreading variety covered with reddish flowers and excellent for spots where grass will not readily grow. *T. chamaedrys,* almost prostrate and similar to *T. serpyllum,* has green foliage and pinkish flower heads. It is a wonderfully satisfying long-napped carpeting thyme and is eager to spread.

Then there are the minty smelling *T. lanicaulis* with long trailing stems of rapid growth bearing gray woolly leaves and bright pink flower heads in June, *T. brittani-cus*, also a grayish green carpeter with roundish woolly leaves and pink flowers, and the "Dalmatian thyme" with low narrow downy leaves and rose colored blossoms. The *T. cimicinus* or red-stemmed thyme is an unusual variety with long stems bearing fine leaves and, by contrast, large pink flowers in August. This is a good variety for trailing down over bare rocks.

The *T. azoricus* forms rounding mounds of vivid foliage resembling softly bristling, very tiny tubes, which gives the impression of a not very compact moss. It bears lilac colored flowers and has a tangerine-orange odor. It is good for stepping stones, or for a spot in the rock garden since it does not spread rapidly, but it tends to winter kill unless protected. *T. jankae* forms loose tumbling mounds of dark green foliage, the leaves rather larger than most thymes, and smells like a whiff of fresh varnish.

Caraway thyme or *Herba-barona* is a great favorite. In the Middle Ages it was rubbed on a baron of beef before roasting, which gave it its name. It has a distinct odor of caraway and forms a high mat of tiny dark green leaves with purplish pink flowers. It spreads rapidly and can be divided freely, which is fortunate, for every visitor will beg a root of it.

T. citriodorus or lemon thyme, definitely fragrant of lemon, is one of the most satisfying and brilliant thymes. It grows into a loosely formed green mound which spreads rapidly by self-layering, and is supposed to be sweeter when developed from divisions than from seed. In his *Paradisus*, the seventeenth century John Parkinson quite accurately describes the variety in the delightfully naïve, unscientific language of those days:

"The wilde Thyme that smelleth like unto Pomecitron or Lemon, hath many weake branches trayling on the ground . . . with small darke greene leaves, thinly or sparsedly set on them, and smelling like unto a Lemon, with whitish flowers at the Toppes in roundels or spikes."

A variegated form of the lemon thyme, var. *argenteus*, or silver thyme, is a shrubby growth in loosely formed clumps, hardly to be called a mound. The leaves are grayish green with white edgings and the pale pink flowers are scattered sparsely over the plants. It forms a notable contrast with the golden thyme, var. *aureus*, one of the most decorative of all. The latter forms a low, open mound and what a breath-taking sight it is, with its vivid green leaves edged with golden yellow. In soil that is too rich and in the heat of mid-summer, it is liable to revert to green; but in poor, gravelly soil and when the days cool in late summer, the golden tints return and in late fall the plant is more gold than green.

In this botanically minded garden age, it is amusing to note how elaborately Parkinson, garden lover of 300 years ago, writes of this variegated thyme and with what grace and charm and in a leisurely way he describes the plant:

"This kinde of wilde Tyme hath small hard branches lying or leaning to the ground, with small party coloured leaves upon them, divided into stripes or edges, of a gold yellow colour, the rest of the leafe abiding greene, which for the variable mixture or placing of the yellow, hath caused it to be called embroidered or guilded Thyme."

Whatever varieties you choose, be sure to have golden thyme, a bright spot from spring to late fall. It can be divided as much as you like at any time to form more clumps or to share with friends.

And now for the many varieties of mints, some fifty in number, and difficult to distinguish one from the other at times because of the centuries of wild growing and cross-breeding. Mints are more adventurous than thymes.

Mint.

From the *German Herbarius,* 1496.

The latter spread on top of the soil by stretching out their running stems but will stay in one place and sulk when balked by other plants. The roots of mint, shallow and persistent, wander about underground, quite hidden from the gardener's view, and often push up among other varieties which may have been planted nearby.

Walafrid Strabo wrote in his *Hortulus,* "Mint I grow in abundance in all its varieties. How many there are I might as well try to count the sparks from Vulcan's furnace beneath Etna." But all mints are fragrant and have a long and honorable line of ancestry reaching far back to the realm of mythology. Their botanical name, *Mentha,* comes from a nymph called Mintha, daughter of Cocytus, who was beloved of Pluto but because of the jealousy of his wife, Proserpine, was changed by her into a plant. Theophrastus in the fourth century B.C. was apparently the first to use the name *mintha* in referring to the mint *Mentha viridis.*

In ancient Greece, where the Saturday night bath was a fragrant ritual, the dandies used to have an after-bath rubdown of herbs, a different fragrance for each part of the body, and extract of thyme was applied to neck and knees, the juice of mints to the arms. Roman Pliny of the first century after Christ claimed, "The smell of Mint does stir up the mind and the taste to a greedy desire of meats." In an emergency, this suggests a stroll in the garden of mints for your dinner guests.

The care of mints is simple and quite set forth in the *Maison Rustique,* even to the danger involved in using manure,

"All sorts of mints, whether garden or wild doe nothing desire the ground dunged, fat or lying open upon the Sunne, but rather a moist ground neere unto Water, for want whereof they must be continually watred, for else they die."

Any form of organic manure will cause a rust but I have found most of the mints will thrive in sun.

Of course the chief characteristics of all mints are square stems, opposite simple leaves and flowers varying from white and lilac to deep lavender and light shades of purple, either in axillary clusters along the stems or in terminal spikes. The flowering tops all contain traces of camphor which produces a fresh, clean, cool effect, and for this reason the mints are used in toilet waters, dentifrices, and mouth washes as well as in refreshing drinks. In the fourteenth century Chaucer's translation of the French *Romaunt of the Rose,* we find:

> "Then wente I forth on my right hond.
> Down by a litel path I fond
> Of mentes ful and fenel grene;"

The perfect place for mints is all along a path so that you brush them in passing, their fragrance filling the air.

I never can understand why plants that spread are looked upon with horror by so many gardeners. You can always restrain them by sinking boundary plates into the ground and easily remove what you do not want as a normal part of gardening. But make no mistake about it, mints do spread. They are delightful around a sundial or by a pool. At the back of the pool will go some of the taller mints such as the English and American varieties of peppermint, spearmint, watermint, woolly mint, curly mint. In front will be the orange mint, golden and silver apple mint, while the area about the pool might be carpeted with the wonderfully fragrant Corsican mint.

My particular favorite among the mints is the American apple mint, *Mentha gentilis,* with two varieties, one with red stems and smooth green leaves and a second or variegated form beautiful with its contrast of vivid green and light gold stripes. The first rises to little more than six inches high and is somewhat bushy. The variegated is a rather sprawling bush welcome to spread all over for its use in potpourris, teas, sandwiches, jellies, and to give to friends.

Next in my favor is *Mentha citrata,* commonly known as orange mint or bergamot mint. The thin broad leaves have a tiny purplish margin. A mixture of the apple mint and orange mint for jelly making is more delicately fragrant than the usual spearmint, and these fruity mints combined with parsley, chopped and mixed with mayonnaise, make a most delicious filling for bread and butter sandwiches to be served with chicken salads. The oil of the orange mint is used commercially for perfume.

M. rotundifolia is sometimes known as apple mint and has light green round leaves which are hairy. There is a much more decorative variegated variety which is known as pineapple mint and is a prize in any mint garden. Both are quite spreading and grow to a height of about 18 inches.

M. spicata, or, according to Linnaeus, *viridis,* grows two feet tall and has narrow crinkly rough leaves tapering to a sharp point. This is the ordinary garden or lamb mint, called spearmint. A variety of this mint, *crispata,* is called curly mint and has broad, crumpled, deeply veined leaves on a stalk scarcely able to bear its leafy burden. It is often used in cooking and there is a kind which is doubly curly.

Peppermint, *M. piperita,* is found in three varieties. One, the "State mint," growing about three feet high and grown in Wayne County, N. Y., was introduced from England and grown commercially here for its oil. A second variety, the white mint, *M. piperita* var. *officinalis,* has slender stems rising to two feet high and light green leaves and produces a high standard of oil. The variety *vulgaris* or black mint, native to England, is about three feet high with stem and leaves both quite purple. It is widely grown here on the peppermint farms in the West because of its resistance to disease and blights. The English call the black "officinalis" and growers here call it the English mint.

English pennyroyal, *M. pulegium,* is a mint of very penetrating odor, prostrate in habits, with small oval leaves and bluish flowers and is not hardy. It is not to be confused with the American pennyroyal, *Hedeoma pulegeoides,* an upright bushy plant with light green leaves, which dies down with the coming of frost but re-seeds prolifically. The true pennyroyal seems to have been given the name "pulegium" by Pliny because of its supposed efficacy in driving away fleas (*pulices*). The plant was also called "Pudding grass" because housewives of early days used to put it into a stuffing or "pudding," as it was called, for meat. Parkinson in 1629 said,

"It is yet to this day . . . used to bee put into puddings, and such like meates of all sorts, and therefore in divers places they know it by no other name than Pudding Grass."

"Lurk-in-the-Ditch" and "Run-by-the-Ground" were also names applied to pennyroyal because of its creeping nature and love of damp soil.

A lovely rock garden plant or carpeter around a pool is the *M. requienii,* a mint native to Corsica and Sardinia, called both Corsican mint and Corsican thyme. It is a flat creeper, almost moss-like, with brilliant green tiny round leaves and mauve blossoms. It spreads in no time at all into a soft, unbelievably fragrant mat. It is not hardy in the cold climates but its beauty is worth the investment in a few plants each year.

There are many other fragrant mints, the *M. longifolia* or European horsemint, white hairy, the leaves not so narrow or pointed as the spearmint, the foliage gray. In spring the leaves are only slightly downy but grow definitely hairy as age increases. There are also the *M. sylvestris,* very hairy with gray-green leaves and growing to a height of three to four feet, the *M. arvensis,* commonly known as field or corn mint, one of the mints preferring a dry location. You may also like the *M. niliaca* var. *alopecuroides,* an Egyptian mint, tall with hairy leaves, or the *M. arvensis* var. *piperascens,* or Japanese peppermint. The *M. arvensis* var. *Canadensis,* known as American wild mint, and no doubt what is frequently called *M. aquatica,* is a stiff low-growing plant found in water at the edge of streams, but grows luxuriantly in the garden.

CHAPTER VI

Old-Time Favorites

Mignonette, heliotrope, lemon verbena, Bible leaf, lavender, marjoram, rosemary. These collected fragrances wafted to us out of the past recall to our hearts half forgotten memories, imagined scenes. Perhaps a whiff of mignonette as our little grandmother in billowy skirts passed near us as she went through the room. Perhaps we held the garden basket as she cut the tips of lavender, or the delicate sprays of lemon verbena, both to be laid between piles of linen. Or perhaps our lovely young aunt with blushing cheeks and starry eyes clasped a tight little nosegay, a tussie-mussie prim and neat with its frilly border. To us the fragrance of the heliotrope in the center was the appeal; to our aunt it was the sentiment expressed by her suitor in the language of the flowers—devotion.

In an old town along the New England coast is one of the loveliest, most restful little walled herb gardens to which I have ever been fortunate enough to be a frequent visitor. This was not planted and looked after by a paid gardener, but loved and cared for by an active little lady. On each side of the central path are rectangular beds, faithful to the tradition of ancient herb gardens. My friend first points out on one side the beds of basil, burnet, chives, but as she turns to the other side her eyes sparkle with a happy light. For this is her tussie-mussie garden, mignonette, rosemary, lemon verbena . . . all of the old-time favorites. Each plant is a personality, each kind of herb a fragrant memory for any visitor to the garden.

Whether rosemary was brought to England by the French at the time of the Conquest in the eleventh century or sent by the Countess of Hainault in the fourteenth century to Queen Philippa, wife of Edward III, we cannot be sure. We do know that it was a plant seen at first only in gardens of royalty and nobility. It reached the modest garden plots only gradually, possibly by cuttings made unobtrusively by gardeners. In Egypt the plant was seen only in the elaborate gardens of the great, and in the gorgeous rose gardens at Algiers and Morocco it served as a fragrant bordering hedge, clipped flat across the top.

Rosemary, however, came to play many rôles in the everyday life of England. It served to symbolize remembrance at weddings and funerals, to deck churches and banqueting halls, to burn in place of costly incense in religious rites, and as a fumigant in hospitals, to cure headache and heartache, to break magic spells and to ward off contagion, to add a piquant touch to salads and to crown the boar's head.

In Anthony Askham's herbal of 1550 we may read, in regard to rosemary, "If thou set it in thy garden kepe it honestly for it is much profytable." And so rosemary was grown and used as the legends and superstitions grew, and these were many and varied. In Portugal and Scandinavia the plant was connected with elves, while in

Sicily baby fairies were supposed to sleep in its flowers. A lovely old legend tells that in the flight from Egypt, the Virgin Mary threw her blue cloak over a bush of rosemary when she lay down to rest. Ever afterwards, in honor of her, the flowers were the heavenly blue of the mantle. A folk proverb has it that where rosemary flourishes, the mistress rules.

We, in the United States, growing a comparatively few bushes of rosemary, and the best of these not very broad or tall, can well be amazed at its growth in southern France, where it was cut and gathered into fagots for firewood; or to read in Bancke's *Herbal* of 1525, "Make thee a box of the wood of rosemary and smell to it, and it shall preserve thy youth." In the sixteenth century, Paul Hentzner in his *Travels* tells of rosemary thriving in the gardens and used to cover the walls surrounding them. At Hampton Court, "it was so planted and nailed to walls as to cover them entirely." The treelike proportions of the growth of rosemary are to be noted in Parkinson's *Paradisus,* 1629,

"In this our Land (when it hath been planted in Noblemans and great mens gardens against bricke wals, and there continued long) as beyond the seas . . . it riseth up in time unto a very great height, with a great woody stemme (of that compasse, that (being cloven out into thin boards) it hath served to make lutes, or such like instruments, and here with us Carpenters rules, and to divers other purposes)."

Besides the useful articles made from rosemary, the bushes were often set "by women for their pleasure to grow in sundry proportions, as in the fashion of a cat, a peacock, or such thing as they fancy." Story has it that rosemary "passeth not commonly in highte the highte of Christe whill He was man on Erthe." After 33 years, the bush broadens out but grows no higher.

As Parkinson says, "The common Rosemary is so well known . . . that it were sufficient but to name it as an ornament among other sweete herbes and flowers in our Garden, seeing every one can describe it." We, too, know the woody little bush with pine-needle-like leaves, dark green above and white beneath. The taste of the leaves is definitely piny and leaves a warm feeling within you. The flowers, appearing in the axils of the leaves, look like tiny orchids, not over a half inch long, usually of a pale blue, but one variety has an unbelievable heavenly blue color which always calls to mind the story of the Virgin.

A prostrate variety is said to be not hardy but I have had it live through the winter in a protected sunny spot. It grows no more than 9 or 10 inches high, and in pots trails over the edge. There is also a gilded variety which, as Parkinson says, "differeth not from the former [common rosemary] in forme or manner of growing nor in the forme or colour of the flower, but only in the leaves, which are edged, or striped, or pointed with a faire gold yellow colour. . . ."

Rosemary, native of the Mediterranean coast, grows best in light, dry soil with quite a bit of chalk dug into the earth. The location should be sheltered, preferably on a south slope. Plants may be grown from seed, but it takes a deal of patience. One good plant will, in time, produce all the plants you want by pegging down the longer branches, allowing them to take root, and then cutting from the mother plant. Slips may be rooted, preferably in the spring, from a branch not in bloom, and kept in pots over the winter.

In northern climates rosemary must be taken in over the winter. Sometimes the plants are kept in a cold cellar with a ball of earth bagged about the roots. They may be left outdoors, if covered and the soil around them kept from freezing—as against a protected housewall on the south.

Strangely enough, lemon verbena, botanically *Lippia citriodora* or *Aloysia citriodora,* is not in English tradition at all, not having been brought to Europe until 1784, although it is one of the all-time favorites, connoting romance in moonlight and old-fashioned gardens. This lovely plant, so popular in colognes, potpourri, finger bowls, refreshing teas, sweet bags, apple jellies, is a perennial shrub from Argentina and Chile, where it grows to a height of ten feet or more. We all know the woody shrub with slightly weak branches having a tendency to droop on the ground if not tied. The tiny, inconspicuous flowers are in terminal spikes, often five or six inches long, and always surprising to me when they appear. The leaf is narrow, entire, and has a heavy central vein. Since the plant is not hardy, it can be cut back severely and kept without watering in a cold cellar, and brought out to a sunny window to revive about February. Or you may abandon the plant, but beforehand take any number of slips, which root easily in sand. Before either step is taken, remove and save every leaf and dry them. They retain their fragrance and can be used in tea or in fragrant boudoir pillows.

In the garden the shrubby lemon verbena grows in northerly climates to a height of three or four feet and should have a very special location where you can readily pluck a leaf or two for its refreshing odor, or gather some for tea or finger bowls. A whole path bordered on both sides by lemon verbena is a wonderful, fragrant experience.

Costmary grows "everywhere in gardens, and are

Costmary.

From Salmon, *Botanologia*, 1710.

cherished for their sweete flowers and leaves," said Gerard in 1597, and "the flowers also are tyed up with small bundels of Lavender toppes, these being put in the middle of them, to lye upon the toppes of beds, presses etc. for the sweete sent and savour it casteth," wrote Parkinson in 1629. But in New England, as well as in Old England, our Pilgrim ancestors also rejoiced in the fragrance which with one whiff would set them down again in the lovely gardens they had left so many miles away. How carefully the roots of this hardy perennial must have been cherished, roots which would make themselves at home in no matter what kind of soil they were planted on this side of the Atlantic. It may be of interest to know that "costmary" comes from *costus,* the name of a spicy Oriental plant, and "Mary," in honor of the Virgin.

Perhaps some of our ancestors did not know that derivation or that costmary bore the imposing name of *Chrysanthemum balsamita,* and they rarely even called it costmary. "Bible leaf" and "mint geranium" were the familiar colloquial names the plant was given. When the staid Puritans went to church, they allowed themselves the indulgence of a fragrant marker for Bible and hymnal and the leaf of this tall plant was chosen, for it retained its minty aromatic scent for years.

Costmary, although it was grown in ancient Egypt, is a native of West Asia. It flourishes best in a dry, warm, sunny spot, although it will grow in the shade and not blossom. Plants set two feet apart will, by eager running roots, cover the space between in two years. It can be divided as much as you like and makes a grand back-of-the-border foil for the multicolored flowers in front of it, but you will surely want a clump near the path where you may pick leaves for a tea or just to crush in your hands as an aromatic restorative on a summer's day. The flowers of the costmary are insignificant yellow rayless buttons flowering late in the season. It is the "alecost" of the ancients, called *Tanacetum balsamita* by Linnaeus from its button flowers and odor, and is called *Balsamita* m as by the early herbalists who gave the name *Balsamita foemina* to another plant known as maudlin, the *Achillea ageratum,* now called the camphor plant and confused by many with costmary. The camphor plant leaves have a strong camphor odor when crushed, the plant does not have running roots, it is low and tidy with small daisy-like flowers which bloom early and even on the young plants. The leaves are blue-green with a wax-like covering and are narrow. The plant must be cut down before seed sets and will come up again in the late summer, fresh and erect.

The odor of heliotrope, more than any other plant, can surround me with memories of other days, other times; can stir my imagination to scenes of dainty ladies receiving courtly gentlemen to afternoon tea, of an opera party in the 'nineties with the guests in full regalia assembling in the box overlooking the stage. There is something intoxicating about the odor and as I bury my nose again and again in the fragrant cluster, more memories, more scenes crowd around me. To some people, heliotrope has a disagreeable, close, musty odor. Some define the odor as that of vanilla. The old-time, colloquial name for the plant was cherry-pie, because of the almond-like odor found in cherry pits which was thought similar to that of heliotrope. Unfortunately, little essential oil can be obtained from the flowers themselves, so that practically all heliotrope perfume is synthetic.

Again we find an old favorite of our grandmother's garden not in the ancient line of English garden tradition, for heliotrope was introduced from Peru to Europe about 1757 and from its source comes the botanical name *Heliotropium peruvianum*. There are some 90 species of the genus to be found in tropical and subtropical regions. In warm climates the plants become bushes rising to a height of 8 or 10 feet and heliotrope hedges are often made.

As we read the old English herbals we find many mentions of heliotrope or "turnsole," the literal translation of the word "heliotrope." But the name was applied to sunflowers and marigolds, which each day followed the course of the sun from east to west, so we must not be misled by our own conception of heliotrope when we come upon the word in the old books.

The fragrant South American plant with hue so distinctive as to give its name to a color was also named from its habit of following the sun from dawn to dark and obtained for itself, in the language of the flowers, the symbolism of devotion. The plant loves warm, light, rich soil and may be propagated by cuttings and by layering. It makes a lovely border, although it is tender.

Mignonette is another plant of our grandmother's garden that spells romance. Bret Harte wrote,

"The delicate odour of Mignonette,
    The remains of a dead and gone bouquet,
Is all that tells of a story; yet
    Could we think of it in a sweeter way?"

It, too, is a plant of comparatively recent importation to England. It was originally a weed in Egypt but was considered an herb of magic by the Romans. Pliny said that it possessed the power to take away disorders. Near an Italian city, now called Rimini, the plant was used to reduce swellings, and when applying it as a remedy the natives repeated the following charm, spitting on the ground three times at each repetition:

Reseda, cause these maladies to cease;
Knowest thou, knowest thou, who has driven pullets here?
Let the roots have neither head nor foot.

Botanically, mignonette is *Reseda odorata,* "reseda" coming indirectly from a Latin verb meaning to assuage. Sentimentally the plant has been called "Herbe d'Amour," a love flower. A spray of mignonette has led the way to many a romance and once to the coat of arms of a noble family in Saxony. This is the story. The Count of Walstheim was in love with the spoilt and coquettish Amelia of Nordburg, while her companion, Charlotte, of humble family, was gentle and modest. At a party one evening, each lady chose a flower and the gentlemen were to write verses for each one. Amelia had flirted disgracefully all evening and the count wrote for her rose, "She lives but for a day and pleases but for a moment." For the gentle Charlotte's mignonette he wrote, "Your qualities surpass your charms." The count became deeply attached to Charlotte, finally married her, and to the ancient arms of his family he added a spray of mignonette with the line he had written to her that evening.

From France, where this sweet plant was called "Little Darling," it found its way to London about 1752, where it was displayed in florists' windows and finally grown in every window box in town until whole streets were almost oppressive with the odor, so it is recorded. Of this popularity in the florists' shops, William Cowper, the poet, wrote:

"... the sashes fronted with a range
Of Orange, Myrtle or the fragrant weed
The Frenchman's darling."

The flower head makes up in odor what it lacks in beauty, really a very inconspicuous display of greenish white spikes made up of tiny blossoms. The odor has been described as a combination of violets and basil, but odors can scarcely be considered abstractly or objectively. They have a personal connotation for each nose.

Lavenders.

From the only known illustrated edition of Dioscorides, printed at Venice, 1558.

In Provençal France mignonette is grown for its perfume. It is an annual, thrives best in cool, moderately rich soil in a partially shaded spot. As it matures, the plant tends to become decumbent but, though it is not a colorful, showy addition to the garden, its fragrance rewards us as no scentless, giant flower ever can.

Lavender and old lace; sweet bags and washing waters; fragrant linens and a clean odor; London cries! Lavender is an old, old herb and, although native to India, it seems to belong peculiarly to France and England, where it has long been used in medicine, cosmetics, decoration, and of late years has been raised commercially by the acre. The first mention of *Lavandula vera* seems to have been in a book by the Benedictine Abbess Hildegarde of the twelfth century, at Bingen on the Rhine, in the chapter "De Lavendula." In a fourteenth century poem on the virtues of herbs, we can read of lavender, while Charles VI of France had made for him cushions of lavender. The name lavender is said to come from the word "to wash," an indication of the ancient use of it in water, not only for washing linen but also the body.

In England the fields of lavender are fields to remember all one's life long; the hedges, the paths bordered with thick, grayish lines topped by lavender, a rose-covered wall with a row of lavender and gray at the base. All are breath-taking. Here in our States with warm climate, we can enjoy such settings as in England, if we will, but in our cooler sections we cannot expect to have such luxuriant growth. John Josselyn in his *New England Rarities*, 1672, says, "Lavender is not for this climate." This, however, is only partly true. We cannot keep the more tender varieties outdoors during severe New England winters but the "true" lavender has weathered even in parts of Maine. Though we may not have borders, we can have clumps of lavender near stands of wild bergamot against the gray artemisias such as wormwood, Silver King, cudweed, or blue chicory.

Lavandula vera, or the true lavender, is the variety from which the English oil of lavender is distilled. It is a narrow leaved, gray-green plant with a short crooked main stalk of yellowish gray and many erect, straight, slender and bluntly quadrangular branches. The leaves are blunt looking, the older ones greener than the younger ones, which are gray. The flowers come in whorls of as many as ten blossoms on long spikes. The plant flourishes in light, dry, calcareous, even stony soil which is well drained. This is true of any plant containing much oil, such as rosemary or lemon balm. It likes abundant sun and air but should have protection from high winds so that the slender flower spikes are not broken off. Each season, late in summer, after the stalks are harvested, prune the plant well. During the growing season dig in a little lime or chalk around the roots every few weeks, but fertilizing will cut down the blooming, although making a more luxuriant leaf growth.

This hardy lavender can be raised from seed but it is a long, slow process for the average gardener, and it is much better to secure a few plants and root cuttings of the younger growth at the end of the summer, leaving a slight heel on the slip. These will root all by themselves in a light moist soil in a shady spot, if it doesn't dry out. In severe weather, a covering of hay or leaves with a basket upside down on top gives good protection.

Lavandula spica is a coarser species than the true lavender and a smaller plant with grayer spatulate leaves. The foliage is clustered about the base of the branches, and the flower spikes are thicker and shorter. The flowers produce much more oil than the *L. vera* but of inferior quality and less fragrant, with a slight piny touch resembling rosemary.

L. stoechas is a variety familiar to lavender lovers from ancient times, mentioned even by Dioscorides in the first century. Gerard says, "These herbs do grow wilde in Spaine, in Languedock in Fraunce, and the Ilands called

Stoechades over against Massilia: we have them in our gardens, and kept with great diligence, from the injurie of our colde clymate." In English, he says, the plant is called "French Lavander, Steckado, Stickadove, Cassidonie, and some simple people imitating the same doe call it Cast me downe." This variety is a shrubby plant growing a foot or two high with short, gray, hairy leaves.

Stoechas Lavender.

From Dioscorides, 1558.

The characteristic feature is the flower head of dark, rich purple with tufts of purple leaflets at the end of the head.

White lavender, of delicate fragrance, is a rare and tender variety. As is true of the other lavenders, it does not take kindly to rich soil and will survive cold better in poor than in rich ground. It once had the distinction of being the name of a literary guild in Amsterdam called the "White Lavender Bloom," but the plant is most noted as having been a favorite with Henrietta Maria, wife of the ill-fated Charles I. In the Parliamentary Survey for November, 1649, of the Manor of Wimbledon, in the inventory of her possessions in the gardens were listed "very great and large borders of Rosemary, Rue and White Lavender and great varieties of excellent herbs."

Other varieties of lavender worthy of note and obtainable in the United States are *L. atropurpurea,* a dwarf, compact little bush hardly the height of this book, blossoming in a haze of blue flowers, and making a grand rock-garden plant. *L. dentata,* a woody plant with rich green, narrow leaves having rounded sawtooth edges resembling babies' teeth, is a most satisfactory, though tender, variety. It blooms all summer and until frost, if the flower heads are kept cut. The *L. vera* var. *compacta nana* is a fine little dwarf bush and blooms somewhat earlier than the true lavender. *L. pedunculata* is a tender Spanish variety with narrow, gray-green leaves and large purple flower heads on short spikes. *L. pinnata* is also a tender variety, usually termed an annual, and readily grown from seed. It is the "jagged lavender" of our forefathers, with light green, finely cut foliage and blue flower heads in profusion on comparatively long spikes. It, too, will bloom until frost if the older flower heads are cut.

Marjoram is a symbol of happiness. The Greeks planted it on graves and thought that only with it growing there could their dear ones rest in peace and happiness. For centuries it has been popular in England in sweet washing waters, in sachets, in soups and in salads, in stuffings for meat, in herbal snuffs, in medicines, in planting mazes. Gerard said, "Organy is very good against the wambling of the stomacke." Could any word be more naïvely expressive of squeamishness than "wambling"? There are some 30 species of marjoram, with the family name *Origanum*. It is characteristic of the entire family to like dry, well-drained soil in a sunny location. *O. marjorana* is the sweet or knotted marjoram, an erect little perennial, but in climates at all severe has to be treated as an annual and in the temperate section is generally thought of as an annual. It has slender, wiry, reddish, woody stems which rise obliquely upward. The white flowers, somewhat like tiny hop blossoms, are hidden in the bracts of the branches. The leaves are longer than the wild marjoram leaves and have a warm balsamic taste and a minty, spicy odor. The germination from seeds is extremely slow and is usually started indoors.

O. onites, pot marjoram, is a strong, hardy perennial and an ever-spreading delight. The flower heads on terminal spikes are curious little formations like four tiny purplish pine cones grouped together at the base. The stems and branches are reddish and so the whole plant at a distance has a reddish tinge. *O. vulgare,* wild marjoram, closely resembles the pot marjoram but smells more like thyme. In fact, oil of thyme is generally called oil of origanum. The flowers of the wild marjoram range in color from purplish to pink and nearly white. *O. pulchellum* is a beautiful, hardy variety with pink flower heads and light green leaves. *O. dictamnus,* dittany of Crete, is a bushy little plant more than a foot high and inclined to sprawl. The wiry little stems are very slender and bear roundish, woolly leaves and spikes of hop-like pink flower heads. It is not hardy but slips easily. *O. heracleoticum* is the winter marjoram, a native of Greece seldom seen in the United States. There are also prostrate and variegated varieties, of interest to collectors, but none of them could be called "old-time favorites."

CHAPTER VII

Scented Geraniums

Parkinson in his *Garden of Pleasant Flowers,* 1629, devotes a chapter to "Geranium. Storkes bill or Cranes bill," opening with the words:

"As was said before concerning the Crowfeet, of their large extent and restraint, the like may be said of the Storkes bil or Cranes bil; for even of these as of them, I must for this worke set forth the descriptions but of a few, and leave the rest to a generall work."

He explains the reason for the name is that after the flowers there come "small heads with long pointed beakes, resembling the long bill of a Storke or Crane, or such like bird, which after it is ripe, parteth at the bottome where it is biggest, into foure or five seedes, every one whereof hath a peece of the beake head fastened unto it, and falleth away if it bee not gathered: . . ."

In this early book he lists but nine, with their virtues, they being great wound herbs (the root is still used medicinally), but eleven years later, 1640, in the *Theatrum Botanicum,* he really outdoes himself, illustrating only 16 but discussing innumerable ones. He says,

"Dioscorides setteth forth but two sorts of Cranes bills, Pliny added a third, Matthiolus hath six, others have encreased the number still more and more, but our age hath found out many more, whereof I have shewed you in my former booke divers sorts, such as are of most delight and beauty, fit to furnish such a garden as you there finde them, of none of these do I intend to speake againe, having given you their descriptions, etc. . . . There are many others fit to be knowne, which shall follow in this place. . . . I will distribute them into three rankes or orders, the first shall be of those that beare broad leaves, . . . the next shall be such as have round leaves like unto Mallowes, and the last of those that have their leaves much cut in and jagged."

It is among the latter that Parkinson described the kinds of scents, savory and unsavory, strong and weak, released from the leaves.

The "two sorts of Cranes bills" set forth by Dioscorides in the first century of the Christian era were identified by Professor Charles Danberry in 1857 as *Geranium tuberosum* and *Erodium malachoides,* both having been drawn by a Byzantine artist of the third century, more than 1600 years ago, and the illustrations lie before me with the comment of Professor Danberry that they are "pretty good." Dioscorides says,

"Geranium (some call it Pelonitis, some Trica, some Geranogeron . . . & on ye tops of ye wings certain excrescencies looking upward, as ye heads of cranes with ye beaks or ye teeth of dogs, but there is no use of it in Physick."

Gerard speaks of many kinds, of some that have scented leaves, of wild kinds; and of others he says,

"These are strangers in England, except in the gardens of some Herbarists: the which do growe in my garden very plentifully."

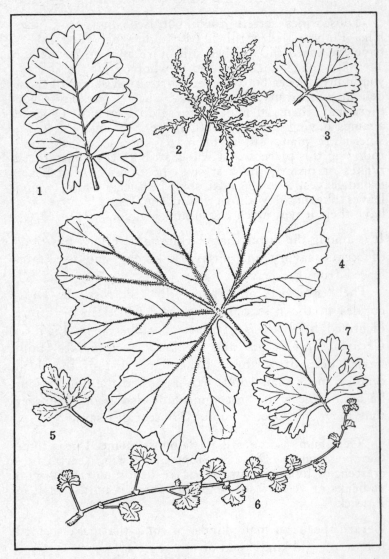

Types of Geraniums.

1. Tuberous rooted. 2. Filicifolium. 3. Lady Mary. 4. Peppermint.
5. Apricot scented. 6. Italian finger bowl. 7. Malva.

Geraniums, like the mints and thymes, are in an almost hopeless state, so far as identification and naming are concerned. They have long been loved and cherished by the people but neglected by the botanists. We do have a family name, *Geraniaceae*, which is all inclusive, and among the genera are: 1. *Geranium*, 2. *Pelargonium* and 3. *Erodium*, respectively from the Greek *"geranion"* from *"geranos"* meaning crane; from *"pelargos"* meaning stork; and from *"erodios"* meaning heron, the origin of the common names of Cranesbill, Storksbill, and Heronsbill. It is the genus *Pelargonium* that appeals to us at the moment, a genus founded in 1787, and it may be divided arbitrarily into climbing, zonal, ivy-leaved, and sweet-scented or scent-leaved pelargoniums. There are some 175 to 200 species.

In the early part of the last century, there was a craze about geraniums, as well there might be, for beginning in 1820 one Robert Sweet, a prolific English garden writer, began to publish his *Geraniaceae, the natural order of gerania: comprising the numerous and beautiful mule varieties cultivated in the gardens of Great Britain, with directions for their treatment.* That year and each second year thereafter until 1830, a huge volume appeared containing text and 100 colored plates. By 1830 there were five such volumes and 500 plates, a mouth-watering publication, still the basis of much of the identification made today.

At an earlier date, 1805, and not always seeing eye to eye with Sweet, H. C. Andrews had published his now rare monograph *Geraniums,* with 124 colored plates, double the size of those in Sweet and some of them double plates. Titles were afterwards issued to make two volumes out of the Andrews book.

Since then, with the exception of an early German

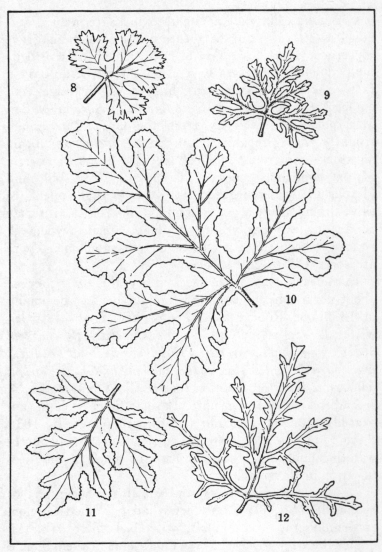

Types of Geraniums.

8. Countess of Scarborough. 9. *P. radula*. 10. Oakleaf. 11. Pheasant's Foot. 12. Dr. Livingston.

treatise and a few random articles of no authority, little
of great value has been found dealing with the sweet-
scented pelargoniums, though reference should be made
to the work of Edward Step, *Favourite Flowers of Garden & Greenhouse,* published in 1896 in 4 volumes with
316 colored plates, and to the almost obscure *History of
Variegated Zonal Pelargoniums* by Peter Grieve, which
was privately printed in London, 1868. Grieve originated
"Mrs. Pollock," "Sunset," "Italia Unita," and many
other beloved varieties.

I suppose we will always call pelargoniums by the name
"geraniums" but there are essential differences, the most
outstanding peculiarity of the pelargonium that can be noticed by the layman, so botanists say, being that it has a sort
of spur joined with the flower stalk, best seen by cutting
through the flower stalk, and a hollow tube will be found
just behind the flower. In the cranesbill the stalk is solid.

Linnaeus described some two dozen or more of the
pelargoniums but as geraniums; those and many others
introduced from the Cape section of South Africa, by plant
breeders and by accident, plus the number of species,
many of which are variable, have all combined in making the most confusing situation imaginable. Few now
have recognized specific names. In the trade and among
the collectors, they have only the pleasing and delightful
common names, some of uncertain origin, others recognized as horticultural hybrids. Mostly the division is by
scent—the pungent group, the lemon group, the rose
group, the spice group—but always there is a large group
called "miscellaneous." There is no agreement in this
classification and little in the various names or even in the
spelling of the names. With this as a proviso, may I list
here a sizable group that I have grown or know in the
gardens of friends.

All by itself is *P. tomentosum,* once named *P. piperitum,* whose peppermint scented, soft, velvety green leaves are so white and silvery in certain phases of the sunlight because of the incredibly downy hairs that cover the large leaves. It frequently grows to great size in a single season in well-drained soil. There is also, among other minty pelargoniums, one of much slower growth called *P. rapaceum.*

In the rose group, perhaps most familiar, are usually classified the deep cut *P. graveolens,* the true rose geranium, and its varieties such as the "camphor-scented"; the Dr. Livingston or "skeleton leaved"; the fern leaved *P. filicifolium;* the *P. denticulatum.* Then, there is the "other" rose geranium with less cut leaves, *P. capitatum,* and of this there are a number of forms.

In the spice-scented group are *P. odoratissimus,* known as "apple-scented," and the variety "coconut-scented." There is *P. fragrans,* nutmeg-scented; *P. odoratum,* known as "Lady Mary"; the "Godfrey's Pride"; *P. scabrum* or "apricot-scented," and a pepper-scented "Rollinson's Unique." There is filbert-scented "Schottesham Pet," and the "Prince of Orange," *P. citriodorum;* and there is a variegated "Prince of Orange."

In the lemon group is the Italian finger bowl or "citronella-scented," *P. crispum;* and there are several varieties, as var. *latifolium* and var. *varigata,* the latter called "Prince Rupert," but there are several forms. Then there is *P. grossularioides* or "gooseberry leaf," *P. mellisimum* or "lemon balm"; *P. limonium,* the "lemon" geranium of which the variety *Scarboriace is* known as the "parsley leaved" or "Countess of Scarborough."

Lastly, there is the pungent group of which *P. quercifolium,* the true "oakleaf," heads the list, but there are

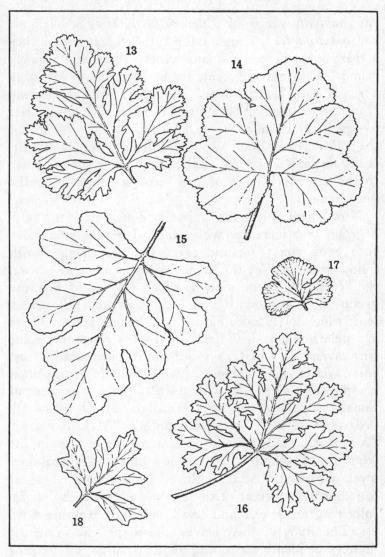

Types of Geraniums.

13. Schottesham Pet. 14. Sprawly round. 15. *P. quercifolium.*
16. Little Gem. 17. Nutmeg. 18 *P. Beauty.*

var. *oakleaf,* var. *Fair Ellen* with dark veined leaves; var. *giant oakleaf,* a huge, tall plant with leaves six inches across; and there are many others such as "Sprawly round." The "almond-scented" or "Pretty Polly" belongs here, as does "Little Gem," named *P. terebinthinaceum* from some thought of turpentine; the "Old Scarlet Unique"; "Clorinda" or "Clorindy" in the old books; the "Pheasant's Foot" or *P. alchemilloides,* which literally means "the crown of the king" and seems to refer to the saw-tooth edge of the leaf (see No. 11 in the illustration).

Now, there is left the "miscellaneous" or "doubtful," a group that increases with every visit that you make, each book you read, and every letter exchanged with fellow growers. For the moment this includes *P. radula,* the "crowfoot" pelargonium, which may be of the rose group; *P. beauty,* with a pungent leaf scent; *P. granelous,* which in its spicy nature may belong above. There are pelargoniums with leaf scent of strawberry, some with lavender-scented leaves, others of pine, musk, tansy, anise, violet, ginger, clove, citron. The *P. extipulatum* has the scent of pennyroyal; the *P. gratum,* the scent of cinnamon. There are the "Duchess of Devonshire," "Mrs. Douglas," "Mrs. Languith," "Mrs. Sargent," "Major Clarke," "Blandfordianum," named from the Marquis of Blandford, to which tuberous-rooted lilies owe their name; "Attar of Roses"; and a hundred others to tempt the collector of these lovely plants with delightfully fragrant leaves and small, colorful, exquisite flowers. The study of their leaves, the shape, the scent, the mystery of identification and of their names, all combine to cast a spell over the most hardened gardener who once gives up and starts "with just a few."

Our grandmothers knew well the "rose geraniums" and

when the jar of apple jelly was filled, placed on the top a leaf of the graveolens or the skeleton leaved, either of which, when dried, is an addition to any pungent potpourri. But these are not plants to grow for use. They are for enchantment. . . .

> ". . . melting heaven with earth,
> Leaving on craggy hills and running streams
> A softness like the atmosphere of dreams."

CHAPTER VIII

The Tooth of Saturn

"And grant me now,
Good reader, thou!
Of terms to use.
Such choice to chuse,
As may delight
The country wight,
And knowledge bring:
For such do praise
The country phrase,
The country acts,
The country facts,
The country toys,
Before the joys,
    Of any thing."
                —THOMAS TUSSER, 1573.

To all tired garden lovers it will be a delight to know that there was a period of perfect happiness, according to mythology, when men lived like gods, without toil, without grief, free from bodily infirmities and the weakness of advancing years. That was the "Golden Age" when earth brought forth abundant harvests without cultivation, an age distinguished for contentment and peace.

Just how the harvest was gathered and utilized without toil still remains unexplained. However, the reigning god in those golden days was called Cronus by the Greeks. Cronus (Kronus) was the father of Zeus, who overthrew him later and reigned instead. The Romans came to identify Cronus with a god of ancient Italy called Saturn (Saturnus). Saturn's emblem was a sickle, perhaps from the story that Cronus waylaid and mutilated his father, the Sky, with a curved sword, at the behest of his mother, Earth. This accounts for the separation of earth and sky, as they are today.

Saturn was the god of agriculture and, as the years passed, his sickle became a scythe in pictures and repre-

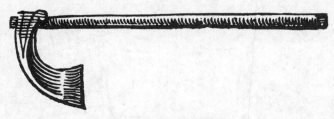

Markham's "Hack."

From *Farewell to Husbandry,* 1660.

sentations, the frontispiece of this book being a reproduction of what is perhaps the earliest of such pictures. In modern times he has become bewhiskered, wings added and ofttimes an hourglass, and through some confusion between the name Cronus and the word "chronus," which means "time," this modified picture has come to signify, within very recent years, the god of time or, briefly, Father Time. Such a picture could scarcely have been known to Ben Jonson (1573-1637) who, in "The Poetaster," speaks of "That old *bald* cheater, Time."

We think of these ideas as being born long, long ago, yet it was shortly before the birth of Christ, and a century or two after Hippocrates, Plato and Aristotle that the

worship of Saturn was conformed to that of the Greek
Cronus. Historians place the date exactly at 217 B.C.,
some 75 years after Theophrastus had written his *Enquiry Into Plants.*

The great festival of Saturn, the Saturnalia, came to
be celebrated in December from the 17th to the 24th;
schools were closed, gifts exchanged, especially wax
tapers and clay dolls, the latter supposed to signify the
children of Cronus who, having been told that he would

The Tooth of Saturn.

From *The French Gardiner,* 1675.

one day be deposed by one of his own children, pro-
ceeded to swallow them one after another until Zeus was
born, the mother concealing Zeus until he grew up, when
he forced the father to disgorge the other children. Many
scholars trace the customs that prevail at Christmas back
to this pagan festival: the Yule log, the trees, the lights.
So, too, a day was set aside as Saturn's day, our Saturday,
a day which week-end gardeners even now devote to the
garden, and well they may.

The story of Saturn, the idea of an ancient god of
agriculture, lends romance to every garden. Yet it is a

strange thing that throughout garden literature I have searched in vain for any mention of Saturn or any representation of his symbol, except in Evelyn (see illustration). On every hand we find the story of Cupid, Apollo, Venus, Jupiter, Minerva, Diana, Vulcan, and too much of Mars, the god of war. Perhaps we need to know more about Saturn, this ancient symbol of a peaceful era, peace and a plentiful harvest. It may be comforting to the occasional gardener to know that the ancient Saxons somehow seem to have lost the sickle and represent "Seater" as carrying a pail of water in which are flowers and fruits, even as you and I.

I say that I have found no mention of Saturn in garden literature. There is one exception, the reference which is given in the chapter on gardening tools, a few words in the very first gardening book we know, the *Hortulus* of Walafrid Strabo, about the ninth century, in which the monk welcomes the approach of spring, being prepared to attack, armed with the "tooth of Saturn," no doubt a reference to his trusty sickle, though the reference to tearing up the clods to rend them from the clinging network of nettle roots might well indicate a far more rugged form of sickle than we use today, perhaps more like Markham's "Hack."

But now we know the "tooth of Saturn" is a symbol of the soil. It appears inconspicuously on the frontispiece of John Evelyn's books on gardening. Just as the plants that it nourishes have entranced mankind, so, too, the romance of the soil itself from the days of Cronus to those of chemi-culture is worthy of many a page. And speaking of chemi-culture briefly, nothing more truly demonstrates that the plant is an entity apart from the soil. Each contributes to the other in many ways and, as long as we do grow our gardens in the soil, it might not be harmful to create a mental picture of the physical conditions under which the plant and soil coöperate.

Another thing that chemi-culture teaches clearly, or so it seems to me, is that the thought of fertilizer as "plant food" is a little misleading. There are many elements required from the soil, as we have learned, that are never found in the chemicals of fertilizers. What we call "plant food" seems, rather, to help the soil than the plant, and by its corrective action on the soil to make possible a less toxic condition, more suitable for a new crop. The various manures, of course, have long been recognized as valuable also because they lighten the soil. Again it is the soil that we are treating, not the plant.

Back in 1594, Hugh Plat was the great authority on soils and manures. I have told of him as a gardening writer in Chapter III and I wish it might be possible to add somewhere a whole chapter on this man who was born nearly four centuries ago, the greatest inventor of the Tudor period and one of the first persons in all the world who sat down to a desk and practiced the trade of author, saw his books printed, and reaped a reward. Between times he promoted all manner of his own inventions from a finger ring for gamblers with a tiny reflecting sphere mounted on it so that one might view the cards the other players held, to the alphabet blocks sold today in every toy store for children to learn their letters. He it was who devised the familiar "turn-spitte" that is used for roasting chickens, hams and beef. He developed methods of preserving foods, various forms of presses for extracting oils from seeds and plants, enlarging devices for draftsmen, secret inks, a method of penmanship, and hundreds of other things. But it was in the matter of soils and fertilizers that he was judged to have most ably served the god of agriculture, and though Elizabeth

seems never to have done anything about it, Plat luckily
outlived her by five years and was knighted by James I of
England.

One of my most precious volumes is Plat's *The Jewel-
house of Art and Nature,* 1594, divided into three books,
the first dealing with many "Diverse new and conceited
Experiments," the last book with the art of distillation
and recipes, some of which is the basis for his later book
Delightes for Ladies, of which I have already spoken.
But in the second book Master Plat writes of "Divers
new sorts of Soyle" and he refers to the "fourth book"
of Kings (now called II Kings) and the miracle of the
second chapter (verse 21) in which Elisha cast salt into
the waters which flowed through the land and thereby
remedied the barrenness of the fields. Plat recognized
that there are salts and salts. He says,

"Coppres is a salt, Niter is a salt, vitrial is a salt,
allom is a salt, Borras is a salt, Suger is a salt, Sublimate
is a salt, Saltpeter is a salt. . . . Tartar, sal Armoniacke,
all these are divers kindes of saltes, and if I would take
uppon me to name them all, I shoulde never make an
ende."

and goes on to say that "although the number of those
men is verie small, which can give anie true reason whie
dungue shoulde doe anie good in arable groundes, but
are ledde thereto more by custome than anie Philosophi-
call reason, . . ." it is apparent to him that it is the action
of the salts on the soil and he condemns those who leave
their fertilizer out in the open for the rains to wash
away all the good. Plat saw clearly that, as we now know,
the valuable salts which do any good in soil must be soluble ones, just those easily lost. He advises the use of
soil beneath a manure heap as a rich dressing for the

garden, after the manure itself has been spread on the fields.

Plat points out that the salt he is writing about is not common table salt but vegetable salts that replace those in the soil, that a field after growing a crop must either be enriched or lie fallow "to the ende that it may gather a newe saltnesse from the cloudes, and raine that

Sir Hugh Plat's "yron presse."

From *The Jewel-house of Art and Nature,* 1594.

falleth upon it." He speaks of the value of lime, of chalk, of ashes, of bone meal, of mulch, of dried blood, of nearly everything we use today. He points out the necessity of allowing animal or vegetable material to become well rotted before use. Moreover, he does not forget, as many modern writers do, that there is a distinction between a field used year after year for new crops and a garden where the same plants grow perennially with constantly increasing root systems and no such abundant fertilizing is needed. I think modern gardeners would do well to consider Plat's advice and not get too stirred up about their soil. The effect of "enriching" the soil is a more luxuriant growth of the plant, sometimes of the flowers; but if you are growing the plant for fragrance or flavor, as in the case of herbs or any fragrant flower, they must not be forced. Bacon throughout his writings, as do other early authorities, stresses the point that excessive nourishment is not good and modern growers of fruit tell us that too rich ground is apt to cause the bushes, vines and trees to "run to wood," except in the case of strawberries and raspberries. The gardener's outstanding exception is, no doubt, the rose. It is hard to do too much for roses.

The type of soil is frequently of more importance than fertilizer, as most good gardeners know. Gerard shows great pride in his ability to adapt the soil to the plant, the plant to the soil. "It groweth in my garden" is his cry of triumph. Tusser, the farmer, speaks of the same thing, as in his lines,

> "Ground gravelly, sandy and mixed with clay,
> Is naughty for hops, any manner of way;"

The same plant in different parts of the garden will give widely different fragrances, as will be quite apparent if you will train yourself to distinguish odors, quite a pleasing hobby in itself.

Why this change of soil should act in such a way is usually a matter of root temperature. Some plants, as southernwood, wormwood, the artemisias, caraway, elecampane, like the stiffer clay with some underlying drainage, thus providing a lower root temperature, a slower growth and more moisture for the extensive foliage they bear. Others seem to be stimulated by the sudden changes of temperature from day to night that a sandy soil provides, such as dill, marjoram and pot marigold. Still

Diuerse new sorts of
Soyle not yet brought
into any publique vse, for
manuring both of pasture
and arable ground, with
sundrie concepted practises
belonging therunto.

Faithfully and familiarly set
downe by H. Plat of Lin-
colns Inne Gent.

LONDON
Printed by Peter Short.

1594

Title page of Sir Hugh Plat's book on soil, 1594.

others love to be against a stone or a wall which carries the heat of the sun well down into the earth at night, providing an even warmth. Most of the creeping thymes grow best on a slope or over a rock or hanging down on a bank or wall. To adapt the plant to the soil, the soil to the plant, is as truly fascinating as any part of gardening.

To get closer to our plant friends, we must sometimes think of the great structure of the soil beneath us that permits air to penetrate and oxidize vegetable matter, to force out gases which are formed, to heat and cool the soil. The same capillary spaces that permit the air to flow also help the grains of soil to retain moisture around themselves in order to dissolve the salts of the soil that are needed by the plants. As the water circulates in the soil and evaporates from the surface layers, it brings to the upper layers some of the soluble matter from the deeper parts, thus renewing to some extent any exhaustion of the upper layers. It was with the idea of loosening up the lower layers that the fad of "deep digging" was preached so vehemently a few decades ago.

Many students of the soil believe that just as the plants give off tons of vapor and gases through their leaves and branches into the air, they also have a similar action through those underground branches we call roots, at the same time as they absorb moisture laden with salts from the earth; that some of the matter thus excreted into the soil by one plant, or left there by its selective absorption, is deleterious to another and so certain plants cannot thrive side by side while other plants delight to be together. Sometimes this is given as the explanation why farmers have always found it best to "rotate" crops.

Even these modern ideas were not unknown to the ancients and explain, no doubt, their belief that rue and basil could not thrive together and that chamomile set near any drooping plant would restore it to health, doing for other herbs what the clovers, for instance, do for timothy and bluegrass. Because of this, chamomile became widely known as the "plant's physician," an idea that may not be unsound but, whether a true idea or not, as William Coles would say, it is pleasant.

There were many of the other gardening writers who devoted pages to the soil, Richard Gardiner, for example, of whose *Profitable Instructions for the Manuring, Sowing, and Planting of Kitchen Gardens,* 1603, I have written in Chapter III. Francis Bacon, whose *Natural History,* 1627, appeared after his death, opens the book with the many tests he made with various sorts of manures and their influence on crops. He tells of making a hot bed exactly as we do it today, and of its great value in "accelerating growth"; he speaks of liquid manures with disapproval, of the use of chalk, soot, ashes, and even the value of wine instead of water, another pleasant thought for devotees of Saturn.

One of the old and well-recommended treatments reminds me of the country custom, so often frowned upon by modern writers, of pouring dish water on the garden. Plat speaks of the wonderful effect of soap ashes liberally used on plants and shows an ear of barley nearly four feet long that was raised that way. W. Carew Hazlitt, writing in 1887, says that in South Australia he has observed the experiments of growing peach trees from planted peach stones, using as a dressing only soap suds applied regularly, and the result was most sturdy trees and an abundance of fruit. Markham, in *Farewell to Husbandry,* 1620, among the discussions on laying "draines" to "ease" the ground of moisture, what grains to take on ship voyages, the preserving of seeds, a new way of harrowing (see illustration), and the multitude of materials for enriching and lightening the soil, includes "sope ashes," "hoofes" and horn shavings, "woollen cloth" torn to shreds by servants and children, the hair of "beasts hides," and

"all your powdred beef broth, and all other salt broths or brines, which shall grow or breed in your house, also all manner of soap sudds, or other sudds, and washings which shall proceed from the Laundery, and this will so strengthen and enrich your manure, that every load shall be worth five of that which wanteth this help. . . ."

Insects and disease aside, a gardener's problem is really a simple one, considering the immense complexity of soil and plant. It is merely one of moisture, air and root temperature, if we reduce it to a visual form. Loose soil and good drainage in nine cases out of ten would seem to be the answer. Drainage is easily given by deep diggings, filling in with upturned sods covered with stones, ashes, sand, gravel. Porosity you can get by mixing in with the top soil a plentiful supply of sand, sifted coal ashes, a little chalk or lime. Add clay to sandy soil and sand to a clay soil and, in gardens, chalk or lime where the soil tends to puddle.

Generally speaking, neutral soil comes nearest to suiting plants, if there is warmth and moisture. There are well-known exceptions, of course; and just as acid soil may be neutralized by chalk or limestone, so a neutral soil may be made acid by digging in sawdust or watering with a weak tannic acid solution.

Elizabethan gardeners solved the problem of drainage, after a fashion, in the most ingenious way of just building up the beds on top of the ground, the familiar raised beds varying in height from a few inches to two feet or

more, even in the same garden. All authentic gardens of
this period have these raised beds but, so far as I recall,
only Lawson ventures to suggest the reason for the raised
beds and in language not unlike that of Hyll concerning
the general ignorance in the use of "dungue." Lawson
says that gardeners "raise their squares . . . if only they
knew it," because soil for plants should be somewhat
dryer than that for trees. Some modern writer has ex-
pounded the same idea in the brief, picturesque and
equally absurd phrase about plants "getting their feet
wet." I wonder how the "wet feet" theory explains the
wonderful results obtained with chemi-culture where the
plant's feet, always in a tank of liquid, aren't merely wet,
they're actually drowned!

But now to gardening tools of early days.

CHAPTER IX

Early Gardening Tools

"Now sets do ask watering, with pot or with dish,
New sown do not so, if ye do as I wish:
Through cunning with dibble, rake, mattock and spade,
By line, and by level, trim garden is made."
—TUSSER, Five Hundreth Points of Good Husbandry, 1573.

In reading the early gardening books, I am always amazed at the great quantity and kinds of tools and at the ingenious devices for carrying forward the cultivation of farm and garden. W. C. Hazlitt, however, in his *Gleanings in Old Garden Literature*, 1887, laments the paucity of information in the early books:

"The bygone gardener had at first a very narrow assortment of tools. The vocabularies mention, so far as I can see, only an axe, a grafting-knife, a spade, and a pruning hook. But later onward—in the Tudor time—he was much better provided, or at all events our information as to his implements grows ampler. We hear of a barrow, a mattock, a spade, a shovel, a short and a long rake, and two kinds of fork, one called in the vocabularies a furca, the other a merger."

Hazlitt goes on to say that the "conduct of horticultural operations . . . involved the employment of many other

155

appliances . . . of which we possess no actual record at first . . . and had become too established and familiar to attract special attention, when the earliest writers on the garden appeared."

Showing the Modern Rake.

From *Ortus Sanitatis,* 1517 edition.

Yet in the *Five Hundreth Points of Good Husbandry,* the rhyming farm treatise written in the reign of Elizabeth, greatest Tudor of them all, much space was devoted to farm equipment. Between stanzas 8 and 9 of the September Husbandry is a "Digression to Husbandly Furniture," of twenty-one 4-line stanzas, listing with slight descriptive embroidery, barn furniture, stable furniture, cart furniture, husbandry tools, plow furniture, harvest tools.

"A brush scythe and grass-scythe, with rifle to stand,
A cradle for barley, with rubstone and sand:
Sharp sickle and weeding hook, hayfork and rake,
A meak for the pease, and to swinge up the brake.

"Short rakes for to gather up barley to bind,
And greater to rake up such leavings behind;
A rake for to bale up, the fitches that lie,
A pike for to pike them up, handsome to dry."

Some of these farm tools are unfamiliar to twentieth century Americans but were used by the sixteenth century English as a matter of course. The rifle, for instance, was a bent stick attached to the business end of a scythe as a handle for striking corn into rows. Tusser's cradle was a three-pronged wooden tool to catch the corn as it falls and lay it in orderly rows. The meak was a hooked handle, five feet in length, to gather up peas. The pike was a two or three pronged pitchfork.

In listing the numerous tools in his 84 lines of verse, Tusser is not content simply to mention rakes, forks, shovels, baskets, ladders, carts, but specifies the kinds for particular uses, as the dung rake, barley rake, the crome to extract weeds from the bottom of ditches; a short pitchfork, straw fork, dung fork, hayfork. Then there were casting shovel, sharp cutting spade, a skuppart, skavel, both for digging in marshy ground, diddall, a triangular spade for keeping the banks of ditches in order. There were hand barrows, carts, tumbrels, and long ladders, gafe ladders from which threshers threw down the sheaves, cart ladders and wheel ladders attached to the sides of the hayrick and to the end of the cart to support huge loads of hay.

These tools and others found today in any implement catalogue were part of the necessary equipment of Tusser's little farm in the parish of Brantham, Suffolk, in 1573. Few of our farms of moderate size could boast of such equipment, a far cry from the pitiful little estimate of tools which Hazlitt claims for the early workers.

Long before Tusser there were many tools described, designed and made only as the need demanded. Neither asparagus bunchers nor potato hook would have been found in the Hammacher Schlemmer & Co. of fifteenth century London, because asparagus had not yet been developed in England any larger, according to Gerard, than the size of large quills, and potatoes had not then arrived.

In the earliest days of nomadic tribes, people gathered food where they found it growing, using shells or pointed stones alone or attached to sticks. When settlements were finally made and the idea evolved of bringing plants from field and forest to a garden enclosed by wattle fence, then those early people constructed more elaborate tools. The crotched digging stick developed into a crude plow drawn by man or beast. Even in Biblical times, certainly, some of those tools were of metal, for we read in Isaiah 2:4, ". . . and they shall beat their swords into plowshares, and their spears into pruning hooks."

By the ninth century, farming and gardening tools were of such quality and quantity as to demand protection from the elements or from neighbors with "borrowing" propensities. As Hazlitt says, "It is only in a casual way that our acquaintance with the contents of the Anglo-Saxon

An Iron Trowel for Lifting Out Plants.

From Ferrarii, *De Florum Cultura,* Rome, 1633.

or later English tool-house comes to us." That holds true for the Continent also, for men there did not write of their tools any more than a gardener now would think of devoting a book to the description of tools in general use. Perhaps one of each kind of our farm and garden implements should be sealed in a huge building which a time lock would open some 5,000 years hence!

To me the very "casual" way we do learn about the tools has a distinct appeal of its own—expense accounts, contemporary pictures, maps and diagrams, diaries, none of these put on display for a wondering student ages hence, but used as part of the ordinary business of life. These little revelations, the happening upon mention or picture of a piece of furniture, gown, cooking utensil, manuscript, gardening tool, all project us back into the times as no detailed account of what must have been, can do.

The medieval monastery, a complete self-subsisting community, is one of our most fruitful sources for information about gardening, because of the detailed records kept by the monks, and the monastery plans kept with equal care, many of them still in existence. The earliest gardening plan is that of the monastery near Lake Constance in Switzerland at St. Gall, coming by the ninth century under Benedictine rule, which exalted manual labor. In this plan, at the end of the central path are the house for the head gardener, one for his men, and a tool house, all plainly labeled. About that time, Walafrid Strabo, abbot of Reichenau, a monastery on an island in Lake Constance, wrote what may well be called the first gardening book, the *Hortulus,* in which he refers poetically to his tools. Speaking of the approach of spring, he says, "I prepare to attack, armed with the 'tooth of Saturn,' tear up the clods and rend them from the clinging network of nettle roots." The tooth of Saturn, no doubt, is the sickle, the symbol of that deity, familiar to us now as Father Time, the sickle changed to a scythe (see frontispiece).

From earliest times, monastery life was well organized, a department for everything and every monk in his department. One was gardening with a hortulanus, gardinarius or garden warder at the head, and other monks as famuli under him, besides hired laborers, their pay derived from the rent of land or buildings. Each hortulanus kept the strictest of itemized accounts for expenses and receipts, not only from the garden departments but from vineyard and orchard.

From such accounts we learn much of the gardening outlay. Records of Ramsey Abbey in the late twelfth century show that 14 loaves and 2 acres of land were paid to two famuli. At Durham, the hortulanus was paid 5 shillings a year, besides other sums which doubled this. From the rolls in 1340 at Norwich, items appear of three pence paid for "iron spades and fixing bills," seven pence for mending an ax and for a new hatchet, 12 pence for two rakes, two spades, and two dung forks new ironed, one penny for the "dentation" of a scythe, a penny for cord, a penny for an earthen pot. In 1402, thirteen and one-half pence was paid for spades, shovels, and other utensils. In 1403, seven pence was paid for gloves, 8 shillings 10 pence for tunics, and in 1427, twelve pence was paid for boots for the gardener.

In early days vineyards, flourishing for the most part in the eastern and southern part, were as important to England as to the Continent. Vines often served as boundary lines, while October, when grapes were harvested, was the "Wyn moneth." In an eleventh century Anglo-Saxon manuscript, a picture shows three men vigorously

pruning vines, two of them working with modest curved
knives, while a third is down on one knee, smilingly wielding over a little tendril what looks like a villainous two-
edged battle-ax with wicked curved blades. In a late
fifteenth century picture, two monks are drinking cosily
together at a table beneath a tree while in the foreground
two laborers are gathering colossal bunches of grapes
from vines that grow bushily straight up, without support.

Any early writer who made any pretense toward gardening subjects, discussed the care of the orchard, and
the necessary tools and equipment. From the beginning of
time, gardeners have been fascinated in grafting fruit
and nut trees and berry bushes. Knowledge of grafting
was, in fact, an essential part of the gardener's education.
In what is probably the earliest original gardening book
in English, *The Feate of Gardening,* a 196-line rhymed
treatise of the early fifteenth century, the author, Ion
Gardener, offers his advice on grafting in a section called,
"Of Graffyng of Treys" and mentions the saw and the
"knyfe" that are required.

Abraham Cowley pays great tribute to the results obtained by grafting, in the tenth verse of his poem "The
Garden," in Evelyn's *Kalendarium Hortense:*

> "We no where Art do so triumphant see,
>   As when it Grafts or Buds the Tree:
> In other things we count it to excel,
> If it a docile Scholar can appear
> To Nature, and but imitates her well;
> It over-rules, and is her Master here.
> It imitates her Maker's Power Divine,
> And changes her sometimes, & sometimes do's refine.
> It do's, like Grace, the fallen Tree restore
> To its blest state of Paradise before:

Who would not joy to see his conqu'ring Hand
O're all the Vegetable World command?
And the wild Giants of the Wood receive
    What Laws he's pleas'd to give?
He bids th'ill-natur'd Crab produce
The gentle Apple's Winy Juice;
The Golden Fruit that worthy is
Of Galatea's purple Kiss;
He do's the savage Hawthorn teach
To bear the Medlar and the Pear;
He bids the rustick Plum to rear
A noble Trunk, and be a Peach.
Ev'n Daphne's Coyness he do's mock,
And weds the Cherry to her Stock,
Tho' she refus'd Apollo's Suit;
Ev'n she, that chast and Virgin-Tree,
Now wonders at her self, to see
That she's a Mother made, and blushes in her Fruit.

As the years marched on, writers became more explicit about the description of tools. In a page of drawings of grafting tools in the sixteenth century, there are several kinds of "chesils," and a "wimble bit," mallets, saws, grafting knives, one straight bladed, another curved, "with each a ryng or butten to hang at their girdell," a pruning knife, a vine knife, a hammer with a file and "pearcer." In the seventeenth century, William Lawson, in seven pages of detailed description, adds to these tools a cleaver and a wedge of wood, iron or bone "two hand-full at least."

John Parkinson in his *Paradisus*, 1629, devotes Chapter V of the section on "Ordering of the Orchard" to detailed description in words and drawing of the necessary tools and the successive stages in the grafting process. The tools are labeled A. the Iron Instrument with chisels at each end, to keep the cleft of the tree open to receive the graft; B. the small "Penne-knife" with a

broad and thin ended "hafte," C. a pen or "quil" cut
half round to take off a bud; D. an Ivory Instrument
made to the same fashion; E. a shield of brass made
hollow before to be put into the slit. The ladder he describes is just like Lawson's—"Stoole on the top of the
Ladder of 8 or more rungs, with two backe-feet, whereon
you may safely and easefully stand. . . ."

In 1670 Leonard Meager in his *English Gardner*
makes claim to have been "above Thirty Years a Practitioner in the Art of Gardening" and says that he is now
setting down the result of his experiences

"very plainly without any deceitful Dress and unnecessary
Flourishes, whereby it may become very useful for all
sorts of Practitioners, yea though of very weak capacities."

His book is full of ingenious devices appealing to the
amateur gardener. To get off tree moss, he says, "scrape
or rub off the Moss as much as you can with an Iron
tool, made in shape like a Howe, or Dough-rake, made
a little hollow on each side, the better to answer the several shapes or sizes of boughs that are to be Mossed; it
is to have a convenient stail or handle, rather short than
long, except you stand on the ground to do your work.
. . ."

At harvest time to gather the fruit carefully, Lawson
suggests, besides the long ladder and the stool ladder
mentioned above,

"a gathering apron like a poake before you, made of
purpose, or a wallet hung on a bough, or a basket with
a sive bottome or skin bottome, with lathes or splinters
under, hung in a rope to pull up and downe; bruise none,
every bruise is to fruit death: if you doe, use them presently. An hooke to pull boughs to you is necessary, breake
no boughes."

Flemish Calendar Showing the Plow and the Harrow.

Reproduced from a fragment of a *Book of Hours,* executed at Bruges in the early sixteenth century, now in the British Museum.

The ingenuity of each age was equal to its needs. In the early fifteenth century *Book of Hours* of the Duc de Berry is a miniature of farm operations taking place beyond castle walls. In the foreground is an amazingly modern plowing arrangement. Two oxen are drawing the plow, the front mounted on two wheels. By pressure the plowman can keep the plow at the desired depth, while release of pressure will lift it to the surface of the ground, the same principle as our tractor plow of today.

In a late fifteenth century picture is a farm scene with one man, knife in belt, and hanging from his neck an apron containing seeds which he is broadcasting. In a nearby field one laborer is cutting grain with an unusually long-handled scythe, while his companion is gathering the crop together with a long fork. Hanging down his back from the waist is a long bag resembling a quiver, full of all sorts of small tools.

On an illustrated Flemish calendar of the early sixteenth century for July, haying is in full progress, the men armed with rakes and scythes with long straight blades, but no place on the straight handle to grip it. For the August days the artist displayed a harvest scene, the field surrounded by a wattle fence. In the distance is an ox-cart bearing a load of grain and a laborer wielding a sickle. Another worker is taking a recess, resting beside a girl busily serving him refreshment. At one side is a cradle for cutting and holding a shock of corn. These scenes remind me of the word picture of June given by M. Stevenson in *The Twelve Moneths,* 1661:

"The Hay-makers are mustered to make an Army for the field, where (not always in Order) they march under the Bag and the Bottle, when betwixt the Fork and the Rake there is seen great force of Armes. The Hook and the Sickles are making ready for Harvest."

The Flemish calendar for September shows the fall agricultural work under way with plowing, planting and harrowing going forward. As in the fifteenth century picture mentioned above, this early sixteenth century plow has an almost modern aspect, a wheel plow drawn by two horses and, amazing as it may be, with removable plowshares. The sower is broadcasting seed from an apron slung about his neck. The inevitable chickens are picking up the grain as he scatters it. The harrow, too, is modern in plan, a two-horse hitch on a tooth harrow, the horses having about their necks very modern looking stuffed collars.

Tusser, of the late sixteenth century, can always be counted on for good husbandly instructions, as the following snatches from the various months indicate:

For September,

> Horse, oxen, plough, tumbrel, cart, waggon and wain,
> The lighter and stronger the greater thy gain.

For December,

> Get grindstone and whetstone for tool that is dull
> A wheel-barrow also be ready to have.

Having thus spent December, a slack month for farming, the laborers in January made the first inroads on the earth untouched for a few months.

For January,

> Let servant be ready with mattock in hand,
> To stub out the bushes, that noyeth the land.

By May weeding is the order of the day, even as now:

> In May get a weed-hook, a crotch and a glove,
> And weed out such weeds, as the corn doth not love.

Tusser's June advice shows his practical husbandry in regard to the farm equipment,

> Provide of thine own, to have all things at hand
> Lest work and the workman, unoccupied stand:
> Love seldom to borrow, that thinkest to save,
> For he that once lendeth twice looketh to have.
>
> . . .
>
> What husbandly husbands, except they be fools,
> But handsome have store-house, for trinkets and tools?

In Markham's *Countrie Farm,* 1616, his edition of Surflet's translation of the *Maison Rustique,* 1600, there is much written of the Plowman's Instruments and Tools in the section on "Arable Grounds." Besides the usual quota of carts, rakes, forks, sickles, sieves, there were two kinds of harrows, one with wooden teeth for simple clay and another with iron teeth for sands or any binding earth. There were also different kinds of plows for each of eight types of soil listed, such as stiff black clay, white blue or gray clay, where the plow may be smaller; red sand, white sand, black clay mixed with red sand, white clay with white sand, black clay with white sand, white clay with red sand. A dull list to read, but we do learn what great attention the early farmers, as well as modern ones, paid to tools, recognizing that upon the implements largely depend successful results. It is a great mistake for us to assume that our early ancestors worked with a few inadequate tools. They had come a long way from primitive digging sticks.

Gervase Markham later in his *Farewell to Husbandry,* 1660, dilates on the problem of what to do with the ground after plowing. He made a drawing of an iron hack, like a curved head mattock, for cutting the clods into small pieces. For making the clods still smaller, he

suggests a clotting beetle. Then if the chunks are not
small enough, the laborer after a rain should apply a
broader and flatter clotting beetle made of thick "Ash
boards more than a foot square and above two inches in
thicknesse."

For the ordinary size garden of the early days, there
were the same sort and variety of digging and raking
tools as for the farm land. Most of the fifteenth century
pictures and woodcuts with a garden setting, show the
gardeners digging with spades of various shapes, square
or curved, some curving so much as to be simply long
handled scoops. It is surprising how very long the handles
of spades were. In one seventeenth century picture from
the *Theatrum Florae,* the gentleman is equipped with
such a long-handled spade while the lady has an impos-
sibly short-handled rake.

The drawings in Thomas Hyll's *The Gardeners Labyrinth,* 1577, and in William Lawson's *New Orchard and
Garden,* 1618, certainly seem to belie Hazlitt's statement
that we learn but in a casual way about the early tools.
These writers and others not only describe tools but
make drawings of them. In both these books the tools,
large as life and twice as natural, are very ostentatiously
laid about the garden. In the Hyll drawing are a reel of
garden line, rake, curved knife, pickax, mattock, and cleft
dibble, all laid carefully and separately around two sides
of the picture, which shows one gardener digging with a
fork while his companion is blithely thrusting a dibble into
a bed preparatory to plunging in a plant firmly clutched
in his fist. In the Lawson picture three men are working
in the model orchard, pruning and setting out young trees.
In the foreground, very neatly laid upon one another but
not to hide any detail, are a very much out of proportion
curved spade, a sickle and a pickaxe.

Other amusing features in the old pictures are the costumes of the well-dressed gardeners. Lawson's laborers work in doublet and hose, odd shaped derbies or high crowned hats with a leaning towards wide brims. Hyll's men also are in doublet and hose, low shoes of the Colonial type, hats varying from the Puritan in design to close fitting cap with tiara-like band with pointed scallops. The gardeners, for the most part, seem very dressy and, I should think, would have been insufferably hot in working, though, in the old accounts, are expense items for tunics, gloves and boots.

But the women in the pictures are really decked out in full regalia. On the title page of the *Herbal* of Tabernaemontanus, 1588, is a scene for all the world like a self-conscious garden setting of the gay nineties.* The three women gardeners are resplendent in full skirts, tight waists with leg o' mutton sleeves, hats of hideous shapes, typical of the nineties or of 1939. One woman, as it seems to be, though it might be a laborer in long tunic, is digging with a long-handled curved spade, another is tending a long-stemmed plant while the third is industriously sprinkling the bed with a watering pot resembling a Victorian urn-like vase with a handle.

The system of carrying on garden operations on private estates was, in general, like that of the monasteries. A head gardener was responsible for efficient management of the gardens, and received for pay as much as 12 pounds a year. As in the monastery of St. Gall, the gardener usually dwelled in his own little house at one end of the garden. In 1600 apparently it was still the custom, for in the *Maison Rustique* we are advised to build at some 20 or 30 paces from the beehives "some little house, if you be so disposed, for him [gardener] to dwell in who

---

* Reproduced in *Magic Gardens*.

hath charge of looking to them [bees] and therein also
to put his tooles."

The head gardener hired day laborers for 3 to 6 pence,
or 2 pence if food was supplied. In the time of Edward I,
in the thirteenth century, an existing record shows payment of only 2¼ pence a day to Roger le Herberur.
Weeding was usually done by women. In Hampton Court

Early Gardening Tools.

From Thomas Hyll, *The Gardeners Labyrinth,* 1577.

accounts is this entry: "Paid to two women rooting up
unprofitable herbs in the garden for three days, 16d."

Much was written in the early days about the art of
weeding. Hyll says that, in weeding, the "Gardener must
diligently take heed that he doe not too boisterously loose
the earth nor handle much the plants in plucking away of
the weeds," but he advises against an iron instrument in
favor of the fingers. Lawson, however, uses tools.

"Weeds in a fertile soile ... will be noysome, and deforme your allies, walkes, beds, and squares, your under Gardners must labour to keepe all cleanly and handsome from them, and all other filth with a Spade, weeding knives, rake with iron teeth: a skrapple of Iron thus formed:" Then follows a drawing of an instrument like a modern long-handled "claw" or scratcher.

Markham advises a session of weeding after a "showre of rain," but not with the hands alone, since "Gorse has exceeding sharp pricks, so that with your naked hands you are not able to touch them, and to arme your hands against them, with strong thick gloves, would be too boisterous and cumbersome, so that sometimes you might either misse the weeds and pull up the corne; or else pull up the Corn and weeds both together; therefore to prevent all these casualties or hindrances, you shall take a pair of long small wooden nippers."

In the early days, there were no clean shaven grass lawns as we have today. In the medieval pleasaunce there was the flowery mede, an uncut meadow dotted with flowers. By the sixteenth century chamomile clipped evenly was very popular, and even in the Victorian Age was still used for ground cover. Not until Markham's *Way to get Wealth*, 1613, is there evidence of anything approaching our lawns, and those were not developed by sowing grass seed but by setting squares of turf out from heaths. In Stephen Blake's outline of a contemplated, but never written, book is a section on "The expert way of laying of Grass work."

However, in John Rea's *Flora*, 1665, are detailed directions for lawn laying. After marking out the plot by painted railings, the ground was carefully prepared. "The best turfs for this purpose are had in the most hungry Common, and where the grass is thick and short."

Square shaped turf was laid out by lines, "then with a straight bitted Spade or Turving-hoe (which many for that purpose provide) and a short cord tied to it near the Bit, and the other end to the middle of a strong staff, whereby one thrusting the Spade forward under the Turfs, and another by the Staff pulling backwards, they will easily be staved and taken up, but not too many at a time for drying, but as they are laid which must be done by a line, and a long level, placing them close together, and beating them down with a Mallet, having covered the quarter or place intended, let it be well watered, and beaten all over with a heavy broad Beater." Often today the edges of a sowed lawn are laid with sod in much the same fashion.

There were no electric hedge clippers in early days, and I am not at all sure the gardeners would have approved of them. In the *Maison Rustique* are specific directions for the time and manner of clipping. "To cut the Border, whether it be of Lavender, Rosemarie, or Boxe, you must use the ordinarie sheeres, which have handles of wood. To cut other smaller and lesse hearbes, you must have sheeres like those which Taylors use."

The early gardening tools were, of course, not manufactured in power-run factories of the best approved materials, and even allowing for the fact that a shilling went farther than it does today, the cost of the tools seems ridiculously low. The price was a matter mostly of pennies. In the Hampton Court records of 1533, an iron rake cost 6 pence, and the same amount for a hatchet. A knife cost 3 pence, six pieces of round measuring line 12 pence; two cutting hooks cost 2 shillings, two other rakes 16 pence, two chisels 6 pence, while a grafting saw cost 4 pence.

Household rolls give us good cross-sections of the daily

life of early times. In the accounts of Thomas, Seventh Earl of Northumberland, 1563-1565, are records of payments for the "sadlyer to the paynter for making viii scutcheons," for colored yarn for carpets, for little "songe bookes," violl strings, virginal wires, crossbow strings, arrows, blowing horns, and some of the largest amounts to settle gambling losses. For garden expenses, there are: a "dyall" for the garden 4 shillings; watering "pottes" (3) 16 pence; 2 "spdes" 2 shillings; "1 shovelles shodde" 8 pence; 2 "Rayke of yron" 20 pence; 1 "Hackes to cut roots" 2 shillings; 1 "Lynes of hemp" 12 pence; seeds 2 shillings.

By the seventeenth century, as can be inferred from the Le Strange household books, prices are higher. A garden spade cost 3 shillings, 2 large garden baskets are 4 shillings, and pumps and pipes for the garden were two pounds four shillings. The gardener's pay was still not to be envied, for two pounds was paid "to the gardener for a quarter's wages wanting 2 weekes."

Many tools were home made, directions for some in the gardening books, and most ingenious were the devices. Sir Anthony Fitz Herbert in his book of husbandry, 1534, tells how to construct forks and rakes. Tools should be made in the winter, he says,

"when the housbande sytteth by the fyre, and hath nothynge to do, than may he make thym redye, and tothe the rakes with dry wethywode, and bore the holes with his wymble, bothe above and under, and drive the tethe upward faste and harde, and then wedge them above with dry woode of oke. . . . They be most commonly made of hasell and withee."

Leonard Meager, seventeenth century writer, contrived a device for the even sowing of seed. After the ground has been prepared "and the furrow made . . . if you put your seeds in a white Paper, you may (if the seeds are small) very easily and equally sow them by shaking the lower end of your paper with the fore-finger of that hand you sow with; the paper must not be much open towards the end. . . ."

Giving the plants artificial rain presented its problems, gardeners being always concerned with how to imitate a shower so the plants would not be drenched. Thomas Hyll tells how to care for transplanted seedlings until, we might say, they were on their feet:

"The best watering which is certain (except your ground be new made, with half dung) is to make a hole with a Dibble a little from the herb or plant, a slope to the root, and so water the root under ground, for water rotteth and killeth above ground."

Some years later this same idea is expressed in John Evelyn's *Kalendarium Hortense,* 1664, for March: "Never cast water on things newly planted nor on Flowers, but at convenient distances so as rather to moisten the Ground without sobbing the Leaves of the Plant, which ends in scorching."

Systems of irrigation were used from ancient times, the gardens divided into rectangular beds with straight intersecting paths through which water was forced by pump or fountain. Hyll carefully describes the best approved Tudor methods of watering, listing the common watering pot, the copper pot-bellied can, the irrigation system operated by a pump, "Squirtes" of tin, the "skiffe" of wood, and last a sort of wick made of wool and set in a container of water placed near each plant. He says:

"The common watering pot for the Garden beds with us hath a narrow neck, big belly, somewhat large bottom, and full of little holes, with a proper hole formed on the head to take in the water, which filled full, and the thumb laid on the hole to keep in the aire, may on such wise be carried in handsome manner to those places by a better help aiding, in the turning and bearing upright of the bottom of this pot which needfully require watering."

The copper pot was "best to be liked," an advantage being that besides the strong handle fastened to belly and head there is "an other strong ring or handle fastened artly to the lips of the pot, much like to the Barbers water-pot carried abroad, . . . this other handle especially serveth to sprinkle forth the water by the long pipe full of little holes on the head, that some named a pumpe, which reacheth from the bottom unto the head of the pot, for the handsomer delivering forth of the water, the handle in the mean time guiding the long pipe of the pot until all the water be spent."

To return again to Hazlitt's statement: "Such men as Evelyn and Worlidge did not dream that we should care to have it in our power to contrast with the present facilities for managing a garden those which prior generations enjoyed." Yet Worlidge in his book, *Systema Horti-culturae*, 1677, dilates on the subject of watering methods, for instance. He first emphasizes that "such ought to be watered by the smallest or rain-like drops as you can, and not too much, for hasty watring and hasty showers discover them." Worlidge advocates Hyll's filtration method—a pot by every plant, each with a woolen wick draining the water over a drop at a time—and also making a hollow ring in the earth around a plant and pouring water into it, the latter much used at Salt Acres during the extreme drought of one summer.

Besides the common type of watering pot, says Worlidge, "There is another sort of Watring pot that hath a small hole at the bottom and another at the Top, so that when you sink it into a Vessel of Water, it will fill by the lower pipe or hole, the air passing out at the hole at the top where the handle is also: when it is full take it by the handle and stop the hole with your thumb, and when you come to the Plant you intend to water, you may ease the hole whereon your thumb lies, and as you please let the water out at the Pipe in the bottom, and so may you stop it, and open it with your thumbs, at your pleasure. . . ." But what concentration on that thumb!

Worlidge also suggests an engine resembling a fire engine that can be placed "in a frame to drive to and fro about your Garden, you may fill it with Water and the Spout or Pipe with a perforated cover like unto the Common watring Pots . . . with this Engine may you intimate Rain, over any of your Beds at a distance. . . ."

It is a pity that Hazlitt did not live to read Evelyn's "Directions for his Gardiner at Says Court" which was not publicly printed until 1932, the manuscript having been held by the family. Although in the *French Gardiner,* 1658, he gives some general directions for making gardening contrivances such as a hurdle for sifting earth; in his "Directions," unknown to Hazlitt, he makes a list of over one hundred "Tools and Instruments Necessary for a Gardiner." These may be divided into four classes: tools for trees; tools for preparing the garden; for the care of seeds and seedlings; for plants and accessories.

The first list contains the customary grafting tools and ladders. Under the second heading are various kinds of spades, scythes, whetstones, shovels, hoes, rakes, forks, sieves, rollers, and beaters, mattock, pickax, measuring chains. In the third division there are plow-rills for seeds, tubs, baskets, barrows, trowels, measure, pair of wooden compasses, dibbles, extracting cases, a net to preserve seeds from birds, mattresses to cover seeds, a case of drawers for seeds, a tin box with divisions for seeds and flower roots, bags and paper hoods for seedlings, shades for newly set plants, melon glasses. The garden accessories are "parcell of Wyres," basket of shreds and felt cuttings, ash pole stakes, flower pots, insect glasses, thread, sawdust, vermin traps, hammer, nails, beehives,

The Thumb-Controlled Watering Pot.

A title-page ornament from Markham, *Countrie Farme,* 1616.

tallies of lead, thread to bind up nosegay, bee calendar, and a paper book "to note what, when and where he sows and plants and to register the successe of tryalls."

Today we have more elaborate and "sophisticated" garden equipment, more complicated farm machinery, but to what good, when in some countries of the world there still prevails the note of Joel, 3-10:

"Beat your plowshares into swords, and your pruning hooks into spears: let the weak say, I am strong."

The gardeners, the farmers, the true dwellers in the land will have none of this. With Isaiah they look forward to the days when these processes will be reversed, when swords will be beaten into plowshares and spears into pruning hooks, and "nation shall not lift up sword against nation, neither shall they learn war any more."

CHAPTER X

Flowers in Food

"What more felicities can fall to creature
Then to enjoy delight with libertie,
And to be Lord of all the workes of Nature,
To raine in the' aire from th' earth to highest skie,
To feed on flowres and weeds of glorious feature,
To take what ever thing doth please the eie?
Who rests not pleased with such happiness,
Well worthy he to taste of wretchedness."

—SPENSER, Muiopotmos, or the Fate of the Butterflie.

In Spenser's poem, the fly "sucking of the sap of herbe moste meete," was not only satisfying his "glutton sense," but was absorbing his daily quota of calories, vitamins, preventive medicines, even as you and I, or our ancestors. Today doctors and dietitians are teaching us that instead of taking doses of iron, calcium, phosphates, iodine, potassium, we may take the much-needed minerals pleasantly at our regular meals in cauliflowers, cabbages, asparagus, celery, raisins, apples.

Our forbears lived in the blackest depths of ignorance about food values or "balanced meals." In those early days of eating, drinking and being very merry, the house-

180

wife served many a tasty dish made from a recipe in her
precious still-room book in which her mother, her grandmother and her "great-greats" had painstakingly written
their choicest "rules." Some of the ingredients also appeared in that same little volume in cures for the head,
for the heart, for weak appetite, for dejected spirits. We
have no way of knowing how closely the housewife compared the culinary and medicinal ingredients, but certain
it is that more by good luck than by good management
did she often serve a dish containing an "herbe most
meete." Not only our ancestors but the herbalists themselves were unaware of calories or the alphabet of vitamins. They simply knew that if you took an herb or
combination of certain herbs, a favorable result would
ensue, and oftentimes it was suggested in still-room book
or herbal that these herbs could be taken in soups, salads
or sweets.

In the *Paradisus,* 1629, John Parkinson says:

"The herbe and flowers [of calendula] are of great use
with us among other pot-herbs, and the flowers eyther
green or dryed, are often used in possets, broths and
drinkes as a comforter of the heart and spirits, and to
expel any malignant or pestilential quality gathered neere
thereunto. The Syrups and Conserve made of the fresh
flowers are used for the same purposes to good effect."

The average housewife seldom came in contact with the
famous herbals we now read with such delight nor could
she have read them if one by chance came her way, but
she felt no need of herbals. Long ago much of the information had become household words, and when Parkinson
speaks of the calendula as being of "great use with us in
possets, broths and drinkes as a comforter of the heart"
that implies long lines of still-room books and word-of-

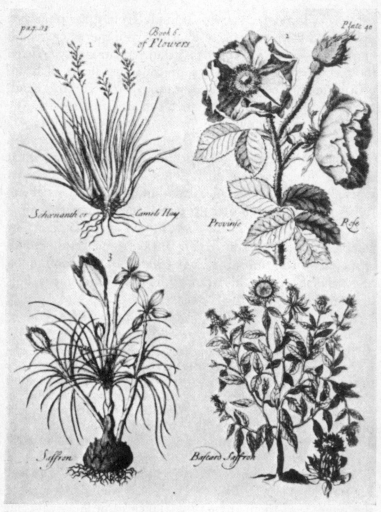

A Page of Useful Flowers, Including Saffron and
Safflower.

From Pomet, *Compleat History of Druggs,* translated from the
French *c.* 1700. The fourth edition was 1748.

mouth hints on healthful cooking, one day far in the future to be dealt with in real earnest.

Preparing a meal in early days was no light matter. The housewife could not call up the butcher, baker and grocer for the makings of dinner which she could hastily throw together after the bridge club. Before me is my much used little pamphlet, "Complete Meals that Cook in 20 Minutes [letters in red], 30 Minutes, 45 Minutes." Our ancient grandmothers, working many hours to prepare a simple meal, would no doubt have liked life in the kitchen to be as easy as those minutes imply, but she had no electric equipment, no gas, nor in early days any coal stove, no commercial helps to cooking. With most of the raw materials such as meat, third or fourth rate in quality, the housewife achieved many of her culinary triumphs by the use of high seasonings and color.

In a fifteenth century book of recipes in a list of herbs considered necessary for the garden are borage flowers, daisies, violets to be used in soup, violets for sauce and gillyflowers for drinks. Almost any gaily colored flowers were added to salads, as rosebuds, violets, cowslips. Thomas Tusser, 1573, lists "violets, of all colours," among the "Herbs and Roots for Salad and Sauce," while in his list of "Seeds and Herbs for the Kitchen," there were "saffron, marigold, primrose and violets of all sorts." A hundred years later Leonard Meager in his *English Gardener,* 1670, lists violets, marigolds and borage among "The Names of divers ordinary Pot-Herbs, call'd also Chopping-Herbs."

From ancient times saffron was an outstanding medicinal herb besides being a culinary herb used in so many dishes, soups, meats, eggs, fish, desserts, that the dinner table must have taken on a yellow cast. By the late fourteenth century saffron was grown in great quantities in

Essex, especially around a town which came to be called Saffron Walden. The only parts used of the herb (*Crocus sativus*) are the stigmas, about 60,000 needed to make a pound, thus making it an expensive coloring and flavoring to buy. Usually a quarter or a half pound was purchased at a time, though an early sixteenth century record shows that 6½ pounds were bought at one transaction for seven pounds, eight shillings (about $37). In America, right now, one pound costs about $45.

In *The Forme of Cury,* a collection of recipes used and compiled by the master cooks of Richard II (1377-1399), and in other thirteenth and fifteenth century cook books, saffron was used in more than one-half the recipes. It still plays its part in English cookery, especially in the saffron buns so characteristic of Cornwall, and in bouillabaisse, a stew of good old French origin. William Makepeace Thackeray honored the dish with a poem, "Ballad of Bouillabaisse":

> "This Bouillabaisse a noble dish is—
>   A sort of soup, or broth, or brew,
> Or hotchpotch of all sorts of fishes,
>   That Greenwich never could outdo."

With the price of saffron so high, and you did need a large area to grow it, in early days of walled castles, towns and generally limited space, the housewife usually substituted petals of the marigold when merely color, not the pungent flavor of saffron, was needed, as in junkets, butter or cheese. The latter was often colored yellow with the juice of the flowers of lady's bedstraw, also used to curdle the milk. Today, in America, safflower, an annual with dark orange flower heads, is often substituted for saffron.

In the *Countrie Farme*, translated in 1600, marigold is considered a very popular herb:

"The yellow leaves of the flowers are dried and kept throughout Dutchland against winter to put into broths, physicall potions and for divers other purposes, in such quantity that in some Grocers or Spicesellers are to be found barrels filled with them and retailed by the penny or less, inasmuch that no broths are well made without dried Marigold."

Perhaps the popularity of saffron was due to its much lauded effect on one's spirits as well as on the body. Francis Bacon said, "It maketh the English sprightly," while another writer, Christopher Catlan, declared, "The Virtue thereof pierceth to the heart, provoking laughter and merriment." Though I have dwelled at some length on saffron, could an herb with such virtues be over-emphasized?

If, perhaps, you would like to serve an herb-flower dinner, you could assemble the entire menu from the old-time cookery books. You probably would not like to begin with such a heavy pottage as the "noble bouilla-baisse," flavored with saffron, but serve, as the medieval housewife often did, a bouillon in which sweet violet pet-als, fennel and summer savory had been cooked. Prim-roses were also a favorite ingredient in soups. John Evelyn said: "The spring buds [of elder] are excellently wholesome in pottage," while Parkinson said, "The simple water of the Damask Roses is put into broths."

Gervase Markham in his *English Housewife*, 1615, gives a recipe for making the "best ordinary pottage" in which the vegetable ingredients are "Violet leaves [petals], Succory, Strawberry leaves, Spinage, Langde-beef [a variety of bugloss], Marygold flowers, Scallions, and a little Parsley," with oatmeal added to the kettle. Besides coloring soup with saffron, alkanet root was sometimes used to give it a reddish hue. In *The Forme of Cury*, it is directed "to make the potage of sangwayne [red] colour for wyntur season." It would certainly be more cheerful than the pervading yellow, but you will use your own discretion about the color for the soup you offer.

To be served at various stages of dinner will be dishes of "sweets and sours." In Markham's edition of the *Countrie Farme* a distinction is made between preserves and conserves.

"I understand by this preserve, taken properly, the preserving of things whole and not stampt and beaten into one bodie" (as in making conserves).

General rules for keeping flowers by both ways follow:

"Take the leaves or flowers of such herbs as you will preserve, make them very cleane, afterward, without anie manner of stamping them, put them whole into some vessell wherein you will keepe them, cast upon them a sufficient competence of fine Sugar made in pouder, and so set them to Sunning in the vessell. Also in this sort boyle them at a small fire with Sugar so long as till the Sugar become as thicke as a Syrrup, and after put them in a vessell."

Or the sugar sirup may be poured over the flowers which have been "diligently cleansed" and put into an earthen pot. "Thus may Roses, Mints . . . and such like be preserved: the flowers of Marigolds, Succorie, Violets, Broome, Sage and other such like: and such preserves are more acceptance than conserves, because the flowers and leaves do in better sort retaine and keepe their natural smell thus, than in conserves. . . ."

As to that delicacy, usually called raw or crude conserve, "make them [the flowers] verie cleane, and bray
[grind] them afterwards in a Marble mortar, or of
other Stone with a pestle," till they become a paste, . . .
"add twice or thrice as much Sugar or Honey."

Honey Was the Great Sweetening of Early Days.

The illustration from Pomet shows the calling of the bees by beating
on a pan.

Then set the mixture in the sun for a month, stirring daily
before putting into jars or, "Set the Vessels upon hot
ashes, to the end they may take a little boyle. . . . After
this manner may the flowers of Rosemarie, Marigolds,
Betonie, Pionie, Marierome, Balme, Scabious, Elder tree,
Mints, Fumitorie, Eye-bright, Succorie, of the flowers of

the Peach-tree, Sage, Broome, Orange, Mallowes, Hollyhocke, and other such like . . ."

Each housewife had her own pet and particular recipe for conserves and preserves, but the general principle was the same, only the details varying. Markham advises three months instead of one for "sunning" violet and rose mixtures. Hannah Glasse directs us to put roses in a sieve to remove the seeds, and for every pound of flowers 2½ pounds of sugar although Markham recommends the time-honored pound for pound proportion. After the conserve, made by Mrs. Glasse's method, has been put into gallipots (earthenware kettles), covered with paper and then with leather, "it will keep Seven Years." It wouldn't have a chance to keep that long, I'm sure, in my family.

Gerard in his *Herball*, 1597, says that besides crude or raw conserves, there are "divers other pritie things made of Roses and Sugar, which are impertinent unto our historie, because I intend neither to make thereof an Apothecarie's shop, nor a Sugar baker's storehouse, leaving the rest for our cunning confectioners." There we see the line of demarcation between herbal and still-room book. While the former merely indicates many concoctions, the details of making them comprised the contents of the latter.

In Hannah Glasse's *Art of Cookery*, 1747, is a recipe for conserve of rose hips which I sent to a friend who is willing to try anything of culinary nature once, but I have not heard about the results:

"Gather Hips before they grow soft, cut off the Heads and Stalks, slit them in Halves, take out all Seeds and white that is in them very clean, then put them into an earthen Pan, and stir them every Day, or they will grow mouldy. Let them stand until they are soft enough to rub thro' a coarse Hair-sieve, as the Pulp comes take it off the Sieve: They are a dry Berry, and will require Paines to rub them thro'; then add its Weight in Sugar, mix them well together without boiling and keep it in deep Gallipots for Use."

A conserve of clove gillyflower (our old-fashioned clove pinks) used to be very popular, one writer claiming, "It is Cordial, chears the Heart and strengthens the Stomach." Conserve of betony was another double purpose delicacy, Parkinson saying that the leaves and flowers "by their sweete and spicie Taste, are comfortable both in meate and medicine."

As for the sours to contrast with the sweets, a few flower pickles might well serve as appetizers according to the old recipes. William Coles in *Adam in Eden*, 1657, says that clove gillyflowers "being pickled with Vinegar and Sugar, are a pleasant and dainty Sawce, stir up the Appetite and are also of a Cordiall faculty." Pickled broom buds were considered so fine a table delicacy as to be served at the coronation feast of James II. Evelyn in his *Acetaria*, 1699, gives a simple recipe for making them. A strong brine made of white wine vinegar and salt is poured over the buds which have been placed in a glass jar. "They should be frequently shaken till they sink under it and keep it [the jar] well stopt and covered." Parkinson in his *Theatrum Botanicum* says that the young buds of broom pickled are

"to be eaten all the yeare after as a sallet of much delight, and are called Broome capers, which doe helpe to stirre up an appetite to meate, that is weak and dejected."

Of the many directions from medieval to modern times for pickling elder buds, those in John Farley's *London*

Art of Cookery, 1801, are about the most workable. The buds "gathered when the size of hop buds" are

"put in strong salt and water for nine days, stirring two or three times a day. Then put them in a pan, cover them with vine leaves and pour on them the water they came out of. Set them over a slow fire till they be quite green, make a pickle of allegar [vinegar made from ale], mace, shalots, and some ginger sliced. Boil them two or three minutes, and pour it upon your buds. Tie them down, and keep them in a dry place for use."

Evelyn suggests pickled nasturtium buds, which would be a colorful and spicy addition to the dinner table.

"Gather the Buds before they are open to flower; lay them in the Shade three or four Hours, and putting them into an Earthen Glazed Vessel, pour good vinegar on them, and cover it with a Board. Thus letting it stand for eight or ten Days; then being taken out, and gently press'd, cast them into fresh Vinegar, and let them so remain as long as before. Repeat this a third time, and Barrel them up with Vinegar, and a little Salt."

Of course, Evelyn was the master mind of the early eighteenth century in regard to salads, to which Chapter XII has been devoted, but we can well take a few lines here to the colorful possibilities in the use of flowers, which also add flavor to our salads.

Among Evelyn's materials for salads, he mentions flowers:

"Chiefly of the Aromatick Esculents and Plants are preferable, as generally endow'd with the Vertues of their Simples, in a more intense degree; and may therefore be eaten alone in their proper Vehicles, or Composition with other Salleting sprinkled among them; But give a more

Primroses and Cowslips.

From Parkinson, *Paradisi in Sole Paradisus Terrestris,* 1629.
He identifies primroses (1-5) as having "but one flower upon a
Stalke" and cowslips (6-13) "that beare many flowers upon a
stalke."

palatable Relish, being Infused in Vinegar; Especially those of the Clove Gillyflower, Elder, Orange, Cowslip, Rosemary, Arch-Angel [dead nettle], Sage, Nasturtium Indicum, etc."

All these flowers may be pickled according to the recipe Evelyn gives for cowslips:

"Pick very clean; to each Pound of Flowers allow one Pound of Loaf Sugar, and one Pint of White-Wine Vinegar, which boil to a Syrup and cover it scalding hot. Thus you may pickle Clove-gilly flowers, Elder, and other Flowers, which being eaten alone, make a very agreeable Salletine."

Parkinson says, "Preserved or pickled Clove Gilloflowers make a Sallet nowadays in the highest esteeme with Gentles and Ladies of the greatest note," while John Worlidge in the *Art of Gardening,* 1677, says that "Nasturtiums . . . are now become an acceptable Sallad as well the leaf as the blossom."

William Coles recommends pickled broom buds for a "sallet of great delight serving all the year which do helpe to stir up an appetite to meat," a custom which would be very acceptable to modern menus, that is, salad as a first course.

As always the "Winter Sallets" were a problem, but easily solved by pickling salad material in summer. Leonard Meager, 1670, recommends the following to be "put with white-wine Vinegar and Sugar for Winter sallets": clove gilly flowers, and flowers of cowslips, bugloss, borage and archangel. Among Markham's material for salads are marigold and violets. The latter flowers in the Middle Ages were much used for salads chopped with onions and lettuce. Dr. Fernie in *Meals Medicinal* quotes a recipe for "Salads des Violettes":

"Take Batavian endive, finely-curled celery, a sprinkling of minced parsley, a single olive, and the petals of a couple of dozen blue Violets, these several ingredients are to be mixed with the purest olive oil, salt, and pepper being the only other condiments; and a dash of Bordeaux wine, and a suspicion of white vinegar."

But perhaps you would like a brighter colored salad, and here again we have yellow, though not the inevitable saffron. This flowery recipe also comes from *Meals Medicinal* and might be called a Nightcap Salad because of its sedative effect:

"The Cowslip and the Primrose, by reason of the delicate flavours which their petals afford, whilst the colours are attractive find frequent admission now-a-days into Salads at refined Tables."

It is said that Disraeli, Lord Beaconsfield, was so fond of primrose salad that the flower became associated with his name. Whatever may be the whole truth, we do know that in England, April 19th, the anniversary of his death, is Primrose Day and his statue in Parliament Square is decorated with primroses and many wear the flower as a buttonhole adornment.

For a colorful touch, Evelyn says that the Germans rolled saffron into little balls with honey, then reduced the balls to powder and sprinkled it over the salad. Many were the varieties of vinegar to be used alone or with oil for salad dressing. From the old-time cook books we can take many a suggestion for our salad dressings in the recipes for vinegars made by steeping in it flowers of rosemary, clove pinks, roses, violets.

As an accompaniment to the flower salad, rose petal sandwiches would be attractive. The night before, place a thick layer of fragrant red rose petals in a glass or earthen jar, lay on top a slab of butter, then another layer of petals, and cover the jar until ready for use. Cut bread into rectangles 2″ by 3″, spread with the butter and place on it several petals. Then either roll up the bread with the petals showing a little, or top the slice with another piece of bread and serve as a flat sandwich. Either way the fragrance is retained.

Perhaps as a vegetable course, you would like a dish of sunflowers. Gerard says that the "heads of the Sunne Flower [which he calls Chrysanthemum Peruvianum] are dressed and eaten as Hartichokes, and are accounted of some to be good meate, but they are too strong for my taste." Maybe this is the beginning of what are now called Jerusalem artichokes.

In Tennyson's "Gareth and Lynette," as the haughty maiden softens toward the "Kitchen knave" King Arthur sent instead of Lancelot as her champion to free Lyonors from the Castle Perilous, she is still angry at the King as she sings:

> "O dewy flowers that open to the sun . . .
> What knowest thou of flowers, except, belike,
> To garnish meats with? hath not our good King
> Who lent me thee, the flower of kitchendom,
> A foolish love for flowers? what stick ye round
> The pasty? wherewithal deck the boar's head?
> Flowers? nay, the boar hath rosemaries and bay."

Flowers always in or about food! The violet indeed was an important ingredient in the stuffing for a hare to be roasted, and Kenelm Digby in *The Closet Opened*, 1669, suggests putting a few marigold petals in a beef stew just before serving it. Here is a recipe from his book, for stewing beef, a really simple one among the complicated directions of the old days:

"Take very good Beef, and slice it very thin; and beat it with the back of a Knife; Put it to the gravy of some meat, and some wine or strong broth, sweet-herbs a quantity, let it stew till it be very tender; season it to your liking; and varnish [garnish] your dish with Marygold-flowers or Barberries."

But what possibilities for "varnishing" did the old-time cooks seize upon that we moderns neglect! Nowadays a few discouraged stems of parsley seem to mark the outer limits of the cook's imagination, and we gingerly lift the limp, drowned-looking sprigs to one side of the plate. The garnish should look and be good enough to eat, social etiquette to the contrary. Hannah Glasse in *The Art of Cookery* suggests a flowery garnish in two of her three recipes for "Salamangundy," a dish of fish, meat, eggs, vegetables, fruit, variously mixed. In one recipe we are to garnish "with Grapes just scalded, or French Beans, blanched or Stertion-flower."

The other Salamangundy is to be dished out "with what Pickles you have, and sliced Lemon nicely cut, and if you can get Stertion-flowers, lay round make a fine Middle-dish for Supper."

Now comes the time for the sweet. What flowery dessert shall we have? The Syrians made a sherbet, the sugar colored and flavored with sweet violet petals. In fourteenth century England, violet jelly and violet fritters were served as an "End-Dish." You might like to serve a custard called simply "Crem boyled," written down sometime in the fifteenth century, although this dessert was served at least 200 years before that:

"Take crem of cowe mylke and zolkes [yolks] of egges, and bete hom wel togedur, and do [put] hit in a pot, and let hit boyle tyl hit be stondynge [stiff] and do thereto sugur, and colour hit with saffron, and dress hit forthe in leches [slices] and plante therein floures of borage, or of vyolet."

As Mrs. Glasse said about one of her recipes, I'm sure we could say about "crem boyled," "It both looks pretty and eats fine."

A cowslip pudding would be a colorful dish to set before your guests, and I offer you two recipes, one from the receipt book, 1654, of one Jos. Cooper, cook to Charles I, the other from *The Art of Cookery,* almost 100 years later. The first recipe calls for two ounces of Sirup of Cowslips boiled in one quart of cream, seasoned with a blade of mace, fine sugar and orange-flower water, and thickened with the yolks of 3 or 4 eggs. This is dished up in "Basons and Glasses" and strewed over with candied cowslips.

Mrs. Glasse's recipe is more lavish, but I think it would "eat fine" if you could overlook the amounts of ingredients required:

TO MAKE A COWSLIP PUDDING

"Having got the flowers of a Peck of Cowslips [a problem in itself], cut them small and pound them with Half a Pound of Naples Biscuit [lady fingers] grated and three Pints of Cream. Boil them a little; then take them off the Fire, and beat up sixteen Eggs, with a little Cream and a little Rosewater. Sweeten to your Palate. Mix it well together, butter a Dish and pour it in. Bake, and when it is enough, throw fine Sugar over and serve it up."

Mrs. Glasse gives a recipe for "Puddings for little Dishes." Four dishes are filled with the pudding. You are to color one "Yellow with Saffron, one Red with

Cochineal, Green with the Juice of Spinach and one Blue
with Syrup of Violet." Sometimes red was produced by
sirup of red roses while a yellow hue was given by saffron
and orange by marigold petals. This simple statement,
however, does not even hint of the hours the housewife
spent in the kitchen for the colorful effects that we can
obtain with no more effort than pouring a few drops
from the little bottles of vegetable compounds the grocer
sends us.

Sirups in early days were often poured over puddings,
cake, creams to point them up and to vary the flavor
or color, just as we have sauces for puddings, and sirups
to make a sundae from a simple dish of ice cream. On
the still-room shelves in early days stood a colorful array
of jars of sirups made from roses, violets, saffron, marigold, peach blossoms, clove pinks, peonies. We cannot try
many of the old-time recipes in their full proportion of
ingredients, dozens of eggs, quarts of thick cream, pecks
and pounds of flower petals, but it is fun and not so reck-
less to experiment with an eighth or even a sixteenth of
a recipe.

Perhaps for dessert you will have plain vanilla ice
cream, and, to be passed about, a tray on which will be
small glass bowls of several flower sirups with which the
guests will make their own experiments in sundaes. If the
season permits, an interesting change from the inevitable
geranium leaves in finger bowls would be a different herb
flower for each guest. Herb flowers placed in the trays
for ice cubes to be put in the water glass at each place
would be another pleasant little emphasis for the dinner.

As with conserves or preserves, a general rule can be
followed for all flower sirups. In Smith's *Compleat
Housewife*, 1728, is a rule for making sirup of any
flower:

"Clip your Flowers, and take their Weight in Sugar, then take a high Gallypot, and put a row of Flowers, and a strowing of Sugar, till the Pot is full; then put in two or three spoonfuls of the same [sugar] Syrup or still'd [distilled] water; tye a Cloth on the top of the Pot, and put a Tile on that, and set your Gallypot in a kettle of water over a gentle Fire, and let it infuse till the strength is out of the Flowers, which will be in four or five hours; then strain it thro a Flannel, and when 'tis cold, bottle it up."

Gerard's rule for making Sirup of Violets would give a more fragrant and colorful sirup: "First make of clarified sugar by boiling a simple sirupe, of a good consistence, or meane thickness, whereunto put the flowers cleane, piked from all manner of filth, as also the white endes nipped away, a quantitie, according to the quantitie of the serupe, to your owne discretion." Infuse 24 hours in a warm place, strain, add more violets, repeating 3 or 4 times. "Then set them upon a gentle fire to simper, but not to boil in any wise . . . some do add thereto a little of the juice of the flowers in the boiling, which maketh it of better force and vertue. Likewise some do put a little quantitie of the juice of Limons in the boiling that doth greatly increase the beautie thereof, but nothing at all the vertue."

Little dishes of colorful confections should grace the table for this last course. The simplest way is to follow a recipe for fondant and, after kneading the mixture, divide into small portions, adding to each a "pretty quantitie" of different colored petals previously pounded in a mortar. You can have orange calendula, blue violets, red roses, clove pinks, blue borage or chicory, purple sage (*Salvia horminum*).

In the early cookery books are many recipes for flow-

ery confections, called lozenges or plates, especially popular from the time of Charles II (1660-1685) who was
particularly fond of them. Hugh Plat in his *Delightes
for Ladies,* 1602, gives "A Way to Make Suger-plate
both of colour and taste of any flower."

"Take violets, and beat them in a mortar with a little
hard sugar; then put into it a sufficient quantitie of Rosewater; then lay your gum [gum arabic] to steep in the
water, and so work it into paste; and so will your paste
be both of the colour of the violet and of the smell of
the violet. In like sort you may worke with Marigolds,
Cowslips or any other flower."

Then there are many recipes for cooked flower candy,
two schools of thought prevailing about the amount of
heat, but the general feeling was that too much heat
spoils the color. In the *Compleat Housewife* is a quite
simple recipe for making rose drops:

"The Roses and Sugar must be beat separately into
a very fine powder and both sifted; to a pound of Sugar,
an ounce of red Roses: They must be mixed together and
then wet with as much Juice of Lemon, as will make into
a stiff Paste. Set it on a slow Fire, in a Silver Porringer,
and stir it well; and when 'tis scalding hot quite thro'
take it off, and drop it on Paper. Set them near the Fire
the next day: they'll come off."

To me the high art of flower confectionery is to candy
flowers neatly. When I was a little girl, I always held my
breath when a box of bon bons was opened. Would the
lovely candied violets be there? To me that "made" the
box, and I still consider them quite beautiful. What could
be a prettier climax than a plate of candied cowslips,
borage, violets, primroses, clove pinks, nasturtium buds?
But take plenty of time. The delicate petals must be

handled slowly, gently and patiently. Very popular in the old days when there was no "store candy," nor even any stores, candied flowers were carefully made by the housewife who was used to taking time and pains to please her family and guests. She was an expert in working with the delicate flowers of borage which, Parkinson said, "of Gentlewomen are candid for comfitts."

There are hot and cold methods for the procedure of candying flowers. There is the time-honored one of brushing the petals with white of egg in which a little water has been mixed and then sprinkling them with sugar. Another method is to dip the petals in rose water in which gum arabic has been steeped, then sprinkle sugar over them and dry them in "an oven after the bread is drawn." Hugh Plat tells how to preserve "Whole Roses, Gilliflowers, Marigolds, etc.," simple directions enough but requiring all the patience of which deft hands are capable:

"Dip half open flowers in a boiling sugar syrup and open the leaves carefully with a smooth bodkin: lay the flowers on paper in the Sun or warm room or oven."

In the *Compleat Housewife* is a fascinating recipe requiring much time, equipment and a "Stander-by." I give but part of the recipe to show how you can make really hard work of a quite simple process. First put the flowers in boiling sugar sirup, "take them out as quick as you can, with as little of the Syrup as may be, and lay them in a Dish over a gentle Fire, and with a Knife spread them, that the Syrup may run from them; then change them upon another warm Dish, and when they are dry from the Syrup, have ready some double-refin'd Sugar, beaten and sifted and strew some on your Flowers; then take the Flowers in your Hands, and rub them gently in the hollow of your Hand, and that will open

the Leaves; a Stander-by strewing more Sugar into your
Hand, as you see convenient; then pour your Flowers into
a dry Sieve, and sift all the Sugar clean from them. They
must be kept in a dry place. Rosemary Flowers must be
put whole into your Syrup."

In early days many flowers were used in making the
contents for the cup that cheers. If sirup of clove gillyflowers or the fresh petals were added to wine to give it
a spicy flavor, the result was called "Sops in Wine," a
cup of which was offered to brides directly after the marriage ceremony. In Chaucer's *Canterbury Tales,* we learn
it was a favorite drink of the Frankeleyn, prosperous
country gentleman . . .

> "Wel loved he by the morwe [in the morning]
>   a sop in wyn."

John Evelyn tells of the elder flowers in his time.
"Small ale in which Elder flowers have been infused is
esteemed by many so salubrious that this is to be had
in most of the eating-houses about our town."

The two great drinks of ancient days and continued
popularity well into the eighteenth century were mead
and metheglin. Dr. Andrew Borde, sixteenth century, in
Regyment of Helth, distinguished between the two in this
way: "Meade is made of honny and water boyled both
togyther; yf it be fyred and pure, it preserveth helth; but
it is not good for them the which have the Ilyacke or the
Colyche. . . . Metheglyn is made of honny and water and
herbs, boyled and sodden togyther; yf it be fyred and
stale, it is better in the regyment of helth than meade."

Sir Kenelm Digby, about 75 years later, seems not to
have made such a distinction and in his hundred and more
recipes many are the herb flowers that entered into the

popular drink: gillyflowers, cowslips, yellow wallflowers, avens, borage, bugloss, elder, hops, St. John's-Wort, marigold, marshmallow, melilot, primrose, roses and violets.

Many and many are the foods in which flowers have played important rôles, and why should they not as well as vegetables, fruit, leaves, seeds? They are the most colorful, often the most fragrant part of the plant. Again we echo Spenser's feelings:

> "What more felicities can fall to creature
> Than to enjoy delight with libertie,
>
>   .   .   .
>
> To feed on flowres and weeds of glorious feature,
> To take what ever thing doth please the eie?"

CHAPTER XI

Flowers in Medicine

"The nature of flowers, dame Physic doth shew;
She teacheth them all, to be known to a few,
To set or to sow, or else sown to remove,
How that should be practised, learn if ye love."
—THOMAS TUSSER, 1573.

Mistress Tusser, she that was Amy Moon, stood looking speculatively over her garden. Hardly more than a
child in appearance as her bright curls danced in the summer breeze, she was rapidly making calculations which
would have done credit to a housewife of much longer
experience.

"Gillyflowers, rosemary, borage, bugloss, balm flowers. Yes, they're there a-plenty," she considered, nodding
towards them. "I have enough primroses and cowslips
saved from spring and the marigolds will be open in a
day or two."

Then she walked rapidly down the garden path fragrant with thyme and quickly inspected the damask roses.
"Buds, too! Oh yes, there'll be enough. Nutmeg and cinnamon I have. Now, if Thomas can get me a thruppence
of saffron when he goes to Norwich tomorrow, I'll have

everything for the Melancholy Water. It does poor old
Mistress Barry so much good. At least, she thinks so!
And this year—," her eyes sparkled in young anticipa-
tion, "Water of Flowers, 20 flowers! What fun!" and
away she sped to the house to consult her precious still-
room book that her mother had given her last year when
she married Thomas. Dear Thomas, so much older, very
staid and serious but very kind, although so hurt when
her sharp tongue became too sharp.

Following Mistress Tusser along the straight paths
separating precisely rectangular beds, gay with some
three dozen flowering herbs, we might have exclaimed,
"What beautiful flowers these will be for the house!"
But that little lady, not understanding our comment,
might have replied, "Yes, I anticipate an abundant harvest. I shall need many herbs this year now that we have
more workers living in the cottages. There's bound to be
sickness."

To us, looking at the hollyhocks, clove pinks, marigolds, nasturtiums, pansies, roses, cornflowers, lilies, wallflowers, or, if we had been there earlier in the season,
violets, peonies, poppies, primroses, iris, we would have
been reminded of our own flower garden from which
we gathered armfuls to brighten up our house. But Mistress Tusser knew no such garden. Hers was ornamental,
to be sure, but made primarily for use. As she proudly
surveyed the oblongs of flowers, she thought of them as
raw materials for cordials, waters, oils, sirups, ointments, powders, lotions, electuaries. What a colorful,
fragrant array of medicine bottles and jars on the still-
room shelves, all in readiness, not only for wounds,
fevers, plague, "dejected appetites," dizziness and so
through the whole gamut of ills of the flesh, but also for
those troubles of the spirit that we moderns find so per-

The Physicians Consult.

Frontispiece from the German *Herbarius*, 1496. Courtesy of
Alfred C. Hottes.

plexing to cope with, but which the doctor and housewife in a matter of fact way treated as just another ailment in Thomas Tusser's times.

Many were the days the housewife and her maids would spend in the still-room, making concoctions of one kind of flowers alone, and others of a veritable potpourri of flowers, as in the Water of Flowers, compounded of twenty different kinds. However, not all of her various flower harvests went at once into medicinal preparations. Some were dried and stored in carefully labeled jars to be used later as occasion demanded.

Ambroise Paré, sixteenth century French surgeon, was famous for his remedy for gunshot wounds, a mixture of sage, rosemary, thyme, lavender, chamomile, melilot flowers, and rose petals, boiled in wine with a lye made of oak ashes and applied as a fomentation on the wound. In seventeenth century Susanna Avery's still-room book there are directions for making "A precious oyle to heal a wound in 24 hours." We are to put a handful each of flowers of St. John's-Wort and rosemary in a glass, pour in "perfect oyle," cover and let it stand in the sun for three days and nights, strain, and put in ginger and saffron dissolved in white wine. After it has set in the sun for eighteen days more, it is ready to be applied warm twice a day to the wound.

From the *Countrie Farme,* 1616, we learn that the "iuce of Marigolds, Scabious [scabiosa] and of the flowers of Betonie . . . causeth the malignitie of the Plague to breake forth by Sweats." Markham in the *English Housewife,* 1615, gives us the recipe for "A cordial for any infection at the Heart," but whether it will mend a heart that has been broken, he does not say. This is the recipe:

"Take of Burrage, Langdebeef [bugloss] and Calamint, of each a good handful, of Hart's-Tongue, Red Mint, Violets, and Marygolds, of each half a handful, boyl them in White-wine, or fair running water, then add a pennyworth of the best Saffron, and as much Sugar, and boyl them over again well, then strain it into an earthen pot, and drink thereof morning and evening to the quantity of seven spoonfuls."

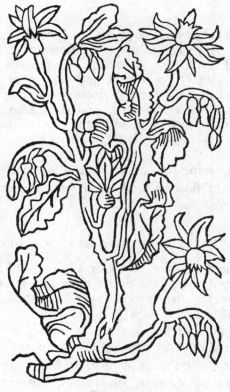

Borage.

From the German *Herbarius,* 1496, *Herbarius zu Teutsch.* Courtesy of Alfred C. Hottes.

In the seventeenth century still-room book of the Fairfax family, handed down through many generations, an ointment for a wen is described as made of a little bouquet of flowering herbs, broom buds, bugloss-flowers, violet petals, red sage, and a little chamomile, mixed with May butter (unsalted butter set in the sun for a month). From this same book we can find "A nonytment for the Palsye":

"Take the flowers of stickades [stoechas lavender], the flowers of ye right spike, the flowers of french, the flowers and cropps of rosemary, ye flowers and cropp of Isop [hyssop]; ye flowers and cropps of maudeline, and a handfull of kowslipp flowers, ye crops of sage, of each of them a handfull, and of Camomill-flowers, three handfuls: put them all into sallet oile, and make it as you make oile of Roses."

Markham's recipe for this oil would apply also for making oils of any flowers, and many were the varieties and uses for them.

"TO MAKE OYLE OF ROSES OR VIOLETS

"Take the flowers of Roses or Violets, and break them small, and put them into Sallet oyle, and let them stand in the same ten or twelve dayes and then presse it."

Oils of many of the flowers commonly used in medicines in early days are to be found on the crude drug lists of today: chamomile, arnica, fleabane, lavender, pennyroyal, orange flowers, marjoram, rosemary, thyme. Quite a flower garden needed for the oils alone; and when we see on the same lists hollyhock, saffron, sunflower, meadowsweet, cassia, calendula, borage, cornflower, cowslip, coltsfoot, elder, we may well think of all those flowers, as Mistress Tusser did, in terms of crops. It is amazing enough to learn of the great variety of medicinal flowers, but it is actually astounding to read to what great extent they are used. When we find from the price lists of the crude drug companies the weight of standard bales in which form they are sold, we can hardly imagine the numbers of flowers used to keep us from all ills—arnica 75 pounds, cassia buds 66 pounds, chamomile 222 pounds, elder flowers 110 pounds, lavender 220 pounds, rose buds 175 pounds. Did you ever try to collect even half a pound of any one kind of flower petals from your garden?

Today we enjoy our flowers for their esthetic value alone and have neither equipment nor plant material enough for making the medicines to be stored against the ills of the flesh and of the spirit. Instead, great manufacturing companies have taken this necessary work for their own and arrange for the medicinal plants to be grown on large areas to supply the families of the nation. In contrast to the great bulb fields of Holland where the flowers are ruthlessly cut and thrown away, on these huge medicinal tracts the flowers are carefully harvested, cleaned, dried and baled. The flowers are the crops that go to market.

Mistress Tusser's physic garden in Norfolk was probably smaller than the area on which a single kind of medicinal flower is now grown for a single drug house, but she had only her family and her household to supply. Many of our gardens are even more limited than Mistress Tusser's, but somehow there is a feeling of continuity from the past to the present, as we ourselves stand and gaze speculatively at our own perennials of medicinal value and contemplate that these very flowers grew in Mistress Tusser's garden.

A roll call of the medicinal flowers gives us a most

revealing cross-section of one phase of life in the early days, the prevailing physical ills, the troubles of the mind and of the spirit, how the housewife coped with them, what materials and what equipment she could assemble for preparing her cures. In the *Family Herbal*, 1755, Sir John Hill tells us that the flowers of archangel (dead nettle) were made into a conserve to be taken for inward weaknesses, while over 150 years before that publication, Gerard, in his *Herbal* (1597) says:

"The flowers are baked with sugar as roses are, which is called sugar Roset: as also the distilled water of them, which is used to make the hart merrie; to make a good colour in the face, and to make the vital spirits more fresh and lively."

In reading the old herbals, we cannot but be impressed how many conserves, sirups and other sweet concoctions were used. Today advertisements recommend chocolate bars and other sweets as a quick energy "pick-up" for that mid-afternoon spiritless feeling; in other words, "to make the vital spirits more fresh and lively." Who are we even to smile at the ancients whose ideas are loudly repeated by modern scientists and dietitians?

Among the ancient herbalists there seemed to be confusion between the identities of borage and bugloss (*Anchusa officinalis*), but seventeenth century John Evelyn, in the *Acetaria,* takes pains to point out the distinction: "What we now call Bugloss was not that of the Ancients, but rather Borrage, for the like Virtue named Corrago [courage]." He says that bugloss in maturity is "much like Borrage, yet something more astringent. The Flowers of both with the intire Plant, greatly restorative, being Conserv'd . . ." The eighteenth century herbalist, Salmon, says that conserve of borage flowers is "chiefly used as a Cordial Sweet-meat, and to restore such as have been long in a Consumption, being often taken with new Cow's milk. . . ." Parkinson, 1640, recommends both the conserve and the candied flowers of

Apothecary and Nurse.

From *Herbarius zu Teutsch,* Augsburg, 1496.

borage for "those that have been long sicke and feeble or in a Consumption, to comfort the heart and spirits and thereby good for those that are troubled with often swooning or passion of the heart."

Thomas Hyll in *Gardeners Labyrinth,* 1577, advises

that the flowers of borage "steeped for a time in the oile
of sweet Almonds, and after the wringing forth of this,
tenderly applied to the stomach, and region of the heart,
do marvellously comfort the weake Patient." Hyll also
says the sirup will preserve a good memory besides being
a specific against the King's Evil (scrofula), heart trouble
and giddiness. Gerard says,

"Those of our time use the flowers [of borage] in
sallads, to exhilarate and make the minde glad. There
be also many things made of them, used everywhere for
the comforte of the hart, for the driving away of sor-
rowe, and increasing the ioie [joy] of the minde."

From little paragraphs like that, we realize the rather
pathetic trust our forbears placed in their medicinal concoctions for curing not only physical ills but for working
upon mind and spirit to preserve memory, increase happiness, and drive away sorrows; such effects as we of today know, coming not from spoonfuls of medicines however sweet, but rather springing from that "hidden
strength" within the mind and heart.

The flowers of Lady's bedstraw (*Galium verum*),
also called cheese rennet in early days, were often used
to curdle milk and to give a yellow color to the cheese.
According to Culpeper, 1652, the bruised flowers thrust
up the nostrils "stayeth their bleeding," while used as
the principal ingredient of an oil or an ointment were
good for "burnings with fire or scaldings with water."
But the chief claim to fame of Lady's bedstraw, medicinally, rivaled that of mugwort as a boon to tired feet.
William Coles in *Adam in Eden,* 1657, says:

"Though Mugwort be an Herb noted amongst the
Vulgar for preventing wearinesse upon sore Travell [the

gentry, of course, did not travel on foot], . . . yet I find
Ladies Bedstraw more celebrated for that purpose
amongst Authors who say that the Decoction of the
Herbe and Flowers being yet warme, is of admirable use
to bath the Feet of Travellers, and others who are sur-
bated by long Journeys in hot weather, and for Lackies
and such like, where running long causeth not onely wearinesse, but stiffenesse in the Sinews and Joynts, to both
which this herb is so friendly, that it maketh them to
become as lissome, as if they had never been abroad."

Broom flowers seemed to be the great specific for gout,
bruises, swellings and skin diseases. Gerard says, "That
woorthie Prince of famous memorie Henerie the eight
King of England, was woont to drinke the distilled water
of Broome flowers against surfets and diseases thereof
arising." The main disease "thereof arising" I take to be
gout, for which William Coles recommends an ointment
made of hog's grease and broom flowers. He adds,

"The Flowers also bruised and mixed with Hony and
Roses or the white of an Egge beaten to gether and
applyed, consume the hard Swellins of the Kings Evil."

Celandine is recommended in the Latin *Herbarium* of
Apuleius, fifth century, for eye trouble: "Take ooze of
this same wort or the blossoms wrung out, and mixed
with honey; mingle then gently hot ashes thereto, and
seethe together in a brazen vessell; this is a special leech-
dom for dimness of eyes."

From ancient times to the present, chamomile has been
one of the most frequently used herbs for producing
sedative effects. We give it in extract form to babies to
quiet them; we take it as a tea ourselves as a nightcap
drink; but in early days there were several other methods
of administering the sedative qualities of chamomile. Not

only was it an ingredient of Ambroise Paré's remedy for gunshot wounds, but it was used with the crushed heads of opium poppy in a poultice for relieving all sorts of aches and pains. Little bags were stuffed with the flowers, steeped in boiling water, and applied to the head for neuralgic pains. Culpeper says, "The flowers boiled in lee, are good to wash the head and comfort both it and the brain," just another instance of the same concoction for producing good effects, whether of a mental or a physical nature. Today a chamomile rinse in a beauty shop is commonplace. But chamomile had other virtues.

Dr. Fernie in *Herbal Simples,* 1897, claims, "No simple in the whole catalogue of herbal medicines is possessed of a quality more friendly and beneficial to the intestines than Chamomile Flowers." Gerard seems to rat chamomile as a runner-up to mugwort and Lady's bedstraw. "The oile compounded of the flowers . . . is a remedie against all wearisomnesse, and is with good successe mixed with all those things that are applied to mitigate paine." A medication of chamomile, as we read about it in Parkinson's *Theatrum Botanicum,* 1640, certainly ought to be effective if the patient were strong enough to endure the process of application. Here is what he says:

"The flowers onely of Camomill beaten, and made up into balls with oyle, drive away all sorts of agues, if the party grieved bee anoynted with that oyle taken from the flowers, from the crowne of the head to the soles of the feet, and after laid to sweat in their bed, with sufficient coverings upon them, and that they sweat well."

Even though clove gillyflowers were as much a part of the early pharmacopœia as chamomile, I have always thought that Parkinson secretly felt very unhappy to have his pet flower, thousands of them, snatched from their stems, pounded and boiled with sugar for sirups. In the early seventeenth century, gardeners were beginning to set aside a space for flowers, which they transplanted from the physic garden, to be a thing of beauty, a delight to the eye and to the nose—the garden of pleasure, as Parkinson called it. Particularly in the smaller gardens, some of the flowers still had to be harvested to supplement the medicinal crop, so no doubt Parkinson may have been philosophic enough to let joy go to smash when joy and duty clashed. He writes quite impersonally of the medicinal value of his beloved gillyflowers, to which he devotes several pages in his *Paradisus,* his book on the *Garden of Pleasant Flowers.*

He says, "The red or Clove Gilloflower is most used in Physicke in our Apothecaries shops, none of the other being accepted of or used (and yet I doubt not, but all of them might serve, and to good purpose, although not to give so gallant a tincture to a Syrupe as the ordinary red will doe) and is accounted to be very Cordiall." John Hill, in the *Family Herbal,* more than a century later, wrote that the flowers "are cordial, and good for disorders of the head; they may be dried, and taken in powder or in form of tea, but the best form is the syrup. This is made by pouring five pints of boiling water upon three pounds of the flowers picked from the husks, and with the white heels cut off; after they have stood twelve hours, straining off the clear liquor without pressing, and dissolving in it two pound of the finest sugar to every pint. This makes the most beautiful and pleasant of all syrups." Gerard claims, "The conserve made of the flowers of the Clove Gilloflower and sugar, is exceedingly cordiall, and woonderfully above measure doth comfort the heart, being eaten now and then."

The virtues of these little clove pinks are many and their uses entrancing but none more so than I found in reading Stephen Blake's *Complete Gardeners Practice*, 1664. There I found out how "To be revenged on a person who steals your tulips." The directions bespeak a bitter dose indeed for the culprit, but it may make your heart merry and increase the "ioie of the minde" just to read of the procedure: Sprinkle dry, powdered Elecampane root on Clove Gillyflowers, "then give your Flowers to the party that you desire to be revenged of, let it be a he or a she, they will delight in smelling to it, then they will draw this powder into their nostrils, which will make them fall a sneezing, and a great trouble to the eyes, and by your leave will make the tears run down their thighs [!]: other things there are which may be bought at the Apothecaries, which I will not give you the receit of, for fear it should come to a malicious mans hand, then the effect would be evil." Master Blake would today have been the life of the party, I fear.

Next in our list are cornflowers, the American bachelor's buttons, which Parkinson said Galen and Dioscorides did not mention in their writings. Gerard said that the faculties of those flowers are not yet sufficiently known, but Parkinson a generation later relates, "We in these dayes doe chiefly use them as a cooling Cordiall and commended by some to be a remedy not onely against the plague and pestilentiall diseases, but against the poison of Scorpions and Spiders." Salmon in the *Botanologia*, 1710, says that cornflowers are "Styptick, and good to Take away Redness, and Inflammation of the Eyes and pains thereof: they cool in fevers, resist Poison, help in Dropsie." Mrs. Grieve in her *Modern Herbal*, 1931, claims that the water distilled from cornflower petals is used for eyes today, while a French eyewash called "Eau de Casselunettes" used to be made from cornflower petals.

A conserve of cowslips was much used in early days as a sedative after nervous excitement, while an ointment made of the juice of them mixed with linseed oil was used as an unguent for scalds and burns. William Coles in *Adam in Eden,* 1657, says,

"An oyntment made of the leaves and Hogs grease, healeth wounds; and taketh away Spots, Wrinkles, and Sunburnings, and so doth the distilled water of the flowers; As divers Ladies, Gentlewomen and she Citizens whether wives or widdows know well enough."

Parkinson also recommends the juice or water of cowslip flowers for clearing the skin of blemishes and declares that they will "take away the wrinkles thereof and cause the skinne to become smooth and faire." I wonder if there is a cowslip lotion or face cream today.

Elder flowers were not only used in food and drink but the water of them, John Evelyn declared, has "effected wonders in a fever," while Parkinson in his herbal suggested other uses: "The distilled water of the flowers, taketh away the heate and inflammation of the eyes, and helpeth them when they are bloud shotten. The hands being washed morning and evening with the same water of the flowers, doth much helpe and ease them that have the Palsie in them and cannot keep from shaking."

Many medicinal herbs used largely for the foliage or roots bore flowers which played a limited but important part in the early pharmacopœia. Both William Coles, 1657, and Mrs. Grieve, 1931, write of the value of the flowers of marshmallow, boiled in water and sweetened with a little honey, as good for a gargle, Mrs. Grieve suggesting the addition of a little alum. A conserve of sage flowers was eaten, according to Salmon, 1710, "to warme and comfort the Brain and Nerves, to help and restore the memory, quicken the Senses," and many other things. Conserve of wallflowers, Parkinson says, "is used for a remedy both for the Appoplexie and Palsie. The oyle made of the flowers is healing and resolving, good to ease paines of strained and pained sinews." A conserve of eyebright was used for dimness of sight.

There were medicinal sirups of peach blossoms, and flowers of peony, pansy, jasmine, for various ailments. An infusion of tansy flowers was a specific for gout, while a wine made of coltsfoot flowers was taken for the stomach's sake. Sir John Hill, 1755, says, "An ointment made of the flowers of foxglove boiled in May butter has long been famous in scrophulous sores."

Reading in the old herbals one continually wonders how it ever occurred to an herbalist, not only to try them for cures, but why a certain one, rather than another, should have been chosen for a particular ailment and, in so many cases, with success, if we judge by the modern use of the same plant. Why some plants were chosen is, of course, clear enough if we understand the ancient belief in the Doctrine of Signatures, that on each medicinal plant is a natural label to indicate what ailment it will cure. This is illustrated by the hawthorn, for example. Distilled water of the hawthorn flowers must have been kept on hand in every manor and cottage. According to William Coles, "it is found by good experience, that if Cloathes and Spunges be wet in the said water and applyed to any place whereinto thornes, Splinters etc. have entered and be there abiding, it will notably draw forth, so that the thorn gives a medicine for its own pricking." But many other plants have thorns. Why was hawthorn chosen? Sometimes I wonder if the Doctrine of Signatures was not merely a means of rationalizing results which had been obtained over the years by trial and error.

Again, St. John's-Wort, with apparent punctures in the leaves, was good for cuts in the skin. Sir John Hill points out that the bruised flowering tops of the plant "are good for wounds and bruises, they stop bleeding and serve as a balsam for one, and take off blackness in the other." Why the plant was particularly good for bleeding is easily explained by Gerard:

"The leaves, flowers and seedes stamped, and put into a glass with oile olive, and set in the hot sunne for certaine weekes togather and then strained from those herbes, and the like quantitie of new put in, and sunned in like maner, doth make an oile of the colour of blood, which is a most pretious remedy for deep wounds. . . ."

Then, again, it would seem probable that the use of iris petals as a poultice on bruises was because of their blue color, often tinged with a faint reddish hue, much like the bruise itself.

The whole study of how the herbalists determined to their own satisfaction, at least, the proper medicinal label, would require a lifetime of work. It would demand more than an unusual quota of imagination for us to ferret out the specific use of certain plants from the label, often quite hidden within the plant. In early days, plants with yellow flowers were made into medicines for jaundice; in Mrs. Grieve's *Modern Herbal* she points out that the yellow flowers of St. John's-Wort are still used for jaundice and the plant is used for hemorrhages. I have not been able to discover, however, why primroses and cowslips have been, as Parkinson relates, "in a manner wholly used in Cephalicall diseases, either among other herbs or flowers, or of themselves alone, to ease paines

in the head and is accounted next unto Betony the best
for that purpose."

As we continue the amazingly long roll of medicinal
flowers, we come upon so many favorites grown in our
grandmother's garden, lavender for instance. Parkinson
in his herbal claims, "It is good to garble the mouth with
the decoction of the flowers, against the paines of the
teeth. Two spoonfuls of the distilled water of the flowers
taken, doth helpe those that have lost their speech or
voyce, restoring it them again." Culpeper, 1657, recommends lavender not only for finding one's lost voice but
also for "the tremblings and passions of the heart and
faintings and swoonings, applied to the temples or nostrils, to be smelt unto; but it is not safe to use it when
the body is replete with blood and humours, because of
the hot and subtle Spirit wherewith it is possessed." Dr.
Fernie, in the nineties, wrote, "A tea brewed from the
flowers is an excellent remedy for the headache from fa-
tigue or weakness."

As Parkinson must have inwardly rebelled against the
thought of having clove gillyflowers pounded into a conserve, so I am sure most of us wince at the idea of mash-
ing up lilies-of-the-valley to be distilled in wine for a
medicinal drink. Their lovely, delicate fragrance brings
a faint nostalgia for childhood days when in early spring
we would part the dark twin leaves to find the dainty
little bells hanging from their primly upright stems.
Or perhaps a whiff of the valley lily odor recalls happy
memories of our high-school graduation or the sweetly
solemn moments of our wedding, or perhaps sorrowful
hours still too unbearably sad to dwell upon. But never,
whatever our feelings, could we bring ourselves to hurt
a single flower.

However, from time immemorial, flower, leaf and root

of lily-of-the-valley have been the ingredients of many a bitter dose. Dr. Fernie in *Herbal Simples,* 1897, says, "Distilled water of the flowers was formerly in great repute against nervous affections, and for many troubles of the head, insomuch that it was treasured in vessels of gold and silver. Matthiolus [sixteenth century herbalist] named it Aqua aurea, golden water." The powder of the dried flowers was used as a snuff to relieve headache, and Henry Lyte in *Niewe Herball,* 1578, reported that the water, "as they say, doth strengthen the memorie and restoreth it againe to his naturall vigor, when through sickness it is diminished." A gout cure recommended by Gerard was certainly made in an unusual way:

"The flowers of May Lillies put into a glasse, and set in a hill of antes close stopped for the space of a moneth, and then taken out, therein you shall finde a liquor, that appeaseth the paine and griefe of the goute, being outwardly applied; which is recommended to be most excellent."

Gerard also recommends the water of valley lilies for strengthening the memory, for an eye wash, for giddiness, for palsy, and for apoplexy. To help the last two ailments most of the early herbalists recommended wine in which the flowers had been distilled. Culpeper says, "The wine [of the flowers] is more precious than gold, for if any one that is troubled with apoplexy drink thereof with 6 grains of Pepper and a little Lavender water they shall not need to fear it that moneth." The reason for this popularity of the flower in medicines is discovered in the statement of William Coles, principal exponent of the Doctrine of Signatures:

"It cureth Apoplexy by Signature; for as that disease is caused by the dropping of humours into the principall

Ventricles of the brain: so the flowers of this Lilly hanging on the plants as if they were drops, are of wonderful use herein, if they be distilled with Wine, and the quantity of a spoonful thereof drunk, and so it restoreth speech to them that have the dumb Palsy."

Sir John Hill, an herbalist himself in the eighteenth century, does not echo the earlier herbalists in their unstinted eulogies of lily-of-the-valley, but is much more moderate in his evaluation of its medicinal virtues. He writes,

"A tea made of them [the flowers] and drank for a constancy, is excellent against all nervous complaints, it will cure nervous headaches, and trembling of the limbs: a great deal too much has been said of this plant, for people call it a remedy for apoplexies and the dead palsies, but though all this is not true, enough is, to give the plant a reputation and bring it again into use."

Something brought it "again into use," for you will find lily-of-the-valley on the crude drug lists of today and the use, as in old days, is for dropsy and heart troubles.

Marigold flowers were used, not only in culinary dishes, but in medicinal preparations. Thomas Hyll in the *Gardeners Labyrinth*, 1577, recommends the juice of the petals mixed with vinegar as a dentifrice to be rubbed on gums and teeth and claims it "a soveraigne remedy for the assuaging of the grievous pain of the teeth." Gerard says that a "conserve made of the flowers and sugar taken in the morning fasting cureth the trembling of the hart; and is also given in time of plague or pestilence, or corruption of the aire."

Marigold tea was a good "thrower-out" of inward corruption, or, as Sir John Hill puts it, "It is good in fevers, it gently promotes perspiration and throws out anything that ought to appear on the skin" as, for instance, "meazles." William Coles a century before had written, "The Flowers of Marigold comfort and strengthen the Heart exceedingly . . . are good in pestilent and contagious Feavers as also in Jaundice, and are very expulsive, and little lesse effectual in the Small Pox and Meazles than Saffron." But of all, according to a poem based on the sixteenth century herbal of Macer, only to look upon marigold will draw "humours" out of the head.

The names of some herbs fall so pleasingly upon the ear that they seem to call up pictures of the old days when time was not at such a premium, when people did not jam into a subway car as though it were the last one ever, when "quick snacks" were unheard of, when a morning cup of coffee was something more than a burning sensation. Rather, the musical connotative sounds recall old-fashioned gardens and, strolling along the paths, courtly gentlemen and gentle ladies in costumes made for leisurely, gracious living. I have always loved the sound of "rest-harrow" and will not let myself admit that it is an outcast from the garden, a noxious weed. And how lovely are Meadow Rue, Daffy-down-dilly, Rosemary, Lords and Ladies, Our Lady's Flannel, Melilot, Meadowsweet. The latter, meadowsweet, is botanically known as *Spiraea Ulmaria,* but I like its other names found in the old herbals, Medesweet, Queen of the Meadow or Lady of the Meadow. Of this herb, Gerard says, "The distilled water of the flowers dropped into the eies, taketh away the burning and itching thereof and cleareth the sight," and he adds that it is reported that "the flowers boiled in wine and drunke, do take away the fits of a quarantine ague, and maketh the hart merrie."

Melilot (sweet clover) flowers entered into the ingredients of a recipe found in the seventeenth century

Arcana Fairfaxiana called "Bath for Melancholy," while William Coles in *Adam in Eden* includes the flowers in a concoction which he calls simply, "Pain in the side." This pain was assuaged in the following manner:

"Take Melilote Flowers, Camomile, Rosemary and Elder Flowers of each half a handful, of Bran an handfull, of Aniseed, Fennel-Seed and Caroway-Seed bruised, of each two Ounces: make a quilted Bag for the side, sprinkle it with Wine; and being made hot, apply it."

When we come to the medicines made of roses, both of early and of modern times, there are such a bewildering number that the task of choosing a few most important ones is hopeless. Parkinson in the *Theatrum Botanicum* says, "Of the red Roses are usually made many compositions all serving to sundry good uses. . . . To entreate of them all exactly I doe not entend for so a pretty volume of itselfe might be composed, I will therefore only give you a hint. . . ." One of his suggestions is, "Rose leaves and Mints heated and applyed outwardly to the stomacke stayeth castings and strengthneth a weake stomache very much." William Coles in *Adam in Eden* suggests roses for a headache. He says,

"If a peece of Red Rose Cake [a mixture of roses and sugar candied] moistened therewith [with vinegar of roses] be cut fit for the Head and heated between a double folded Cloth, with a little beaten Nutmeg and Poppy Seed, strewed on the side that must lie next to the Forehead and Temples and bound so thereto for all night."

In Smith's *Compleat Housewife*, 1728, is a sort of rose poultice for a swelling in the Face: "Take a handful of Damask-rose Leaves [petals], boil them in running

Water till they are tender; stamp them to a Pulp, and boil white Bread and Milk till 'tis soft, then put in your Pulp with a little Hogs Lard and thicken it with the Yolk of an Egg, and apply it warm." Anthony Askham in his *Herbal*, 1550, gives a recipe for "Melrosette" which we would call Honey of Roses and would consider of culinary, as well as medicinal, value. It follows:

"Melrosette is made thus, take faire purified hony and newe redde roses, the white endes of them clypped away, than chop them smal and put them into the hony and boile them menely togither, to knowe whan it is boyled ynough, ye shall knowe it by the swete odour and the colour redde. Five yeres he may be kepte in his vertue, by the Roses he hath vertue of comfortinge, and by the hony he hath vertue of clensynge. In Wynter and in Somer it may be given competently to feble sycke, flumatike melancholy, and colorike people."

In contemplating the myriad uses of rosemary, I find it as difficult to choose but little to say as in the great subject of roses. Again I am one with Parkinson who says the medicinal uses of rosemary are so many "that you might be as well tyred in the reading, as I in the writing, if I should set down all that might be said of it."

According to the herbalists, rosemary would seem to be the one plant we must have in our gardens, because of its ability to raise our spirits. Little cakes or drops made of the flowers and sugar were supposed to comfort the heart and quicken the spirits. A conserve of the flowers was "singular good . . . to expell the contagion of the Pestilence"; the oil was "accounted a soveraign Balsame"; the distilled water was used for halitosis; the flowering tops were good for "head-ach, tremblings of the limbs and all other nervous disorders"; the flowers alone were eaten "to procure a cleare sight"; and if they were laid on the bed, kept the sleeper from nightmares; the powder made of the flower, if carried about one, made him "merry, glad gracious and well-beloved of all men." Anthony Askham, 1550, takes care of the ills which rosemary will cure, in one recipe:

"Take the flowers and put them in a lynen clothe, and so boyle them in fayre cleane water to the halfe and cole [cool] it, and drynke it for it is much worth against all evyls in the body."

Saffron is one of the most ancient of all the flowers, used as a sedative for nervous afflictions, for palpitation of the heart, fainting spells and, most naturally because of its yellow color, for yellow jaundice. Thomas Hyll says, "Taken in meat it causeth a long and easie breathing, and helpeth the Asthma," while William Lawson in *Country House-wives Garden*, 1617, advises housewives to "gather the yellow (for they shape much like Lillies) dry, and after dry them, they be precious, expelling diseases from the heart and stomacke."

But William Coles really comes to the fore in praise of saffron. In *Adam in Eden* he says, "There is not a better Cordial amongst herbes than Saffron is, for it doth much comfort the Heart, and recreateth the Spirits and makes them cheerfull that use it."

Violets alone or made up into sirups, cordials, conserves, have been used for centuries for all sorts of ailments, accidents and weaknesses of the flesh and spirits. In *Proprietatibus Rerum, c.* 1280, Bartholomaeus Anglicus says, "Violet is a little hearbe in substance, and is better fresh and newe, then when it is olde, and the flower thereof smelleth most, and so the smell thereof abateth heate of the braine, and refresheth and comforteth the spirites of feeling and maketh sleepe, for it cooleth and tempereth and moysteneth the braine. . . ." The ancient Romans drank a wine in which violet flowers had been infused, for epilepsy. In the *Countrie Farme,* 1616, Markham said the sirup and conserve of violets were "good for inflammation of the Lungs, the Pleurisie, Coughs and Agues."

In the *Grete Herball,* 1526, a most simple recipe for sirup of violets is given: "Syrope of vyolettes i mach in this maner—Sethe vyolettes in water and lete it lye all nyght in ye same water, than poure and streyne out the water and in the same put sugre and make your syrope." Gerard tells us that there is "made of Violets and sugar, certaine plates called Sugar Violet, Violet Tables or plate; which is most pleasant and wholesome, especially it comforteth the hart and the other inward parts." These "plates" or lozenges, which became especially popular after being praised by Charles II, were also used for sore throat, headache and insomnia. They were common as late as 1900.

Among the ancient Welsh there was a curious preliminary test to decide whether a man who had been beaten would live. A bruised violet was bound about his forefinger. If he fell asleep it was a sign he would recover; if not, he would surely die. In the *Countrie Farme* is a sort of violet cure for the victim of an assault:

"He that shall have taken a blow upon the head, so that it hath astonished him, shall not have anie greater hurt, if presently after such a blow he drinke Violet flowers stampt, and continue the same drinke for a certaine time."

Most of us would feel that we needed more than a drink of violet water on such an occasion, and it must be remembered that the word "astonished" in those days really meant knocking a person out "cold." Away back there the British were given to understatement!

Also in Markham's book are directions for what to do for a "hangover." It reads:

"The flowers of March Violets applied unto the brows, doe assuage the headach, which commeth of too much drinking and procure sleepe."

If that were a popular remedy nowadays, I suppose a large violet patch in anyone's garden would be looked upon with definite suspicion.

Let it not be supposed that in this discussion I have exhausted the entire list of kinds or uses of medicinal flowers. In fact, we can scarcely imagine the color, the fragrance, the quantities of blossoms that poured into the still-room from early spring to late autumn, all to be efficiently taken care of by the housewife, always solicitous for the health of her family and household. Although we now look to doctor and druggist to cure our bodily ills, when we find ourselves confused and bewildered by defeat, confronted with perplexing problems that must be solved, we may well turn to our perennial garden to heal many a wound of mind and spirit. As we look into the depths of a newly opened rose, scan the personalities in the funny little faces of the pansies, bend over to catch the fragrance of violet or lily-of-the-valley, do we not for a moment, at least, cast aside the world pressing too hard upon us? In the picture of a medieval garden in the "Frankeleyn's Tale," Chaucer describes that particular effect in a few lovely lines:

> "The odour of floures and the fresshe sighte
> Wolde han maked any herte lighte
> That ever was born, but if to greet siknesse,
> Or to greet sorwe held it in distresse;
> So full it was of beautee with pleasaunce."

CHAPTER XII

A Prelude to Salads

"She also produced (besides a cabbage) a handful of mustard and cress, a trifle of the herb called dandelion, three bunches of radishes, an onion rather larger than an average turnip, three substantial slices of beetroot, and a short prong or antler of celery; the whole of this garden-stuff having been publicly exhibited but a short time before as a twopenny salad, and purchased by Mrs. Prig, on condition that the vendor could get it all into her pocket."
—DICKENS, Martin Chuzzlewit, 1844.

Mrs. Prig then recommended "that these productions of nature should be sliced up, for immediate consumption, in plenty of vinegar." This mixture seemed to Victorian Betsey Prig and Sairah Gamp an adequate salad. In reading Boulestin and Hill's *Herbs, Salads and Seasonings,* 1930, I found its counterpart in a description of the present English salad:

"It consists of Shredded Lettuce, half a dozen Radishes, three slices of Tomatoes, two of Cucumber, a little Beetroot, Watercress and Spring Onions whole; there is at the bottom of the moulded glass bowl, so small that one could not possibly mix the salad if there was a chance of doing so, a certain amount of water. A bottle of 'salad dressing' stands handy, next to the purely ornamental cruets. . . . No wonder salads are not, as a rule, much appreciated by the population."

In most country hotels and in some London restaurants such salads are, indeed, the "salad du jour" and I might add, with beet juice running unpleasantly about the salad and giving it all a purplish tinge.

On the Continent, however, even the smallest of inns serve the freshest of green salads, while America is a country of salad eaters who appreciate all the subtleties of taste and texture. But salads are looking up again in the better eating places in England and, with the new interest in herbs, perhaps the old cookery books will start a new era of salads.

From those ancient books the whole story of salads may be gathered, from the simplest dish of greens in spring to the elaborate cooked salads for winter. In very early times, the housewife and cook did not self-consciously gather one herb for its calories, another for its vitamins, nor balance one kind against another as later herbalists did, for its effect on body or soul. In spring the fresh young shoots of mint, of purslane, of cress and the whole family of alliums simply "touched the right spot," while in winter when fresh greens could not be gathered from field or garden, vegetables were boiled, sliced and an oil-and-vinegar dressing poured over them, in response to that desire for something to offset the heavy meats. Nowadays when we can choose several kinds of fresh greens at the vegetable market, we scarcely realize how hard put our ancient grandmothers were in winter time to find variety of food for our grandfathers and often for his sisters, and his cousins and his aunts.

One "green salad" fit for a king is found in *The Forme of Cury,* a roll of ancient English cookery, compiled about

1390 by the master cooks of Richard II. The recipe is called quite simply, "Salat":

"Take parsel, sawge, garlec, chibollas [young onions], oynons, leek, borage, myntes, porrectes [kind of leek], fenel, and ton tressis [cresses], rew, rosemarye, purslarye [purslane]; lave, and waisshe hem clene; pike hem, pluk hem small with thyn [thine] honde, and myng [mix] hem wel with raw oile. Lay on vynegar and salt, and serve it forth."

A list of herbs in a fifteenth century book of culinary recipes gives us an idea of summer salad ingredients:

"Buddus of Stanmache [perhaps black lovage], Vyolette flourez, Percely, Redmynt, Syves [chives], Cresse of Boleyn, Purselan, Ramson [bear's garlic], Calamynt, Prime Rose buddus, Dayses, Rapounses, Daundelion, Rokette, Red Nettle, Borage flourers, Croppes of Red Fennell, Selbestryn, Chykyn-wede."

Herbs of the field, most of them, full of more medicinal virtues than the housewife dreamed, in spite of her skill in dosing.

As my tiger cat, Orphie Whiffendorfer, goes browsing about Salt Acres until he finds just the herb or grass he wants, so our primitive forbears experimented with one herb after another. Some were found good and culled for the dinner, some unpalatable and rejected by the salad connoisseur which the clown in *All's Well That Ends Well,* IV-5, definitely was not:

LAFEU: 'Twas a good lady, 'twas a good lady; we may pick a thousand salads ere we light on such another herb.

CLOWN: Indeed, sir, she was the sweet marjoram of the salad, or, rather, the herb of grace.

LAFEU: They are not herbs, you knave; they are nose herbs.

CLOWN: I am no great Nebuchadnezzar, sir; I have not much skill in grass.

In Thomas Tusser's list of "Herbs and Roots for Salads and Sauce" in *Five Hundreth Points of Good Husbandry*, 1573, a thought is given to the winter salad as well as to the early greens. The salad materials are: alexanders, artichokes, blessed thistle, cucumbers, endive, mustard, musk-million, mints, purslane, radish, rampions, rocket, sage, sorrel, spinage, sea holly, asparagus, skirrets, chicory, tarragon and violets of all colors. At the end of the list, Tusser adds, capers, lemons, olives, oranges, rice, samphire; but since they commonly are not dwellers in the English garden,

> "These buy with the penny,
> Or look not for any."

Neither could the ingredients for the salad dressing, except the vinegar, be had unless with the penny, so a thoughtful gift they made. On April 30, 1466, Sir John Paston sends from Wales to his brother, "two Pots of Oil for Sallads, which oil was good as might be when I delivered it [to the bearer of the letter] and shall be good at the receiving, if it not be mishandled or miscarried." Sugar was not to be obtained in the country, except rarely, and then not granulated as today, but in a loaf from which it was scraped as needed. In 1461 Margaret Paston writes "to my right worshipful Husband, John Paston," who at the time was in London, "I pray you that ye will vouchsafe to send me another sugar loaf, for my old is done." If you were living in London you could buy the materials in small quantities at the stalls and markets. In the domestic accounts of a gentleman who was summering in London, there are frequent items of 3d (6¢) for oil and sugar, the same amount for salad and eggs and 2d for herbs.

By the sixteenth and seventeenth centuries, the great herbalists and gardening writers had the salad situation well in hand and had given it a clinical cast. Now the housewife could know why and how she used each of the dozen kinds of greens and vegetable herbs. Many of the salad materials, such as blessed thistle, nettles, sea holly, are a bit too harsh for the modern tongue, but many of the herbs used then are still relished by the modern gourmet. Asparagus was a great salad favorite. Gerard, 1597, says: "Asparagus should be sodden in flesh broth, and eaten, or boiled in fair water, then seasoned with oil, pepper and vinegar, being served up as a salad." Thomas Hyll, 1577, adds to similar directions, "I think it necessary to be remembered that the Sperages require a smal boiling, for too much or long boiled, they become corrupt or without delight in eating." And some of us think that the thought of not wearing out a vegetable in cooking is a wholly modern idea !

Beetroots were, even then, salad material, sliced and served with oil and vinegar, and were used, as Parkinson says, "to trimme up or garnish forth manie sorts of dishes of meate." Evelyn, the early salad maker without peer, and writer of the *Acetaria*, 1699, says: "The Roots of the Red Beet, pared into thin Slices and Circles, are by the French and Italians contriv'd into curious Figures to adorn their Sallets." Sweet Chervil (Sweet Cicely) was a valuable salad, good in every part. The roots, Gerard claimed were "most excellent in a sallade, if they be boiled, and after dressed, as the cunning Cooke knoweth how better than myself; notwithstanding I do use to eat them with oile and vinegar, being first boiled, which is very good for old people that are dull and without courage, it rejoiceth and comforteth the hart, and increaseth their lust and strength."

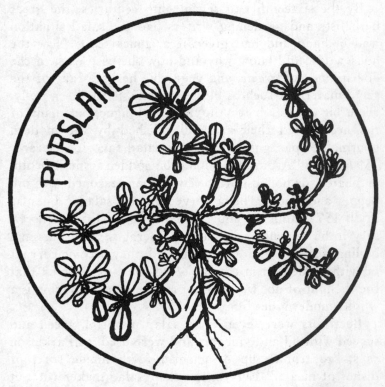

Purslane.

Formerly planted in the garden for salads, now found everywhere.

"The seedes," Gerard says, "eaten as a sallade whilest they are yet greene, with oile, vinegar and pepper, exceede all other sallade by many degrees, both in pleasantnes of taste, sweetnesse of smell, and holsomnesse for the cold

and feeble stomach." Gerard continues the praise of Sweet
Cicely: "The leaves are exceeding good, holsome, and
pleasant among other sallade herbes giving the taste of
Anise seede unto the rest"; while De la Quintinye, famous
gardener to Louis XIV, says that sweet cicely gives a
"perfuming relish" to the salad and "ought never to be
wanting in our sallets for it is exceeding wholesome and
charming to the spirits." Any housewife of those days
who did not grow sweet cicely in her kitchen garden
must have felt somewhat less than a good salad maker.

Evelyn also recommends spinach, cooked but not fresh,
for salads. In the old days, he says, spinach was not used
in salads and "the oftner kept out the better; I speak of
the crude: But being boil'd to a Pult [pulp] and without
other Water than its own moisture, is a most excellent
Condiment with Butter, Vinegar or Limon, for almost all
sorts of boil'd Flesh, and may accompany a Sick Man's
Diet."

Almost any vegetable boiled and served with oil and
vinegar was accepted as a matter of course as a salad, but
the opinions expressed about fresh greens are often most
startling although delightful. Evelyn makes a special note
that "Persley is not so hurtful to the Eyes as reported,"
while basil "imparts a grateful Flavour, if not too strong,
somewhat offensive to the Eyes; and therefore the tender
Tops to be very sparingly used in our Sallet."

The cucumber was quite generally frowned upon and
begrudgingly admitted to salads. Parkinson says, "The
usuall manner to eate them is with pepper and salt, being
pared and sliced, and to drowne them in wine for feare of
doing more harme." Evelyn claims that it has not been
long "since Cucumber, however dress'd was thought fit to
be thrown away, being accounted little better than
Poyson." Many people of today also feel that no matter

how you prepare a cucumber, it is still a cucumber. In the *Countrie Farme* are sounded still further alarms and warnings. "Furthermore, there may not come neere unto their bed, any vessell full of oyle, because the cucumber, of all other things hateth oile, and cannot thrive if he which doth till them, have handled oyle."

Parkinson in his *Theatrum Botanicum*, 1640, divides plants into 17 classes or Tribes. The sixth Tribe is "Cooling and Succory-like Herbs," purslane, sorrel, orach, beets, chickweed, borage, bugloss, endive, chicory, dandelion, lettuce. Other herbs, as tarragon and rocket, were considered heating, and on that basis did the herbalists toss their scientifically combined salads. Lettuce then, as now, was considered "tops" among salad materials. Evelyn claimed that we "meet with nothing among all our crude Materials and Sallet store, so proper to mingle with any of the rest, nor so wholesome to be eaten alone or in Composition." Although Gerard felt that lettuce was more digestible cooked than raw, he approved of it either way:

"It is served in these daies, and in these countries at the beginning of supper, and eaten first before any other meat, which also Martialis testifieth to be done in times past, marveiling why some did use it for a service at the end of supper . . . being taken before meate it doth many times stir up appetite; and after supper it keepeth away drunkenness which commeth by wine; and that is by reason that it staieth the vapors from rising up in to the head."

It is said that lettuce was introduced into England from Flanders for Catherine of Aragon, and in the expense accounts, 1531, for Henry VIII is a record of payment to the gardener at York Place for "lettuze" delivered at Hampton Court.

Another cooling herb was endive, which Gerard claimed "doth comfort the weake and feeble stomacke and cooleth and refresheth the stomacke over much heated." Evelyn recommends dandelion leaves being "Mace-

Salad Burnet (*Sanguisorba minor*).

From Parkinson, 1629.

rated in several Waters to extract the bitterness," while Parkinson says that the roots bleached to remove bitterness, and "eaten as a sallet are more effectuall than the leaves used in the same manner." Thomas Hyll lauds the ubiquitous purslane that causes us many a headache in weeding; "The Purselane is one of the Garden herbes, served first in Sallets, with Oyle, Vinegar and a little Salt as well at the mean or rich men's tables." De la Quintinye says that "the thick stalke of Purslain that is run to seed are good to pickle in Salt and Vinegar for Winter Sallads."

In the *Countrie Farme,* 1616, we may read that leeks, cibols, and chives were "wont to be used in Sallads to helpe to temper the coolness of other hearbes used in Salads," while tarragon, according to Gerard, is not to be "eaten alone in salades, but ioyned with other herbs, as lettuce, purslane, and such like, that it may also temper the coldness of them." Hyll says that rocket is like tarragon and is "added to the Lettice in Sallets, to the end it may temper the contrary vertue of the same, so that the Lettice is seldom eaten with meat without the Rocket." Garden cress, still another cooling herb, Parkinson says, was eaten with lettuce and purslane, or sometimes with tarragon or rocket "with oyle, vinegar, and a little salt, and in that manner it is very savoury."

The lesser burnet (*Sanguisorba minor*), so Gerard says, "is pleasant to be eaten in sallade, in which it is thought to make the hart merry and glad." What we all today surely need is more burnet and oftener! Evelyn recommended, for another salad ingredient, orange mint (*Mentha citrata*), one of my most used herbs: "The gentler Tops of the Orange-Mint enter well into our Composition, or are grateful alone (as are also the other sorts) with the juice of Oranges, and a little Sugar."

Oftentimes a salad on the dinner table, a salad is to us, and it is nothing more, but in the early days, according to Gervase Markham's *English Housewife,* 1615, "Sallets and Fricases" were the first of the five parts of cookery, the others being "boyled meats and Broths; Roste meats and carbonadoes (broiled fish); Bak't meats and Pyes; and banquetting and made dishes, with other conceits and secrets." A housewife of the Restoration period took her salads seriously, Markham classifying them as simple, compound, some "onely to furnish out the table, and some both for use and adornation." The simple salads were just dishes of greens or vegetables, such as cibols, chives, scallions, radish-roots, boiled carrots, skirrets, turnips, lettuce, purslane, samphire, bean-cods, asparagus, cucumbers, "with a world of others too tedious to nominate."

"Your compound Sallets are, first the young Buds and Knots of all manner of wholesome Herbs at their first springing; as red Sage, Mint, Lettice, Violets, Marigolds, Spinage, and many others mixed together, and then served up to the table with Vinegar, Sallet-Oyle and Suger." Markham also included directions for making "Strange Sallets," truly named:

"THE MAKING OF STRANGE SALLETS

"Now for the compounding of Sallets, of these pickled and preserved things, though they may be served up simply of themselves, and are both good and dainty; yet for better curiosity, and the finer adorning of the Table, you shall thus use them. First, if you would set forth any Red flower, that you know or have seen, you shall take your pots of preserved Gilliflowers, and suting the colours answerable to the flower you shall proportion it forth, and lay the shape of the Flower in a Fruit dish; then with your Purslan leaves, make the green Coffin of the Flower, and with the Purslan stalks, make the stalk of the flower, and the divisions of the leaves and branches; then with the thinne slices of Cowcumbers, make their leaves in true proportions, jagged or otherwise: and thus you may set forth some full blown, some halfe blown, and some in the bud, which will be pretty and curious. And if you will set forth yellow flowers, take the pots of Primroses and Cowslips, if blew flowers, then the pots of Violets, or Buglosse flowers; and these Sallets are both for shew and use, for they are more excellent for taste, then for to look on."

An excellent compound boiled salad was made by washing and boiling two or three handfuls of spinach until "it be exceeding soft and tender as pap," draining it, chopping it fine, then cooking it up in a pipkin (small earthen pot) with butter. Then a handful of currants was stirred in; "then put to as much Vinegar as will make it reasonable tart, and then with Sugar season it according to the taste of the Master of the house, and so serve it upon sippets [small pieces of toast or fried bread]." Perhaps this salad would suit the master of your house but the master of my house feels about this "sallet" as Gerard did about parsnips, "I have made no tryall of, nor mean to do."

These boiled salads, as well as "Bak'd, Pickl'd, or otherwise disguised, variously accommodated by the skilful cooks, to render them grateful to the more feminine Palat, as Herbs rather for the Pot," did not interest Evelyn since he was concerned rather with the fresh salad material, but Markham takes all kinds in his stride:

"Your preserved Sallats are of two kinds, either pickled, as are Cucumbers, Samphire, Purslan, Broom and such like; or preserved with Vinegar, as Violets, Primrose, Cowslip, Gilly flowers of all kinds; Broom-flowers, and for the most part any wholesome flower whatsoever."

"Now for the pickling of Sallats, they are only boyled," and then he tells how they are drained, spread on a table, thoroughly salted and, when cold, placed in an earthen pot and a pickle made of water, salt, and vinegar added, and the jar sealed. Flowers were preserved with sugar and vinegar.

"Now for Sallets for shew only, and the adorning and setting out of a table with number of dishes, they be those which are made of Carret roots . . . cut into many shapes and proportions, or some into Knots, some in the manner of Scutions and Armes, some like Birds, and some like Wild Beasts, according to the Art and cunning of the Workman; and these for the most part are seasoned with Vinegar, Oyl, and a little Pepper."

Markham then leaves the subject of salads with a not altogether modest thought. "A world of other Sallets there are, which time and experience may bring to our House-wifes eye, but the composition of them, and the serving of them, differeth nothing from those already rehearsed."

The housewife's labors were not over when she had prepared a fine dinner, but she must see that it was served up with some degree of elegance. I am sure we all feel with Markham the importance of offering food in a manner appealing to the eye as well as to the palate:

. . . "For what availes it our Good Hous-wife to be never so skilfull in the parts of Cookery, if she want skill to marshall the dishes, and set every one in his due place, giving precedency according to fashion and custome . . . she shall first marshall the Sallets, delivering the Grand Sallet first, which is evermore compound: then green Sallets, then boyled Sallets, then some smaller compound Sallets."

A new note to salad is introduced by Sir Kenelm Digby in his *Closet Opened,* 1669, by his recipe for "Sallet of Cold Capon Rosted," certainly a forerunner of our popular chicken salad: "It is a good Sallet, to slice a cold

Capon thin; mingle with it some Sibbolds, Lettice, Rocket and Tarragon sliced small. Season all with Pepper, Salt, Vinegar and Oyl, and sliced Limon. A little Origanum doth well in it."

There seem to have been no really inspired writers on salads from Markham to Evelyn. For the most part the green and the boiled mixtures and concoctions remained about the same. Leonard Meager in the *English Gardner,* 1670, gives the usual list and adds, "Also some make a very acceptable boil'd Sallet of the young and tender stalks of both Turneps, and of Cabbages when they first run up in the Spring, they boil them and peel them and put Butter, Vinegar and Pepper to them." John Worlidge in his *Systema Horti-culturae,* 1677, also recommends the old standbys of lettuce, cooling and refreshing, purslane, asparagus ("crude or boyl'd"), endive, chicory, beets, orach, sorrel, borage, bugloss, chervil, alexanders, tarragon. Mints, however, really draw Worlidge's attention:

"Garden mints were universally used for sauces in Pliny's time; and much commended for their singular Vertues, especially the young red buds in the Spring with a due proportion of Vinegar and Sugar, refresh the Spirits and stirreth up the appetite, and is one of the best Sallads the Garden affords. There are divers sorts of Mint but the red Garden Mint [*Mentha citrata*] is the best."

Evelyn, the nonpareil of all early salad makers and writers on salads, says that "the more frugal Italians and French to this Day, gather Ogni Verdura, anything almost that's Green and Tender, to the very tops of Nettles." Yet, "anything almost" seemed to be grist for Evelyn's own salad mill, for in his *Acetaria,* in the section on "Furniture and Materials" are listed 73 materials and "to all which might we add sundry more," some of them discussed for three pages more. Later, however, in the book, Evelyn says upon being asked "what Herbs were proper and fit to make Sallets with," he had with the assistance of Mr. London, the King's gardener, "reduc'd them to a competent Number, not exceeding Thirty-Five: but which may be vary'd and enlarg'd by Taking in, or leaving out, any other Sallet-Plant, mentioned in the foregoing List [of 73]."

Evelyn makes a distinction between boiled and raw salads; that is, "the Olera [which were never eaten Raw] from Acetaria, which were never Boil'd." He goes on to say that "we are by Sallets to understand a particular Composition of certain crude and fresh Herbs, such as usually are, or may safely be eaten with some Acetous Juice, Oyl, Salt, etc. to give them a grateful Gust and Vehicle."

To make the Perfect Salad, Evelyn discusses nine details that are of the utmost importance to be taken into consideration:

1. "Let your *Herby Ingredients* be exquisitely cull'd ... discreetly sprinkl'd, than over-much sob'd with Spring-Water, especially Lettuce . . . let them remain awhile in the Cullender to drain the superfluous moisture: And lastly, swing them altogether in a clean course Napkin." (And we call ourselves modern with our "swing!")
2. The *"Oyl"* must be "very clean, not high-colour'd nor yellow: but with an Eye rather of a pallid olive green, without Smell, or the least touch of rancid, or indeed of any sensible taste or Scent at all. . . ."
3. The *"Vinegar* and other liquid Acids, perfectly clear, neither sawre, Vapid or spent. . . ."
4. The *Salt* should be "detersive, penetrating, quickning" and of the "brightest Bay grey-Salt."
5. *Mustard* ("another noble Ingredient") should be

"of the best Tewksberry; or else compos'd of the soundest and weightiest Yorkshire Seed."

6. *Pepper* should "be not bruised to too small a dust."

7. The *"Yolks* of fresh and new-laid Eggs, boil'd moderately hard, to be mingl'd and mash'd with the Mustard, Oyl and Vinegar: and part to cut into quarters, and eat with the Herbs."

8. The *Knife* "with which the Sallet Herbs are cut (especially Oranges, Limons etc.) be of Silver and by no means of Steel, which all Acids are apt to corrode, and retain a Metalic relish of."

9. The *Saladiere* (Sallet Dishes) should be "of Porcelane, or of the Holland-Delft Ware."

A special note at the end of these nine details explains, "That by Parts is to be understood a Pugil; which is no more than one does usually take up between the Thumb and the two next Fingers. By Fascicule a reasonable full Grip, or Handful." As anyone conversant with the "Language of the Sallets" would know, if you take a fascicule of Herby Ingredients, a pugil of salt, a little Acetous Juice and of Sallet-Oyl, you will have a simple green salad.

As time marched into the eighteenth century, household "receipt books" written for the public made their appearance, but directions for making salads were conspicuously absent. Directions were given for complicated procedures like pickling, preserving, ragoos, soups, pastries, pudding, jellies, bills of fare and table settings. Practically every writer of cookery books was greatly concerned with table settings. The "marshalling of dishes" was still a performance not to be taken lightly. In the *Royal Cookery, or The Compleat Court-Book,* 1716, by Patrick Lamb, Esq., there are diagrams for some forty tables correctly set, a definite spot for each dish. There are tables for large and small dishes, some set for the First Course in which the soup, salad and

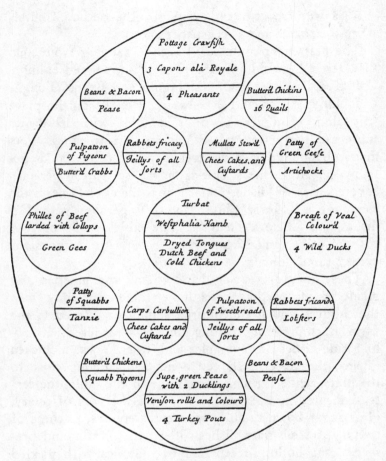

My Lady Arran's Daughter's Wedding Supper, June 6, 1699.

From Patrick Lamb, *Royal-Cookery*, 1716. Lamb was Master-Cook to King Charles II, King James II, William and Mary, Queen Mary, and Queen Anne.

entrees were served, and some for the Second Course, when the roasts and sweet dishes entered.

The first chart contains 51 dishes, ranging from soup to "Desert," including potage, crawfish, sowced Salmon, Coloured Pigg, Veal Olives, Hamb and Beans, Tongue and Udder rosted and 2 Gees à la Royale, but no place for salad. However, on another table with 19 dishes there are two green salads and two white salads, geometrically placed in a square, identical colors in diagonally opposite corners. One table was set for 38 persons, covered with 43 dishes and 24 hors d'œuvres, one in the shape of a "Horse Shoe" for 120 persons with 114 dishes and 83 hors d'œuvres. The table for 20 persons with 21 dishes and 12 hors d'œuvres must have been for a cozy family dinner.

These diagrams bring back to me the nineties and memories of grandmother's dinner table on Sunday when the children and grandchildren simply gravitated to the farm. Each place on the long table was bordered with oblong side dishes of vegetables and, when it was a chicken dinner, the crescent shaped bone dish clinging close to the plate, while through the middle of the table, the center indicated by the lazy Susan, were the vase of celery, glass sugar bowl, tumbler with extra spoons, pitchers of cream, pressed glass dishes filled with pickles and preserves, the hollow green leaf of majolica with pickled peaches. And what food! The mouth waters even to recall those dinners climaxed by the lemony-tasting homemade custard ice cream.

In Patrick Lamb's day, the bills of fare for "every Season in the Year" listed among first course food "Grand Sallad with Pickles," both green and boiled salads being devised. In Elizabeth Raffald's *The Experienced Housekeeper,* 1782, in "A correct List of everything in Season, in every month of the Year," salad greens are present, while in Chapter XVI, "Observations on Pickling," materials for the winter salad are taken care of. Against that winter time when fresh greens are no more, the housewife pickled cucumbers, mangoes, codlins (green apples), kidney beans, samphire, walnuts, barberries, parsley, nasturtiums, radishes, elder shoots and buds, beets, cauliflower, red cabbage, grape, artichokes, mushrooms, onions.

Late eighteenth century William Cowper devoted a poem to "The Salad," but speaks of the green salad material in none too flattering terms:

> "There at no cost, on onions rank and red,
> Or the curl'd endive's bitter leaf he fed."

The ancient vegetable-herb, sperage, gradually changed its name to asparagus, later to be dubbed "grass," as in rural sections we even now hear it familiarly called. In eighteenth century Hannah Glasse's *Art of Cookery*, I came across a recipe called, prosaically enough, "Asparagus forced in French Rolls," but when I read the directions I was amazed at the inventor's ingenuity. Having taken off the top crust and scooped out the rolls, the cook was to fry the shells thus made. Then a thick sauce was made of cream and egg yolks, seasoned with nutmeg and salt. Then comes the amazing part:

> "Have ready a Hundred of small Grass boiled, then save Tops enough to stick the Rolls with, the rest cut small and put into the Cream, fill the Loaves with them. Before you fry the Rolls, make Holes thick in the Top crust to stick the Grass in; then lay on the Piece of Crust and stick the Grass in, that it may look as if it was growing. It makes a pretty Side dish at a Second Course."

The *Housekeeper's Receipt Book,* 1813, contains a monthly memorandum for gardening in which green salad material is taken into consideration. In February and March, the gardener was to begin to sow lettuce and other greens. In April, "Sow young sallads once in ten days and some Cos and Silesia Lettuces." In May salads were to be sown once in two days; "and at the same time choose a warm border and sow some purslain." (At Salt Acres this year, purslane was, with no encouragement whatever, one of our best crops. In every plot, in every nook and corner, shady or sunny, purslane grew with all its might and main, completely encircling the tender seedlings whose roots would be disturbed by weeding.) In June we are told, "Endive should be planted out for blanching."

In this comprehensive compendium of useful knowledge for housewives, directions are given for raising salad in two days, by steeping seed of mustard, cress, lettuce in "uqua vitae" (alcohol) and sowing them in fine mould mixed with pigeons' dung and slaked slime. "This process will produce a sallad in eight and forty hours." This quick method is practically the same as that described in the *Systema Horti-culturae,* 1677, although in the early book the author claims no definite time for the appearance of the "Sallad," vaguely in a few hours, although the herbs would sprout immediately if the process were followed.

Since the *Domestic Oracle,* 1826, was written by a doctor, Alexander Murray, "the whole drawn from the best sources, and the experience of forty years," we may rightly expect recipes for the most healthful salads. Salads are:

"proper for all seasons, but particularly from the beginning of February to July, in which period they are in greatest perfection, and consequently act most effectually in cleansing and attenuating the blood. . . . So again from the middle of September to the end of January, fresh salading of every kind is grateful to the stomach, and will have the effect of removing obstructions, relieving shortness of breath and correcting the humours generated by gross food."

The French, Dr. Murray says, "are famous for their salads and compound them of a great variety of herbs, which the English despise as useless. In Italy salads are eaten with all kinds of meats, particularly poultry. The Dutch mince with their salads cold boiled turbot or lobster, and add thereto grated Parmesan or old Cheshire cheese, and sometimes they mince some fine tarragon, chervil, burnet, young onions, celery, or pickled gherkins. But after all, the wholesomest way of eating salads is with bread only."

"In dressing salads," Dr. Murray continues, "the best way is to arrange them in the dish, then to mix the sauce in a bowl, and pour it on the salad, so as to let it run to the bottom, and not stir it before it goes to the table. . . . If mustard in salads occasion nausea, cayenne pepper should be substituted in its room." Another word of advice is given by Dr. Murray: "All salads require to be thoroughly chewed, otherwise their salubrious qualities will be lost." Dr. Murray suggests many kinds of herbs for his wholesome salads; such as spinach, parsley, sorrel, onions, pennyroyal, mint top, tarragon, sage, balm, endive, coleworts, cabbage, and as Evelyn would say, "to the very tops of Nettles."

Some 20 years after Dr. Murray's "wholesome Salads," came the salads de luxe, throwbacks to the eighteenth century made dishes, constructions justly deserving the whole-hearted approval of Gervase Markham. The architect and builder of many of these edifices was Charles Elmé Francatelli, born in London, of Italian extraction, pupil of the celebrated Frenchman, Carême, and having the great honor to be chief cook and maître d'hôtel to Queen Victoria. As we learn from his book, *The Modern Cook*, 1845, the secret of forming his elaborate salads was aspic jelly, which we also now use with great success but with more restraint to produce attractive dishes.

Francatelli's recipe for Italian salad calls for a border of mixed vegetables in aspic, while in the center is a mixture of vegetables cut in fancy shapes. In the center of the Russian salad, also with a vegetable aspic border, is a mixture of cut up lobster, anchovies, "thunny," tails of crayfish, prawn tails, stuffed olives, and French capers. Red mayonnaise, however, is the dressing, and not sour cream. The vegetable border of the German salad calls for a mixture of Dutch herrings, Hambro' beef, olives, beetroot, crayfish and celery.

We have come a long way in salads from the simple "Salat" made for Richard II by his chef to those complicated salads made for Queen Victoria by her maître d'hôtel, Francatelli. With the latter, the prelude to salads finds itself where it began. Dickens' *Martin Chuzzlewit* appeared just a year before Francatelli's *The Modern Cook*. In the one we find the simple green salad arranged with little ado, while in the latter are displayed all the cunning contrivances of culinary art that could be summoned to make a salad worthy of "Her Most Gracious Majesty, the Queen." Francatelli's directions for making a lobster salad and his accompanying drawing of it are offered as an example of what a royal chef can do when occasion demands an extra special salad:

"LOBSTER SALAD

"Break the shells, and remove the meat whole from the tails and claws of the lobsters; put this into a basin, with a little oil, vinegar, pepper and salt, and reserve the pith and coral to make some lobster-butter (No. 182), which

A Lobster Salad.

From Francatelli: *The Modern Cook,* 1845

is to be thus used:—First, spread a circular foundation of the lobster-butter upon the bottom of the dish, about seven inches in diameter, and the fourth part of an inch thick; then, scoop out the centre, leaving a circular band. Drain the lobster on a cloth, cut the pieces in oval scallops, and with some of the butter (to stick the pieces firmly together), pile the salad up in three successive rows, the centre being left hollow; fill this with shred lettuce, or salad of any kind seasoned with oil, vinegar, pepper and salt; pour some scarlet remoulade (No. 95) or mayonnaise sauce (No. 100) over the salad, without masking the pieces of lobster; garnish the base with a border of hearts of lettuce, divided in halves, and around these place a border of plover's eggs, having a small sprig of green tarragon stuck into the pointed end of each; place a white heart of lettuce on the top, and serve."

CHAPTER XIII

The Witches' Garden

"From Witches and Wizards, and long-tailed Buzzards,
And creeping things that run in hedge-bottoms
Good Lord, deliver us."
—Celtic Litany.

Do you always look at the new moon over your right shoulder, walk around instead of under a ladder; avoid setting three lights in a row; pick a four-leaf clover, but if you see a five, do you let it thrive? If you observe these traditions and perhaps others, you are one with all the past, from the primitive ancients to the immediate present.

Quite possibly, all of us are not very serious in these little observances and probably we think of witches but once a year, and then only in connection with Hallowe'en fun. But ancient people lived in constant fear of witches and evil spirits always hovering around them, day and night, year in and year out, waiting, waiting for just the right moment to pounce on a victim with sickness of mind or body. Consequently, everyone was always on the alert, ready to deal with these unseen enemies.

From earliest times medicinal cures have been com-

plicated with superstitious practices. Before medical re-
search had established a profession on a scientific basis,
there was already a system of popular medicine which
has never wholly disappeared. Primitive people, colossally
ignorant of the cause of disease and of curative processes,
attributed to supernatural agencies any causes and effects
for which their simple minds could give no natural explanations. Whether a person be afflicted by a toothache,
seized with an epileptic fit, or become delirious from a
high fever, it was all laid to demons and witches. From
Biblical writings we read much of people being possessed

Endpiece from an old book of witchcraft.

of the devil, and of demons being driven out from many
a victim's body. Strangely enough, some of the weapons
against these supernatural forces were what would seem
to us natural ones, herbs of the field.

But a belief in animism in plants lifted them above the
merely vegetable life into an existence even higher than
human beings. Plants not only lived and died, but were
attacked by the unknown, even as people themselves. A
tall plant of mugwort would suddenly be broken off and
laid low by some malicious demon hiding in a devastating
tempest, or be stricken with what we now call a blight.
The life of one plant would be affected by another. Rue
was definitely hostile to basil, rosemary to hyssop, but
coriander, dill and chervil lived on the friendliest of

terms, while chamomile exerted such a good influence on other plants that, set beside an ailing herb, it would soon cure the sick neighbor.

It seemed obvious then to the ancient mind that plants could and did similarly affect human beings. Rampion grown in the cottage garden made the children of the house quarrelsome; breathing deeply into a handful of mint refreshed your senses, but aconite could cause your death. So plants and trees were treated with much respect, mutilation of them was unthinkable and before one was cut down, propitiatory rites were performed in the presence of the spirit of the plant, often thought to be its scent. Ceremonies were performed before fruit trees to induce the spirits to produce a bumper crop.

From long experience gained by trial and error, the spirits of some plants proved themselves effective fighters of disease demons and consequently, in case of sickness, were reverently gathered, prepared and administered, with appropriate incantation and ceremony at each stage. When, however, the plant spirits were not strong enough in themselves, then the family called in the Medicine Man. He appeared, a "monster of so frightful mien," with noise-making apparatus which produced such a terrifying din that even the hardiest demon was likely to flee.

The Chaldeans had great faith in Ea, their god of healing, to whom prayers were said in case of sickness, but herb remedies were also given the patient by the god's representative in the community. Many of the incantations to Ea are still preserved, one of these "Magic Texts," when translated, reading thus:

"Flea-bane on the lintel of the door I have hung
St. John's wort, caper and wheat ears."

Among the early Egyptians, a more or less common-sense medical procedure obtained, as in most other countries, but along with it flourished deceptive practices of magicians and, to a greater extent, of sorcerers who co-operated with mentally sick people in causing fear and

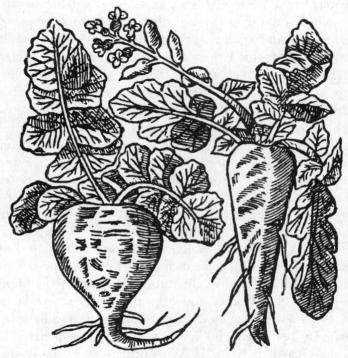

The "Black Raddish" and the "Common Raddish."

From Parkinson, 1629.

trouble to helpless victims. Great mystery surrounded those dreaded practitioners of evil, hiding themselves from the light of day. We do not know how far back in history the name of witch became attached to them, but in as ancient folk-lore as concerns us, at least, witches, supernatural in power, unearthly in appearance, and evil in intention, were as much to be feared as demons of disease or other unseen spirits. In Rome, witches were rampant. The poet, Horace, described the visit of witches, when the moon was new, to a cemetery where bones and noxious herbs were gathered. In Greece, witches worked for people's undoing through the medium of poison.

It was from Persia that magic medicine came, so called because it embodied the doctrines of the Magi, ancient priests. It is through the writings of the Roman, Pliny, who was interested in that literature, that we can be informed of many of the rites and the formulas. Many a time in later centuries, when scientific medicine failed, the family resorted to the old magic remedies, as primitive people had summoned the medicine man. There were conjurations, rites, exorcism of each disease. This system later found its way into the Anglo-Saxon Leech Books, which were compilations of medical cures, a most surprising mixture of good old home remedies and magic healing. With the introduction of Christianity to England, the Church forbade such goings on, but the decrees were neatly handled by substituting portions of the litany, prayers to the Trinity and appeals to the saints in the place of the heathen charms and incantations. The spirit, however, remained 100% pagan, as is seen in the Nine Herbs Charm, written in Wessex dialect in the characteristic Anglo-Saxon meter, and dealing with popular herbal medicine administered with a background of Norse mythology starring Woden, but with frequent interpolations of Christian doctrine.

Primitive people have nothing to do with the abstract, the terms "evil influence" or "forces" meaning nothing to them, but "long-tailed Buzzards," crawling monsters, flying demons, weather-beaten old witches, they could and did vividly picture, and these evils they understood. In Britain, the great forests could not even be penetrated by human beings; but since the primitive people could not imagine any place uninhabited, they conceived of denizens of the forest with suitable qualities, thus the goblins, elves, sprites, the "little folk." Witches took on characteristics and appearance according to local imaginations, for each country had its own particular "wykked sperytes."

So besides the fear from attacks of wild men and animals in savage, uncivilized England, the Anglo-Saxons entertained many fears in regard to the harm these unseen but plainly visualized enemies could do to body, mind and soul. These attacks were, as in very ancient times, warded off or counteracted by natural means, the herbs of the field, with the proper incantation at each step in the procedure, but with due respect to the Church. One of the old Leech Books gives the formula for a salve against the "elfin race and nocturnal goblin visitors." Fourteen herbs, including wormwood, viper's bugloss and fennel, were first gathered. The directions continue thus:

"Then set under the altar, sing nine masses over them, boil them in butter and sheep's grease and much holy salt, strain through a cloth, throw the worts into running water. If any ill tempting to a man, or an elf or goblin night visitor come, smear his forehead with this salve, put it on his eyes and where his body is sore, and cense him with incense and sign him frequently with the sign of the cross; his condition will soon be better."

An amusing remedy is recorded for what might be considered flying demons, if thus we regard winged words. It is: "Against a woman's chatter, taste at night fasting, a root of radish; that day the chatter cannot harm thee."

After reading pages and pages of the Anglo-Saxon

Leech Books, I would conclude that the people often decided that what was good to drive away one kind of evil spirit would be just as effective for another. Potentilla, for instance, used to drive out the demon of fever, was also good against witches. In fact, it is most interesting to observe that among lists of plants abhorrent to witches a good share of them were also used in cures for bodily ailments. A recipe for curing "head melancholy" took care of troubles from both natural and supernatural causes. St. John's-Wort should be "gathered on a Friday in the hour of Jupiter, when it comes to effectual operation. So gathered in the full of the moon and borne about the neck, it mightily helpeth this affection, and drives away all fanatical spirits."

The natural elements were important tools of evil spirits in bringing trouble to human beings, as we learn from *Macbeth*. One of the witches planned to take her spite out on a sailor whose wife had refused to give her some chestnuts. Each of the other two witches promised a wind to toss his boat, while the first one said:

> "I myself have all the other,
> And the very ports they blow,
> All the quarters that they know
> I' the shipman's card
>
> . . .
>
> Though his bark cannot be lost
> Yet it shall be tempest-tost!"

Certain plants could be used to avert catastrophe by the elements. Peony would keep away any kind of storms. Mugwort hung over doorways on Mid-summer's Day, June 24, would keep off lightning, as St. John's-Wort would if gathered before sunrise on that day. The Chinese protected themselves from lightning by growing orpine *(Sedum telephium)* on the roofs of their houses. Our ancient ancestors kept thunder away by planting on their housetops the variety of sedum the Dutch called "Donderbloem" or houseleek.

By the Renaissance period, medical science had so far advanced that unauthorized practitioners were frowned upon, decreed against and generally feared. Great frauds were worked upon ignorant victims, irreparable harm and catastrophe often caused by quacks, quite willing to accept a pretty "tuppence" for a love potion or perhaps for a packet of poisonous herbs not bought with intent to do away with vermin.

The arts of sorcery and witchcraft were employed to a great extent by poor old women, considered beyond the pale of village society because of their practices, and consequently they lived as hermits, furtively venturing abroad for food after dark, thereby avoiding any possible insults from villagers. Because of the similarity to the much feared witches of darkness, in their rarely being seen and in their working harm to human beings, these social outcasts came to be thought of as witches, many innocent old women suffering for the sins of their unfortunate sisters. It was thought these "earth-witches," in order to get even with the world for wrongs done them, had made a compact with the devil that in exchange for their souls they would be endowed with certain supernatural powers in carrying out their petty spites.

Queen Elizabeth appointed a commission to seek out these witches, and an act of Parliament was passed against "those who shall use, practise or exercise any witchcraft." Even learned men admitted the power of witches and inveighed against them. Thomas Browne, author of *Vulgar Errors,* said, "I have ever believed, and do now know that there are witches." So, in fact, did all of Europe and New England where great campaigns were launched to do away with witches, much more easily assailed than the rarely seen witches of the air.

Reynolde Scot, a Kentishman whom we recall as gardener and author of the *Hoppe Garden,* 1574, wrote the *Discouerie of Witchcraft* in 1584. He felt that not all women who were tried as witches were guilty, stating, "Now the witches are mortal women, which be commonly old, lame, blear-eyed, pale, foul and full of wrinkles, poor, sullen."

James of Scotland, to become in 1603 King James I of England, was a violently fanatic believer in witches. In July, 1589, he married Anne of Denmark by proxy, but her coming to Scotland was delayed by stormy seas. James, impatient to see his bride, finally joined her on the Continent but the next May crossed to Scotland in a terrific storm, caused, obviously, by witches. James then ferreted out the old women in Linlithgow, the county of his birth, and personally supervised their trial as witches. Tortured beyond endurance, one woman confessed that she and two hundred others had been responsible for the storms, and thereupon these unfortunate victims were burned to death at the stake in Edinburgh Square.

In 1597 James answered Scot's book by the publication of *Daemonologie,* discussing the fact that these "detestable slaves of the Devil" abound in Scotland and should be punished, Scot to the contrary, notwithstanding. One of James' first acts upon his succession to the English throne, was to have Scot's book burned.

Shakespeare in *Macbeth* catered to this pet hate of James and introduced witches for the monarch's benefit, although in the source of the play, Holinshed's *Chronicles of England, Scotland and Ireland,* the three who met Banquo and Macbeth upon the heath were "three women in strange and wild apparel, resembling creatures of an elder world," although "afterwards the common opinion was that these were either the weird sisters, that is (as ye would say) the goddesses of destiny, or else nymphs or fairies inbued with knowledge of prophecy by their necromantical science; because everything came to pass as they had spoken." So the tactful Shakespeare took the benefit of the doubt, and pleased everybody by giving to "the three" the physical characteristics of the village "Wise Women Witches" and also the supernatural attributes of the traditionally much feared witches.

By the sixteenth and seventeenth centuries this wide interpretation of the term "witch" had come to be accepted, perhaps to the confusion of modern readers of literature of that period, but not to the people themselves. Their imagination was sufficiently vivid to combine in a way satisfactory to them, at least, the outstanding features of the witches both of air and of earth.

There were supposed to be three kinds of witches: the black variety that always worked evil; the white, always good and rendering human beings great services; and the gray ones, good or bad as they saw fit. The black witches are the most interesting since they are figuratively more colorful, with a definite personality, ill disposed as they are.

The celebrations on Hallowe'en, the eve of All Saints' Day, go far back to a Druidical autumn festival when bonfires were lighted in honor of the Sun God who had made possible an abundant harvest. The Druids believed that on the eve of this festival Saman, lord of death, called together the wicked souls that within the past twelve months had been condemned to inhabit the bodies of animals, while in parts of Ireland, too, occurred the Vigil of Saman. This sort of conclave would appeal to

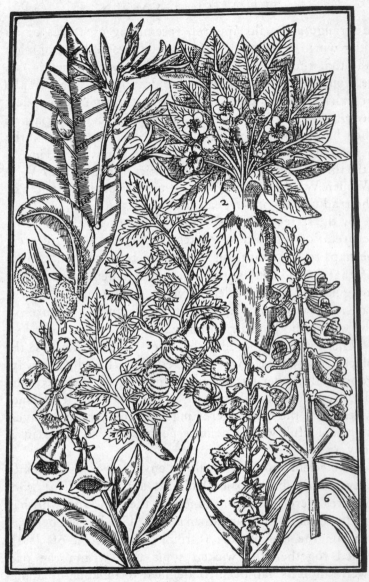

Witches' Thimbles (Foxglove), 4, 5, and 6; Love
Apples (Tomatoes), 3; Mandrake, 2.

From Parkinson, *The Garden of Pleasant Flowers.*

witches who, sure enough, rode abroad that night, and under just the right conditions could be seen by human beings. In the ceremonies for the autumn festival, some observances had their origin in a corresponding Roman festival of Pomona in which nuts and apples, representing the store of winter fruits, played an important part. Nowadays on Hallowe'en, we still have the survival of the autumn rites in bonfires, grinning jack-o'-lanterns made of pumpkins, bobbing for apples, roasting nuts, and we also take note that the witches are hovering near Saman's assembly of wicked souls by divination stunts and by the custom, fortunately on the wane, of setting things topsy-turvy, as witches do.

In the early days, people were obsessed with the desire to catch a glimpse of witches. In the old literature every once in a while up crop directions for surely seeing the wicked old hags. In Germany a person carrying a four-leaf clover on Christmas Eve would see them. In the Tyrol was a belief similar to an English one, that sprigs of rue, broom-straw, agrimony, maiden hair, and ground ivy bound together or sewed up in a bag and worn next to the heart would be effective in bringing a witch into view. In Swabia it was thought that if you made a three-legged stool of fir wood and looked through the three holes made for the legs, into a church on Christmas Eve, you would see all the witches sitting inverted with milk pails on their heads. Certainly it would be an adventure worth the effort, if successful. I wonder whether the witches would be wearing on their fingers their ornaments of foxglove blossoms, often called witches' bells or harebells, sometimes known as witches' thimbles.

The head of the Sororate Order of Witches was Hecate, Grecian name for the Goddess of Hades. She knew the properties of every herb, as would be supposed,

The Art of
SIMPLING.
AN
INTRODUCTION
TO THE
KNOVVLEDGE
AND
Gathering of Plants.

VVherein the Defini-
nitions, Divifions, Places,
Defcriptions, Differences,
Names, Vertues, Times
of flourifhing and gathering,
Ufes, Temperatures, Signatures
and Appropriations of Plants, are
methodically laid down.

Whereunto is added,
A Difcovery of the Leffer World.

By W. COLES.

LONDON,
Printed by *J. G.* for *Nath: Brook* at
the Angell in Cornhill, 1657.

The Title Page of Coles' Tiny Volume.

(The rare corrected issue.)

since she relied upon them for concocting poisonous doses, love philtres, and potions to produce dreams that would reveal the future. With Medea and Circe, her daughters, she shared her knowledge, the three working, as mythology tells us, to the undoing of practically every well-meaning person with whom they came in contact.

Hecate felt the importance of her position as Queen of the witches, for in *Macbeth* she is very angry with the three underlings of no rank at all who had addressed Macbeth and Banquo.

"How did you dare
To trade and traffic with Macbeth
In riddles and affairs of death
And I, the mistress of your charms,
The close contriver of all harms,
Was never call'd to bear my part
Or show the glory of our art?"

For use in their nefarious enterprises, the witches particularly liked these herbs: "Root of hemlock, digg'd i' the dark," deadly nightshade, vervain, dill, mandrake, meadow saffron, poplar, opium poppy, tobacco, monkshood, feverfew, sesame, cudweed, dyer's alkanet, plantain. In this short list of witches' herbs, we observe how many have soporific or deadly qualities. In studying some 200 other plants, it may not be a matter of surprise that they are the ancient medicinal herbs surrounded by an aura of mystery, secrecy and superstition, transmitted through the ages in the practice of popular medicine. Indeed, it would appear that any Anglo-Saxon leech-doctor had all the equipment necessary to step right into the profession of witches.

To be effective, the herbs to be administered both in medicine and in witchcraft must be gathered at certain phases of the moon. For the latter black purpose it must be taken from a place the sun had not touched, because witches' work cannot endure the light of day. An odd number of herbs or of sprigs of the same herb was preferred, seven or nine in witchcraft. Three kinds of wood were necessary to boil the water, while charms and incantations were said as the brew strengthened.

Once in a while at a secret place, was held a sorority meeting called the Witches' Sabbatical. The witches first had to be anointed with a magical preparation concocted by Hecate. Rumor hath it that this was made, as William Coles tells us, of the juice of smallage, wolf's bane and cinque-foil, mixed with the meal of wheat, all this to be absorbed into the fat of children. For the most part, our old herbalist friends, Gerard, Parkinson, Coles, do not commit themselves about the supernatural but repeat what, perhaps, Fuchsius saith, or some other ancient. Certainly Coles is not one to confess belief or disbelief in witches, as we see by Chapter XXII of his "Art of Simpling," which is given here complete:

"The Oyntment that Witches use is reported to be made of the fat of Children digged out of their graves; of the Juices of Smallage, Woolfsbaine and Cinquefoyle mingled with the meale of fine Wheat. But some suppose that the soporiferous Medicines are likeliest to doe it, which are Henbane, Hemlock, Mandrake, Nightshade, Tobacco, Opium, Saffron, Poplar Leaves, & c. They take likewise the roots of Mandrake, according to some, or as I rather suppose the roots of Briony, which simple folke take for the true Mandrake, and make thereof an ugly Image, by which they intend to exercise their Witchcraft. Many odde wives fables are written of Vervaine, which you may read elsewhere, as Master Gerard saith. Those that are used against Witchcraft, are Mistletoe which if one hang about their neck, the Witches can have no power of him. The roots of Angelica doe likewise availe much in the same case, if a man carry them about him, as Fuchsius saith. The common people formerly gathered the Leaves of Elder upon the last day of Aprill, which to disappoint the Charmes of Witches, they had affixed to their Doores and Windowes. Matthiolus saith, that Herbe Paris takes away evil done by Witchcraft, and affirms that he knew it to be true by experience. I doe not desire any to pin their Faiths upon these reports, but onely let them know that there are such which they may believe as they please. However there is no question but very wonderful Effects may be wrought by the Vertues which are enveloped within the compasse of the green Mantles, wherewith many Plants are adorned."

As we all know, witches ride through the air on a broom, but sometimes their means of locomotion was a bulrush, a branch of thorn, mullein stalks, cornstalk, or ragweed, called fairies' horse in Ireland. The broom we commonly visualize is the neatly manufactured kind we buy at the corner grocery, but the witches' broom was a limb of the broom bush which people did often use for sweeping the hearth. If these brooms, usually called besoms, are laid across the threshold of your house, country people will tell you no witch can enter. Instead, I imagine, unsuspecting members of the household might stumble inadvertently over the obstacle and plunge into the house in none too pleasant state of mind themselves.

In spring the witches do penance for their wrongdoings, as is poetically described in Spenser's *Faerie Queene*, Book I, Canto II:

> "Till on a day (that day is everie Prime,
> When Witches wont do penance for their crime)
> I chaunst to see her in her proper hew
> Bathing her selfe in origane and thyme."

To carry out their evil schemes witches were, of course, obliged to make themselves invisible. This they often did by carrying fern seeds. Apparently they had no trouble in obtaining them although many a human being went through a long involved process in a fern seed hunting adventure on Midsummer Eve.

The black witches were greatly feared since no one could resist their enchantments, but help from witches, perhaps from the gray sisters, was often sought in an effort to look into the future, come what might. From translations by scholars from the old books of magic and witchcraft, much of the folklore so firmly established in people's minds must have come. Certain it is, that the complicated processes for divining the future, for instance, never originated in the simple ignorant minds of the common people, and, furthermore, the nature of the great body of folklore smacks of the old witch lore.

An expectant mother would avoid cyclamen, stepping over it being an ominous sign. If she ate onions or beans, her child would be a fool; but if she tasted quinces or coriander seed, the offspring would be ingenious and witty.

Herbs played a great part in divination proceedings by lovers. In Denmark, between the rafters of the house, two sprigs of St. John's-Wort were sometimes set. If they grew together, a wedding was imminent. In Italy, on Midsummer's Eve, girls gathered buds of houseleek and named a bud for each suitor. In the morning the bud most fully opened would obviously indicate the future husband. A plant of orpine was often set by a young girl on her window sill on Midsummer Eve. The next morning she would rush to see which way the stalk had turned, for from that direction her future husband would come. To determine constancy of lovers, on that same mystic eve, pots of orpine were placed on a table and two stalks named for the lovers. These stalks were watched with trepidation to see whether they turned away from each other and thereby indicated inconstancy.

Love philtres were the great stock in trade of witches, who labored diligently in making potions sure to inspire everlasting love in those who drank them. Sometimes the results were tragic, as with Tristram and Iseult who, on the journey to Cornwall where she was to become the bride of King Mark, together drank the love philtre intended for Iseult and Mark. Though the scheduled marriage took place, the love potion instilled such love in Tristram and Iseult that it finally ended in tragedy for them.

Cumin was often an ingredient of such love potions since it produced the effect of retention in whoever ate it. So girls often gave to their lovers, departing on a journey, a cake in which cumin had been scattered. Perhaps, once in a while, some girl induced her lover to eat the cake then and there. Basil was also put in love philtres since it was thought to cement friendship and also to produce sympathy between two people. In Moldavia, if a girl gave a young man a sprig of basil, even though she had never seen him before, he would fall in love with her. Suppose that same young man had, upon leaving home, eaten a cumin cake made by his sweetheart. Could even Hecate, Queen of Witches, straighten out that complication?

Vervain was a highly esteemed herb for love potions, as was endive seed, which had to be dug up with a piece of gold or with a stag's horn and then only on the saint's days, June 27th and July 25th. Here we have folklore originating in Christian religion mingled with witchcraft so hated by the Church. Sometimes witches had to achieve deadly effects in their potions and these they brewed with hemlock, belladonna, monkshood and other herbs, always to the number of seven or nine.

People of early days, as of all times, were curious about the future and went to great lengths to know all before the due time. Magic wreaths, pills, garlands and nosegays, were supposed to be very efficacious both in divination and in curing physical ailments. A Scotch witch would pass her patient nine times through a wreath of woodbine. One kind of magic pill was made of nine fresh mistletoe berries steeped in a mixture of wine, beer, vinegar and honey. This concoction was to be taken fasting and then the person was to retire before midnight, but the procedure, to be effective, must take place only on Christmas Eve, or on the first or third night of a new moon. Then he would dream of his future.

Another process was to make a bouquet of many colored flowers, of nine kinds, but only one sprig of a kind, with the left hand sprinkle it with oil of amber, bind the bouquet around the head, underneath the nightcap, and retire to one's bed, which must be made up with clean linen. If these directions were followed dreams of the future would surely come to the person. I would think he would be more apt to have a visit from a good old-fashioned nightmare, such as terrified our Anglo-Saxon forbears.

In Thomas Moore's *Light of the Haram,* the enchantress, Namouna, instructs Nourmahall to gather certain herbs that, made into a wreath, could be used to recall her Selim's love:

> " 'Twas midnight. . . .
>   'Tis the hour
> That scatters spells on herb and flower
> And garland might be gathered now
> That turn'd around the sleeper's brow. . . ."

With the introduction of Christianity, the devil, of course, had entered the ranks of evil spirits to be combatted. He had his favorite plants, as the witches did— yarrow, vervain, belladonna *(Atropa Belladonna),* the first part of the botanic name, appropriately enough, from Atropos, eldest of the three Fates, the one who cut the thread of life, an act accomplished also by the plant. Tradition has it that parsley seed, which is supposed to go nine times to the devil and back before coming up, is so much liked by him that he keeps some of it, so we human beings never can expect to have a 100% germination of parsley seed.

Because of the close association which was generally understood to exist between devil and witches, people did not always feel sure from which source came the ills that befell them. In the long run, however, it did not matter, so the same precautions usually taken against one were used against the other.

If we read through the old books, we will conclude that fear of the Evil Eye held great terrors. Various measures were taken to avoid it, most popular being the suspension of certain herbs and tree branches over the doorways of dwellings and stables. Commonly used greenery were tansy, honesty, garlic, St. John's-Wort, mountain ash, roadside verbena. As a sort of general precaution against witch or devil, people also hung up rosemary, cinquefoil, olive branch, valerian, alyssum, scilla, hawthorn, hyssop, plum tree branches, elder. Incidentally, an elder stick notched for every wart on the hands and rubbed over the warts was recognized as a sure cure for them.

Trailing woodbine was hung in the stables in Scotland on May 2 to keep cattle from being bewitched. Reynolde Scot in his *Discoverie of Witchcraft* says that it was believed that hunters and their dogs would not be bewitched if branches of oak were laid on the ground and then both men and dogs walked over them. The oak was used in many other ways against evil spirits, since it was sometimes thought to be the tree from which the Holy Cross was made.

Christmas rose (black hellebore), strewn on the floor or burned, drove away witches, and if cattle had been bewitched, this broke the wicked spells. No witch would enter a house where rue had been rubbed on the floors. Perhaps such beliefs arose from the old custom of placing pots of basil on the window sill to keep away flies, or of strewing shelves and floors with mint, tansy, rue, to prevent vermin. Certainly our ancestors must have regarded vermin as evil.

Pimpernel (poor man's weather glass) was also a protection, but as the gatherer collected the herbs, he must chant a certain incantation and continue to do so twice a day for 15 days, in the morning fasting and in the evening after supper. Fumitory (earth smoke) was a favorite to keep off the Evil Eye. It was thought the presence of strongly scented flowers and plants in the house would ward off the devil and all his cohorts. Onions hung up within doors would attract disease demons which otherwise would fasten themselves on the inhabitants. Water lilies gathered with incantations were also used to counteract evil influences, as were strongly scented varieties of artemisia, hyssop and rue. If a person had become bewitched, Devonshire people had a cure for it. Herbal medicines were given internally but also this procedure was used: They put certain herbs into a paper which was slowly burned, along with bay leaves and rosemary, over hot coals, all the while the first verse of the 68th Psalm and the Lord's Prayer were being said.

In planning your own Witches' Garden, you must first choose the location near some tree significant in witch lore, or else in a spot near which young trees can be planted. Have a tree or two the witches particularly like, such as the alder, larch, cypress and hemlock; then, to counteract any possible evil effects, there must be a holly, yew, hazel, elder, mountain ash or juniper. It is supposed that witches are obsessed to count all the tiny leaves of the juniper, so innumerable that they would inevitably make mistakes and have to begin over again. Having great control, they flee before they become so preoccupied in counting that they get caught.

The English mountain ash (*Pyrus Aucuparia*), usually called rowan, is one of the greatest dreads of witches.

> "Rowan-tree and red thread
> Put the witches to their speed."

If a branch of rowan held by a baptized person touches a witch, she is in terror for she will be the next victim claimed by the devil.

You will surely want an elder, for although it holds great fascination for witches, it is hated by them because any baptized person touched with it can see what any witch is doing in any part of the world. A cross made of it and hung over stables was supposed to protect the cattle from being bewitched.

Witches particularly loathe yellow flowers because it reminds them of the wholesome health-giving sun, to which they are adverse. It is said that witches will never cross a hedge that blossoms in green or yellow flowers, so an appropriate enclosure for your garden would be a hedge of rue that has such bright yellow flowers. After all, you don't want your garden swarming with witches even though it contains plants they could use in their evil profession.

There are some other plants and trees suitable for a witches' garden, some with soporific effect, others quite deadly but only if dug or picked and made into potions. Then there are others with no effect at all unless certain charms are said while they are being gathered. Still others will have no effect unless the removal is done at certain times of the moon, on certain days of the week or month, or at certain hours of the day. So the uninitiated need have no fear of stirring up the wrath of the evil spirits. The plants you choose may be grouped according to deadly effects, and elaborately labeled, others that ward off the evil eye, those effective in divination, those that keep away thunderstorms, and those used in love philtres. When all has been said, you must still use your imagination, a quality which needs must be powerful when dealing with witches.

At Christmas time, give your bird neighbors a gift by tying pieces of suet on the branches of the witches' trees. Witches may yearn towards their beloved plants and trees, but as Marcellus says in *Hamlet*,

> "Some say that ever 'gainst that season comes
> Wherein our Saviour's birth is celebrated,
> The bird of dawning singeth all night long;
> And then, they say, no spirit dare walk abroad;
> The nights are wholesome, then no planets strike,
> No fairy takes nor witch hath power to charm,
> So hallowed and so gracious is the time."

CHAPTER XIV

Herbs That Never Were

"But this is to be reckoned among the old wives fables ... touching the gathering of Spleenewoort in the night, and other most vaine things, which are founde heere and there scattered in the old writers books from which most of the later writers do not abstaine, who many times fill up their pages with lies and frivolous toies, and by so doing do not a little deceive yoong students."

—GERARD, 1597.

Vegetable Lamb.
From Parkinson, 1629.

From our childhood, when we were very "yoong students," we all have cherished the old stories by which we were not a little deceived, enchanted tales of wonderful animals such as unicorns, dragons, centaurs, sea serpents. But if you read the old herbals and books of folklore, you will find much more of fabulous note in vege-

275

table life, even if you exclude such mythical items as the symbolic Yggdrasill of Scandinavia. This was an ash tree with branches embracing the earth and aspiring to heaven, and with roots piercing the lower world. An eagle, whose powerful eyes were supplemented by those of a hawk perched on his forehead, was given information by a squirrel of the universe beyond his sight. A huge snake ever tried to climb up to kill him and other reptiles ate at the roots where spurted the fountains of destiny. Under this strange tree was a horn, perhaps corresponding to the trumpet of the Angel Gabriel, which would sound at the end of the world.

The many supposed phenomena of plant life in early days were not fabricated from figurative whole cloth, but originated in undated antiquity when primitive peoples did not worry about precisely placing everything in classes. They would have been unable to play the old game of "animal, mineral or vegetable," an impossibility for people who believed in the existence of trees with iron where sap ought to be, in plants that produced fruit containing living lambs.

In early days devoid of science, no reasonable, natural explanations to extraordinary phenomena were attempted. When people with their own eyes could see fire belching forth from a mountain peak, could witness the blotting out of the sun by day and the moon by night, could discover huge bottomless fissures made instantly in the earth after mighty rumblings and quakings from within, truly anything might happen. And surely it did, according to the uncomplicated minds of those naïve people, when a forked twig from a certain kind of tree, held just so in a person's two hands, would be an infallible guide to springs of water deep within the ground, or when little branches of plants when simply bent down and stuck into the soil would strike root and form a new plant or tree. Our remote ancestors had a good healthy respect for nature which was so truly wonderful, and in their untrammeled imagination they entertained a rather unhealthy awe of the supernatural.

Playing upon the simple credulity of the people were the shrewd rhizotomoi or root-diggers of ancient Greece who made their living by collecting medicinal herbs. They frightened off would-be intruders upon their profession by concocting fantastic tales of the difficulties and dangers attendant upon obtaining the coveted plants. Theophrastus (fourth century B.C.), in Book IX of his *Enquiry into Plants,* relates some of the cautions supposedly necessary. In cutting some roots, one must stand to windward or his body will swell up, or, as in gathering the fruit of the wild rose, his eyes will be in danger. Peony must be dug at night, for if a woodpecker catches a gatherer at work during the day, woe to the man's eyes.

So firmly did the insidious scare-stories take hold upon the imagination of the people that an herb much in demand would be made to assume an appearance that struck terror to the timid soul. Such a plant was the shrieking mandrake.

To be sure, there is a mandrake plant, botanically *Mandragora officinarum* or, according to Linnaeus, *Atropa mandragora.* The plant has large entire leaves spreading out upon the ground, a long taproot sometimes one and one-half feet long which, as the plant matures, often takes on weird forms reminiscent of human limbs, just as branches of trees assume most life-like attitudes. The fruit is a yellowish apple, like our American May apple.

In Lyte's translation, 1619, of Dodoens' *Cruydt-Boeck,* 1554, we find,

"The roote is great and white, not much unlike a Radish root, divided into two or three parts, growing one upon another almost like the thighes and legges of a man."

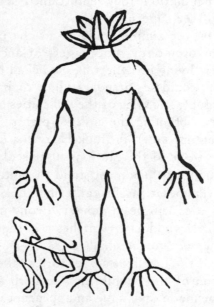

Mandrake and Dog.

From an edition printed in Rome (*c.* 1480) of the herbal of Apuleius (*c.* 500), of which ninth and tenth century Saxon translations still survive.

The traditional picture of the mandrake showed the definite form of a man with body, limbs and even fingers. The swollen top of the root developed into the head from which the broad leaves of the plant radiated as a halo of hair. In the famous sixth century manuscript of the first century Dioscorides, is a drawing dated from the second century B.C. showing the Goddess of Discovery handing Dioscorides a mandrake root in human shape, its hair being broad radiating leaves. The dog used for digging is in the inevitable throes of death. In the herbal of Apuleius Platonicus, originating in the fifth century and translated into Anglo-Saxon in the early eleventh century, the mandrake-man is colored a madder red with leafy hair rising from the neck, and a dog tied with heavy ropes to both legs of the plant root. In the title page device of Brunfel's *Contrafayt Kreuterbuch,* 1537, is a most depressing figure of a weak-kneed, hirsute, down-at-the-mouth old man with dragging feet and with hair composed of three large leaves and two apples.

The herbalists about 1600 showed infinite scorn for such conceptions of the mandrake, and Gerard spoke for them. He said that the resemblance of the root to a man

"is no other wise then in the rootes of carrots, parsneps, and such like, forked or divided into two or more parts, which nature taketh no account of. There have been many ridiculous tales brought up of this plant, whether of olde wives or some runnagate surgeons or phisickmongers, I know not, (a title bad enough for them) :"

Because of the long taproot and its brittleness, it was with great difficulty even an experienced gatherer could dig up an unbroken mandrake. One plant after another might be abandoned in the attempt and this would lead to a great waste of roots for which the rhizotomoi were paid well. Hence, their zeal in spreading terrifying stories.

If you pulled at the taproot itself, the mandrake would shriek so that you would go insane. Shakespeare says, in *Romeo and Juliet,* IV, 3:

"And shrieks like Mandrakes torn out of the earth,
That living mortals, hearing them, run mad."

Caput. cclxxvj.

MAndragora vir. Jſi. Spēs ei⁹ oue
ſunt. Maſculus ſcʒ ʒ femina. De
maſculo in iſto cap̄.tractaf. Man
dragora ſil'is ē paruo peponi:oicta cʒ bʒ ma
la ſuaue olētia : magnitudine malimatiani:
vñ ʒ latini eã malũ terre vocāt:eo cʒ radiceʒ
bʒ formã boîs ſimilātē. Antropos cm homo
oʒbui⁹ cortex in vino miſſa oaf ad bibendũ

Mandrake.

From *Ortus Sanitatis*, 1517 edition.

It was believed that a gatherer would die soon after he pulled the main root, so a dog was used instead. Great ceremony was connected with the performance, the details varying with different legends. There is a graphic description of it in Apuleius Platonicus:

"Thou shalt in this manner take it, when thou comest to it, then thou understandst it by this; that it shineth altogether like a lamp."

Thomas Moore speaks of this same light in *Laila Rookh* but refers to it as a deadly lustre:

"Such rank and deadly lustre dwells,
    As in those hellish fires that light
    The mandrake's charnel leaves at night."

But to return to the description given by Apuleius:

"When first thou seest its head, then inscribe thou it instantly with iron lest it fly from thee; its virtue is so mickle and so famous, that it will immediately flee from an unclean man, when he cometh to it; hence as we before said, do thou inscribe it with iron, and so shalt thou delve about it, as that thou touch it not with the iron, but thou shalt earnestly with an ivory staff delve the earth. And when thou seest its hands and its feet, then tie thou it up. Then take the other and tie it to a dog's neck, so that the hound be hungry; next cast meat before him, so that he may not reach it, except he jerk up the wort with him. As soon as thou see that it be jerked up, and have possession of it, take it immediately in hand and twist it and wring the ooze of its leaves into a glass ampulla."

There are found, in old literature, many variations on the above. Sometimes the dog simply loosened the root and the gatherer did the rest. Theophrastus says that the gatherer is enjoined to draw "3 circles round mandrake with a sword, and cut it with one's face towards the west; and at the cutting of the second piece, one should dance round the plant and say as many things as possible about the mysteries of love."

The mandrake was used, not only for its narcotic and anaesthetic properties but also as aphrodisiacs and for charms against sterility. In the King James translation of the Bible, in Genesis, chapter XXX, we read of its being used for the latter purpose by Rachel after she had wheedled from Leah the plant brought by Reuben, though the apples and not the root seemed to be the effective part. The correctness of translating the Hebrew word as mandrake was often debated. Parkinson says:

"The strong sent of these apples is remembered also, Cant. 7.13. although some would divert the signification of the Hebrew word . . . unto Violets, or some other sweet flowers, in the former place of Genesis, and the fruit of Musa, or Adams Apples in this place of the Canticles."

William Coles, however, says,

"I know not how the translators of the Bible came to mistake, but the word in the Originall is a common word, signifying amiable and sweet smelling flowers [and is used, Cant. 7.13 in the same sense] which Reuben brought home for their beauty and smell rather than their virtue, whereas in the flowers of Mandrake, there is no such delectable or amiable smell. This is the judgement of Mr. Gerrard, whose reasons for the same you may see if you consult his Herball."

Coles also says that though the popular belief is that the roots of the mandrake grow "in proportion like a Man's body which make a wonderful skreeking at their pulling up . . . and cause fruitfulness in women, if they carrie the same near the body . . . in Mandrakes there is no such proportion, skreeking, or vertu, as everyone that knows them can tell."

The mandrake was often thought to bring good fortune to a household. It was left untouched for three days, then placed in warm water later used to sprinkle possessions of house and barns. Four times a year this bath was given to the mandrake, which was kept at other times in a silk cloth among one's best belongings. Although sometimes only a part of the root was used, the whole plant was usually demanded. As the years passed the demand became so great that mandrake gatherers bettered the instructions of their predecessors and made up convincing forms either from plain roots of mandrakes or of briony.

In the *Grete Herball,* 1526, we may read,

"Nature never gave forme or shape of mankynde to an herbe. But it is of troughe that some hath shaped such fygures by craft as we have fortyme herde say of labourers in the field."

The fake was exposed after it became too obvious with the raising of "hair" on the mandrake's head by planting grass seed in the top of the root. But in spite of this, the practise continued and people went on buying the charms, much to the disgust of the herbalists. William Turner, 1568, said:

"The rootes which are conterfited and made like little puppettes and mammettes, which come to be sold in England in boxes with heir, and such forme as a man hath, are nothying elles but folishe feined trifles, and not naturall. For they are so trymmed of crafty theves to mocke the poor people with all, and to rob them both of theyr wit and theyr money."

Gerard, 1597, berates the "idle drones that have little or nothing to do but eate and drinke" and "have bestowed some of their time in carving the roots of Brionie forming them to the shape of men and women." Salmon, 1710, says:

"Sometimes (tho not often) three of those Roots have been observed, which some by Transplanting have Occasionally cut off for humor or admiration sake, and to amuse Fools . . ."

But not to tricky root gatherers alone are we indebted for our herbs that never were. Many times, a good many others besides the "poor people" and "yoong students" were not a little deceived by tales of wonderful plants. There was an amazingly easy credence by most surprising people in the barnacle tree, although the idea of trees producing living beings is as ancient as the world. We read of a race of dwarfs hanging like fruit from the Indian fig tree (probably monkeys), of birds flying out of vase-shaped fruit of another Indian tree (Have you even seen an oriole come out of her nest?), of human heads crying "Wak! Wak!" on a tree on an island in the Indian Ocean.

Pope Pius II, in one of his writings published in the fifteenth century, describes from reports a tree in Scotland that bore fruit like ducks. Those dropping on the ground died, those chancing to fall into the water developed into living birds. But during his eager search for witnesses to such phenomena, he was always told that they were found only in the Orkneys. I have nowhere read of his following up that hint. But a writer, named Martin, claimed to have seen the inmature birds still in their shell hanging by their bills to the tree, but in the Orkneys when the sun was high, the birds at that stage were said to have showed signs of life. The sixteenth century Sebastian Munster in his *Cosmographia Universalis* claims that in Scotland on certain trees, overhanging the water, the leaves curl about the fruit which finally drop into the water and develop into living tree-geese. The great sixteenth century botanist, Caspar Bauhin, adds his bit to the legend by declaring that if the leaves fall on land, they turn into birds; if on the water, into fish!

A late fourteenth century writer, whose real identity is unknown but who at any rate, in print, called himself Sir John Maundeville, claimed to have had excellent proofs of the barnacle tree, that

"beren a fruyt that becomen briddes
fleiynge: and thei that fallen on the erthe
dyen anon: and thei ben right gode to mannes mete."

But then, Sir John, that Baron Munchausen of his time, tells of his travels for thirty years in innumerable countries, travels that would take an experienced world-traveler with advantage of airplane many lifetimes to achieve.

Gerard himself, who scoffed at the shrieking mandrake, believed in the barnacle tree. He shows us a picture of it, gives it a Latin name "Britannica Conchaanatiferae" and vouches for these shellfish which turn into feathered fowl "bigger than a Mallard and lesser than a Goose." There is no connection between this barnacle and the things that collect on ships' bottoms. The name of the fowl, says Gerard, "whom we call Barnacles, in the North of England Brant Geese, and in Lancashire tree Geese." Aldrovandi's *Dendrologia,* 1667, shows a tree resembling a myrtle growing amid a clump of reeds at the water's edge and leaning over the water. Along the branches are

The Barnacle Tree. It bears fruit
like ducks.

From *Gerard,* 1597.

fruit like elongated bleeding heart flowers and skimming along the surface of the water are four excited birds.

All along the centuries disbelievers in the strange barnacle geese would crop up. Albertus Magnus, German monk of the thirteenth century, although he did not be-

The Lamb Tree.

From Sir John Maundeville, *Travels,* 1633.

lieve in the barnacle tree did, funnily enough, believe in the geese but insisted they were hatched from eggs like other birds. Geraldus Cambrensis of the twelfth century railed against eating barnacle geese during Lent, and all through the Middle Ages the conflict waged whether barnacle geese should be considered as fish or flesh for Lenten menus.

Now we turn from the problem of whether it's fish or flesh to whether it's animal or vegetable—The Vegetable Lamb! That strange animal-plant appearing on the title page of Parkinson's *Paradisus,* 1629, as a plant found in the Garden of Eden, is shown supported in the middle of her body by a single leafless stem growing out of a clump of grass.

In a figure of the lamb from Zahn's *Speculae Physico-Mathematico-Historicae,* 1696, we see rising from a rosette of huge leaves a straight stalk with three pairs of opposite leaves, topped by an animal more resembling a lifeless boar than a gentle lamb. Zahn, however, claims that the animal does resemble a lamb except for horns, which are supplanted by tufts of hair. The body is covered by thin bark which is often removed to be used as head coverings by the inhabitants of Tartary. The flesh is like lobster meat, considered a particular delicacy by wolves but by no other animals. I should think the lamb's conspicuous position on the top of a three-foot stalk would make her easy prey for wolves.

The belief prevailed that the lamb ate all around the stalk, and when the vegetation was all gone the stalk withered and the poor lamb died. The Vegetable Lamb was also called the Scythian Lamb and the Barometz, the latter coming from the Tartar word for lamb. In Erasmus Darwin's poem, *The Botanic Garden,* 1791, we may read:

> "Cradled in snow, and fanned by Arctic air,
> Shines, gentle Barometz! thy golden hair;
> Rooted in earth, each cloven hoof descends,
> And round and round her flexile neck she bends;
> Crops the gray coral-moss and hoary thyme,
> Or laps with rosy tongue the melting rime,
> Eyes with mute tenderness her distant dam,
> Or seems to bleat, a Vegetable Lamb."

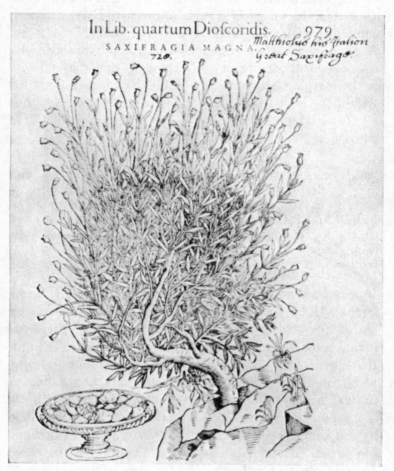

A Bowl of Stones with Saxifrage, Illustrative of its Virtue.

From Matthioli, *Commentarii Dioscoridis,* 1565.

There were other versions in the old days such as in the sixteenth century Scaliger's *Exotericae Exercitationes,* where it is claimed that the plant itself resembled a lamb. Then we read of an account by the Indian traveler, Odorico da Pordenone, who had been told that on an island in the Caspian Sea there was a plant with melon-shaped fruit like a lamb. This plant is described by the ubiquitous Sir John Maundeville who in his travels found a tree with gourd-like fruit,

"and whan thei ben rype, men kutten hem a to, and men fynden with inne, a lytelle Best, in flessche, in bon, and blode, as though it were a lytylle Lomb with outen walle. And men eten bothe the Frut and the Best; and that is a gret marveylle. Of that Frute I have eten; alle thoughe it were wonderfulle; but that I knowe wel that God is marveyllous in his werkes."

Springwort was also called blasting-wort. The name might well be applied, too, to saxifrage (from the Latin words for "rock" and "to break") because the little plants grow in clefts of rocks, thus giving rise to the idea that they had split the stone. Going on that premise, people in olden days used the saxifrage plant to "break" or cure bladder stones. But the blasting-wort was much more powerful, since it had magical qualities not held by the simple little saxifrage. Many differences of opinion prevailed about its identification. One writer seems to associate it with *Euphorbia Lathyrus,* caper spurge or sometimes mole plant, said to drive away moles and because of that planted in many old-time gardens. But yet again, blasting-wort probably belonged to that great luxuriant mythological garden. However, people searched for this rare plant continuously, some hitting upon an ingenious way of finding it with certainty.

The first essential was to locate a black woodpecker's hole at nesting time and, when the mother bird was off the nest, to block up the hole so she couldn't return. The anxious bird would search and soon return with a plant of blasting-wort which, applied to the plug, would blast it out with violent force. The watcher would scare the bird into dropping the plant to the ground.

Pliny notes that this phenomenon is accompanied by fire, and since the woodpecker was called the lightning bearer, we find the association of lightning with the plant. The Swabians believed that if the plant were set down in a mountain peak, it would draw the lightning and scatter the storm. It eludes man's grasp, is luminous at night, and altogether seemed to have electric qualities. In this respect it makes one think of Dr. Fernie's comment on the nasturtium flowers' giving out sparks of an electric nature at sunset. The blasting-wort will open entrances to treasure caves and chests, a useful plant but unfortunately very rare.

There were many plants and trees which were supposed to have a deadly effect upon anyone coming within the radius of their influence. One was the Bausor tree, which gave off a narcotic exhalation, sure death to passers-by. In the *Ortus Sanitatis*, 1517, there is a terrifyingly graphic picture of such victims, two men lying stiffly side by side, the head of one to the feet of the other.

The Yew tree, so universally used in ancient funeral ceremonies because it is an evergreen, was planted in or around churchyards. It was claimed by some authorities that it was placed on the west side because the branches absorbed "poysonous vapours," believed to come forth from the yawning graves after sunset. Most of the early writers thought that a tree which inhaled poison would certainly be poisonous itself. Dioscorides believed in a

lethal quality of the leaves of yew. Virgil, Latin poet of
classic times, warned against planting the yew near beehives for he felt that the honey would be spoiled if bees
should feed on yew. In Lyte's translation of Dodoens we
may read:

"Yew is not profitable for mans bodie, for it is so hurt-
full and venemous, that such as doe but onely sleep under
the shadow thereof, become sick and sometimes they dye,
especially when it bloweth."

Dodoens believed the berries to be poisonous and also
the bark which, he says, "the Ignorant Apothecaries of
this Country" use instead of Tamarisk and daily commit
wickedness by "ministering of naughtie hurtful medicines
instead of good."

Gerard, however, who took most of his herbal from
Dodoens, pooh-poohed the whole idea of the poisonous
dangers of eating the berries or sleeping under the
branches, for he and his schoolfellows had many times
done both without any harm to themselves. Parkinson is
quite noncommittal, simply reporting,

"Ancient Writers have ever reckoned it to
be dangerous at the least, if not deadly."

We find many herbs in our gardens that need moisture
such as the mints, while others such as rue and fennel sus-
tain a drought with equanimity. We read of the Japanese
Palm that shuddered and withered away if the tiniest
drop of water touched the trunk. But if such a catastrophe seemed imminent, the tree could be saved if you dug
it up and set it in the ground again. But it was essential
to surround the roots and lower part of the trunk with
sand and iron filings, and to cut off the old leaves with an
iron tool and fasten them again to the tree.

Then again there was a tree near Mt. Olympus in Greece that seemed to need a dry heat and flourished luxuriantly with flames licking away at its roots.

The Bausor Tree.

From *Ortus Sanitatis*, 1517.

Some herbs had most peculiar habits of growth. One is described by Sir John Maundeville who saw it when he was near the Dead Sea on one of his travels. The tree produced fruit like beautiful apples but if one of them was cut open, it would reveal only "Coles and Cyndres." The tree called Mesonsidereos, instead of having pith in its middle as any self-respecting tree should have, contained iron wires starting at the root and extending to the top of the tree, of great value (no doubt) for fence posts. In Italy is a plant, *Conjugalis herba* or Concordia, very scarce and extremely difficult to find. The root is divided into two parts, each resembling a complete hand. Prospective brides and grooms used to try to obtain one of these plants as an omen for their marriage. If the two root hands are together, happiness will result; if separated, the marriage will go on the rocks. A most fascinating plant, called the Boriza or Lunaria, governed by the moon, is distinctly my favorite herb that never was. It developed one leaf each day during the increase of the moon until the 15th day; then shed one leaf each day till all were gone. During the period of darkness, the plant was said to keep out of sight, and I should think it would.

It was the accepted belief, even among herbalists in the early days, that ferns produce no seeds or else that they were impossible to find, except on Midsummer's Eve, June 24th. At midnight on this date the fern blossomed and then seeds appeared which were invisible and had the power to make the finder of them invisible. Diligent was the hunt and complicated the procedure. Legend has it that 12 pewter plates must be brought. The seed would go through 11 and be deposited on the 12th plate. The searcher must go barefoot and wear only his shirt. The preparation, ceremony, and formality of collecting the seed varied with different countries.

Hieronymus Bock, author of the *New Kreütter Buch,* 1539, determined to find out about the fern seed situation. He made the attempt on Midsummer's Eve and, sure

enough, just before daybreak he found the seed, small
and black.

"I went about this busynes, all figures, coniuryinges,
saunters, charms, wytchcrafte; and sorseryes sett a syde,
Takynge wyth me two or three honest men to bere me
companye."

Thus Bock proved to his own satisfaction that on Midsummer's Eve fern seed could be gathered, as specified.
As Mrs. Arber remarks in her *Herbals*, it is too bad he
didn't extend his investigations further and find out
whether the seed could be gathered at any other time just
as well as on Midsummer's Eve at midnight.

Gerard was much fascinated by the stone tree.

"Among the woonders of England, this is one of great
admiration, and contrarie unto man's reason and capac-
itie; that there should be a kind of wood alterable into
the hardness of a stone, called Stonie woode, or rather a
kinde of water which hardneth wood and other things,
into the nature and matter of stones. But we know that
the works of God are woonderfull, if we do but narrowly
search the least of things which we daily beholde."

When Gerard went to the sacred well of Newman Regis
in Warwickshire to which people flocked to be cured of
all diseases, he beheld this wonder.

"I founde growing over the same [well] a faire Ash
tree, whose boughes did hang over the spring of water,
whereof some that were seare and rotten, and some that
of purpose were broken off, fell into the water & were all
turned into stones. Of these boughes or parts of the tree,
I brought unto London, which, when I had broken in
peeces, therein might be seene that the pith and all the
rest was turned into stones."

Gerard said the buds and flowers had also petrified. His
main reflection was that if this

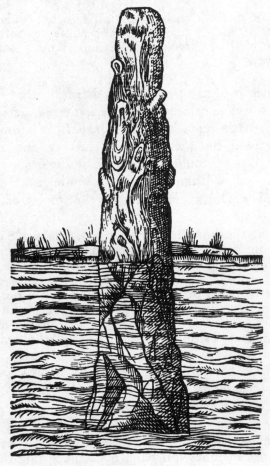

The Stone Tree.

From *Gerard,* 1597.

"water was prooved about the hardning of some kinde
of confection Phisicall, for the preservation of them, cr

other speciall ends, it would offer greater occasion of admiration for the health and benefit of mankinde, than it doth about such things as already have been experimented, tending to very little purpose."

So we find Gerard characteristic of mankind of high or low estate of all centuries, from great writers to ignorant people, from those who scoffed at the shrieking mandrake but had complete faith in the barnacle tree, from those of us who laugh at the old custom of sowing cumin with a curse to ensure a good crop, and at the same time believe rue and basil will not grow side by side.

CHAPTER XV

The Modern Role of Ancient Herbs

Today in a spacious office in Wall Street six bottles
stand on a rack, and in those crystal containers are sam-
ples of the six products that have most profoundly affected the world of commerce. One is a jar of little
berries, just a handful of pepper, one of the spices to
which history attributes the beginnings of world trade.
It holds a place of honor from which, because of its
past, it can never be dislodged. America itself owes its
discovery to the search for just such aromatic herbs.

We moderns are amazed at the dependence of early
peoples on herbs in every phase of their existence. Yet
with all our science and invention, we base many of our
activities still on these same ancient plants. We grow in
the garden a large proportion of what was once food and
medicine, of plants that brought health and created industry. Most of the subjects in our flower border . . .
iris, rose, larkspur, calendula, peony, foxglove, and hundreds more . . . are the crude drugs of commerce, the
foundation of today's huge botanical drug industry. They
are medicinal herbs, long since set apart for their beauty,
but for thousands of years grown as crops for the relief

Sesame has been used in cooking, medicine, arts, and trade for more thousands of years than books and manuscripts record. The Chinese, it is known, have used it since 5000 B.C. The illustration here was published in 1565 in Matthioli, *Commentarii Dioscoridis,* and accompanies a description of the plant and list of its uses. In 1935 the United States imported 146,394,158 pounds of sesame seeds . . . more than all other drugs, herbs, leaves, and roots together, and also imported 11,088 pounds of sesame oil.

of the ailments of man, as they still are grown today in some sections of the world.

Then there are the thymes, the mints, the lavenders, artemisias, the basils . . . a multitude of friendly little plants grown the world over for fragrance and for culinary purposes. These too are herbs and the basis of enormous industries dealing with soaps, perfumes, gargles, lotions, extracts, chewing gums, and a multitude of liquors and liqueurs and other products which require flavoring.

There are the herbs of the field . . . boneset, tansy, dandelion, milkweed . . . and the savory seeds such as anise, cumin, coriander, mustard, sesame, caraway and dill. These are herbs, some medicinal, some culinary, all with innumerable technical and industrial uses as well and some forming the basis for a world-wide trade in spices and condiments. Lastly, there are the ancient herbs we now call vegetables . . . carrots, onions, parsnips, spinach, beans and beets, now raised on huge farms for food and industry. Little did the Anglo-Saxons, gathering at times the root of beet to cure the bitings of mad dogs, know that this "wort," as Apuleius calls it, would become the basis for an important branch of the sugar industry. It is hard to realize that as late as Elizabethan times, Gerard was timidly suggesting that the roots of beets, as well as the leaves then used in salads, might possibly prove good wholesome food. It must be remembered that the word vegetable, denoting a food, has been in use less than 200 years.

No chart of small proportions can more than suggest how these various divisions of our modern industries, professions, and sciences arose. They form a sort of family tree with roots in the dim past and the branches beginning when the discovery of printing made the knowledge of the herbalists available to all who could read. It helps to show how the gardener, the farmer, and the botanist are one with the doctor, the druggist, the brewer and the cook. It is symbolic that the story of the Bible begins and ends in a garden. The garden and the herbs grown there loom large in all recorded history.

From the Chinese Herbal of Ching-Nong we learn, among other herbs, of ephedra, which was used in Asia 5,000 years ago and is used again today in this country in sinus troubles; we read of rhubarb, also of sesame seeds, the first oil seeds, which are now used by bakers and candy-makers, and in a multitude of industries aside from food. The black of the finest Chinese drawing ink, for instance, comes from burnt sesame; thus herbs enter into the drafting rooms of every factory as well as into the studios of artists and illustrators and thence to magazines, newspapers, and books.

The very existence of the cosmetic, distilling, brewing, perfumery, and tobacco industries is due to herbs. Also based on herbs are many of our food industries and much of farming and husbandry. Surgery, medicine, botany, household science, part of chemistry, can be credited to the study of herbs for more than 7,000 years. Before the printing process was invented, the findings were laboriously entered on parchment manuscripts, copied one at a time over a period of years, and kept in the possession of a few scholars and in monasteries. Many of these manuscripts still exist. Some were reproduced among the first of printed books. Then, as the process of printing became known, new authors appeared. In Elizabethan years some of them wrote of the garden, taking over the description and culture of plants from the herbalists. At about the same time the casting off of superstition and the rise of medicine as a profession did away with the

popular treatises on the medical uses of herbs. Thus the
content of the herbal was gone and after 1710 there appeared no herbal of importance.

The Virtues.

X. *The Liquid Juice.* *Parkinson* says that it is
effectual to cure the Dropsy, by taking 4 or 5
Ounces of the *Juice* fasting, which will strongly
purge the Body both upwards and downwards.
I have had no experience of it, but 'tis very probable that it may cure the Dropsy, if given by a wise
Hand and in a due Dose. I should be afraid to give
4 or 5 Ounces at a time, by reason of its Violence;
but it is a continued use of it, beginning with a
small quantity, and gradually increasing it, that
must determine how much may be safely given at a
time. *Monardus* says it is an *Alexipharmicon* a-
gainst the Stinging or Biting of any Venomous
Creature, being immediately applyed to the hurt
place.
XI. *The Syrup of the same.* It is found by good
Experience to expectorate tough Flegm out of the
Stomach and Lungs. It kills Worms in the Stomach and Belly, eases the Head-ach and Megrim,
as also the Cholick and Griping pains in the Bow-
els; tho' for some time it may seem to cause more
trouble in them, and disaffect the Stomach. It is
profitable for those who have the Stone or Gravel in

Tobacco, once it was introduced from America into Europe, became a popular subject of discussion, especially in herbals. Many
medicinal uses were suggested, as can be seen by the few lines
reproduced here from Salmon, *English Herbal* (London, 1710).
Under the heading, "A Powder of the Leaves and Stalks," occurs
the only reference known in the early herbals to the use of tobacco
as snuff solely for medicinal purposes. The author says: "Used as
a sternutatory, it opens the Head, and cleanses it of the Recre-
ments of the Brain; Strewed upon old Ulcers, it disposes them to
a speedy healing: It also kills Lice in the Head."

The gardening books continued and eventually the science of botany was born in the search for methods of classification and identification. But with the gardening books to direct the culture of plants and the medical profession to prescribe the application of them, there was need for a source book of materials to use—*materia medica*—and the old herbals were adopted for the beginnings of a pharmacopœia, printed in Latin. Great was the hubbub when Nicholas Culpeper, obtaining a copy, published an English translation with comments of his own. However, the establishment of an approved list of herbs for medicine began the great drug industry. Tobacco, early an ingredient of medicinal snuff, was soon recognized as having a narcotic effect and its use for pleasure, apart from medicine, brought edicts, laws and decrees against its use in smoking; but it persisted as a snuff through the centuries, to emerge in the last generation as a giant industry in the New World.

Coincidentally with the decline of the old herbals, a new type of book came into being and it marked the entrance of woman into the role of author. Strangely enough, it too grew out of ancient manuscript books and unconsciously opened up a whole new field for industry. It was to become as powerful an influence in daily life as the herbal had been before it. This was the "still-room book."

From early times there was no question about woman's place being in the home. The business of men was war. There was no industry and little trade. Everything was made on the premises. The lady of the house not only directed the meals but in the "still-room," a place set apart, she distilled oils of the herbs, made medicines, liqueurs, jellies, jams, household preparations, and preserved foods. All this was from formulas and recipes handed down from generation to generation, mother to eldest daughter, in a "still-room book," many preserved unto this day, with changing handwriting, changing methods, notes along the margins, certain favored rules

Pomet's *Compleat History of Druggs,* of which several editions were printed in London in the early eighteenth century, speaks of tobacco as "Holy Herb," because of its great virtues. Many remedies made of tobacco are suggested, and snuff is mentioned, but only indirectly, because ". . . there are so many Sorts." The use of tobacco for smoking is only inferred in Pomet's discussion, though Parkinson in his *Theatrum Botanicum,* a century earlier, speaks of Sir Walter Raleigh and the kind of tobacco he chose while he was a prisoner in the Tower. The illustration above is from Pomet's book, which was originally written in French.

marked with an X, denoting good. Such are books of Lady Sedley, Mary Doggett, Susanna Avery, Mary Cholmeley, and many others not known to fame. Here are the beginnings of many of our modern industries, the formulas for all manner of cosmetics, soaps, perfumes, tinctures, gargles, lotions, powders. Here are the ways to preserve, to can, to drive away flies and moths, to bathe tired eyes, aching feet, a gaping wound, a complete compendium for daily living.

These were the manuscripts from which came the printed "household receipt" books which only a generation or two ago were common in every home and from which all cook books stem. From them, too, come our beauty preparations which today we buy in the drugstore, still made with herbs by the old formulas familiar to Elizabethan ladies. Furniture oil still has the scent of lemon balm, as their books advise; thymol is still the oil in bronchitis remedies; the root of alkanet still gives us its red coloring matter with which court ladies dyed their lips and gave to the plant its symbolism of deceit. It is widely used to stain rosewood and mahogany and to color spurious port wine.

Our dentifrices today, as then, are flavored with anise, peppermint, sage, caraway and thyme, as are our chewing gums. Our soaps are scented with rosemary, lavender, dill and fennel. In any drugstore in the land, you can buy "Hungary water," a lotion scented with rosemary, first made in the fourteenth century by the Countess of Hainault and the recipe sent to her daughter, the wife of Edward III. Thus, for more than 600 years this simple toilet water has appealed to women.

Of great age also, and full of herbs, are many of our liqueurs, particularly those which took their names from the monasteries where they originated. Chartreuse, for example, contains tansy and angelica; benedictine is amazingly herby with tips of hyssop, cardamom seeds, angelica, peppermint, thyme and arnica flowers. Anise is the basis of anisette, wormwood of absinthe, caraway of kümmel, peppermint of many liquors. Angelica stalks are used as an adulterant of juniper berries in real gin and the seeds are used in muscatel and in vermouth. Clary sage, the oil of which is the best fixative for blending fine perfumes, is infused with elder flowers and added to Rhenish wines to convert them into muscatel wines.

Innumerable are the perfumes in which herbs give the fragrance . . . basil in "mignonette" and in "jonquil"; celery seed in the perfume called "sweet pea"; coriander in "lily" perfume and, with cumin, furnishing the flavoring for the American "hot dog" as well!

Lastly, the true art of cookery, so little practiced nowadays, depends upon the use of ancient herbs, for with modern refrigeration we no longer need the Oriental spices to mummify our food or hide the flavor of decay. The country people still know the savour of home grown sage and marjoram, of fennel, mint and parsley, of savory and thyme. Salad lovers call more lustily than ever for chervil and for tarragon . . . French tarragon, that amazing plant that has spread throughout the world by root division, no seeds being available, although the Russian tarragon, which grows from seed, is often foisted on an unsuspecting purchaser. The pickle maker knows the value of the ancient dill and mustard for his products. They are as universally used throughout the industry as sage in sausage, tarragon and burnet in vinegar, cumin and coriander in frankfurters, caraway and poppy seeds in breads and rolls.

Beverages, liqueurs, breads and snuffs; tobaccos, fixatives and dyes; polishes, tinctures, extracts and lotions; insecticides, medicines, sugar and drawing ink . . . there is no end to the importance of ancient herbs in modern industry and home.

CHAPTER XVI

Garden Designs

"The severall situations of mens dwellings, are for the most part unavoideable and unremoveable; for most men cannot appoint forth such a manner of situation for their dwelling, as is most fit to avoide all the inconveniences of winde and weather, but must bee content with such as the place will afford them; yet all men doe well know, that some situations are more excellent than others: according therfore to the severall situation of mens dwellings, so are the situations of their gardens also for the most part.

"And although divers doe diversly preferre their owne severall places which they have chosen, or wherein they dwell; As some those places that are neare unto a river or brooke to be best for the pleasantnesse of the water, the ease of transportation of themselves, their friends and goods, as also for the fertility of the soyle, which is seldome bad neare unto a rivers side; And others extoll the side or top of an hill, bee it small or great, for the prospects sake; And againe, some the plaine or champian ground, for the even levell thereof: every one of which, as they have their commodities accompanying them, so

307

The round form, "the outermost Walk being adorned with Cypress Trees, the inner parts of the Grass Plats with Firr Trees, and the Quadrants within the lesser Circle, planted with variety of Fruit Trees, and the principal Walks round and streight, bordered with Flowers, and delightful Shrubs and Plants." From Worlidge, 1677.

have they also their discommodities belonging unto them, according to the Latine Proverbe, *Omne commodum fert suum incommodum.*"

These are the opening words, printed more than three hundred years ago, of what is generally considered the grandest of all the gardening books in the English language, the massive *Paradisi in Sole Paradisus Terrestris* by John Parkinson, Apothecary of London, 1629. They meet our situation today so aptly that I am moved to yield still more space to what he says, and give you now the whole of Chapter II that you may read the words that the great of London were reading in the years the Plymouth colony was being established, the charter of the "Company of Massachusetts Bay" issued, Boston founded.

The frame or forme of a Garden of delight and pleasure, with the severall varieties thereof.

"Although many men must be content with any plat of ground, of what forme or quantity soever it bee, more or lesse, for their Garden, because a more large or convenient cannot bee had to their habitation: Yet I perswade my selfe, that Gentlemen of the better sort and quality, will provide such a parcell of ground to bee laid out for their garden, and in such convenient manner, as may be fit and answerable to the degree they hold.

"To prescribe one forme for every man to follow, were too great presumption and folly: for every man will please his owne fancie, according to the extent he designeth out for that purpose, be it orbicular or round, triangular or three square, quadrangular or foure square, or more long than broad. I will onely shew you here the severall formes that many men have taken and delighted in, let every man chuse which him liketh best, or may most fitly agree to that proportion of ground hee hath set out for that purpose.

"The orbicular or round forme is held in its owne

The square form "each principal Corner with Flower pots, and
the middle of the greater Square with Statues. . . . Fountains
would be placed with more delight." From Worlidge, 1677.

proper existence to be the most absolute forme, containing within it all other formes whatsoever; but few I thinke will chuse such a proportion to be joyned to their habitation, being not accepted any where I think, but for the generall Garden to the University at Padoa. The triangular or three square is such a forme also, as is seldome chosen by any that may make another choise, and as I thinke is onely had where another forme cannot be had, necessitie constraining them to be therewith content. The foure square forme is the most usually accepted with all, and doth best agree to any mans dwelling, being (as I said before) behinde the house, all the backe windowes thereof opening into it. Yet if it bee longer than the breadth, or broader than the length, the proportion of walkes, squares, and knots may be soon brought to the square forme, and be so cast, as the beauty thereof may bee no lesse than the foure square proportion, or any other better forme, if any be.

"To forme it therfore with walkes, crosse the middle both waies, and round about it also with hedges, with squares, knots and trayles, or any other worke within the foure square parts, is according as every mans conceit alloweth of it, and they will be at the charge: For there may be therein walkes eyther open or close, eyther publike or private, a maze or wildernesse, a rocke or mount, with a fountaine in the midst thereof to convey water to every part of the Garden, eyther in pipes under the ground, or brought by hand, and emptied into large Cisternes or great Turkie Jarres, placed in convenient places, to serve as an ease to water the nearest parts thereunto. Arbours also being both gracefull and necessary, may be appointed in such convenient places, as the corners, or else where, as may be most fit, to serve both for shadow and rest after walking.

"And because many are desirous to see the formes of trayles, knots, and other compartiments, and because the open knots are more proper for these Out-landish flowers; I have here caused some to be drawne, to satisfie their desires, not intending to cumber this worke with over manie, in that it would be almost endlesse, to ex-

A multitude of simple garden forms "amongst which it is possible you may find some that may near the matter fit most ordinary grounds." From Meager, *English Gardener*, 1688.

presse so many as might bee conceived and set downe, for that every man may invent others farre differing from these, or any other can be set forth. Let every man therefore, if hee like of these, take what may please his mind, or out of these or his owne conceit, frame any other to his fancy, or cause others to be done as he liketh best, observing this decorum, that according to his ground he do cast out his knots, with convenient roome for allies and walkes; for the fairer and larger your allies and walkes be, the more grace your Garden shall have, the lesse harme the herbes and flowers shall receive, by passing by them that grow next unto the allies sides, and the better shall your Weeders cleanse both the beds and the allies."

Such is the "ordering" of the Garden of Pleasure. I have given you so many of the knots and "trayles," hedges, walls, mazes, mounts, and borders in *Magic Gardens* and, like Parkinson, do not intend "to cumber this worke" with any more, but of the garden designs most useful for authentic forms, I include plates from Worlidge's *Systema Horti-culturae: or, the Art of Gardening*, 1677, published 50 years after Parkinson, from Leonard Meager's *The English Gardner: Or, a sure Guide to Young Planters & Gardeners*, 1688, together with some of the old nineteenth century garden forms at Salt Acres and a triangular form we have worked out in recent years because on this plot, as Parkinson says, we "may not make another choise . . . necessities constraining [us] to be therewith content."

Worlidge sets forth that of the forms "The Round is very pleasant, and some curious Gardens there are of that Form in foreign parts. . . . The Walk that circundates that Garden is not unpleasant" because you can keep going as long as you please "always forward without any short turning" which might be of advantage, no doubt,

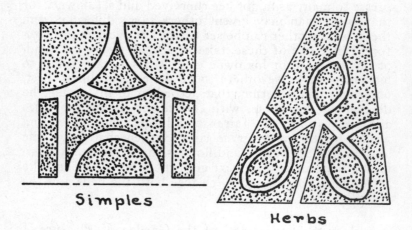

Simples

Herbs

Spring Flowers

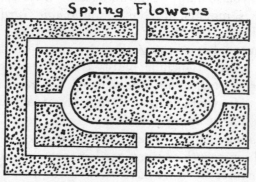

The gardens at Salt Acres, including the triangular herb garden with clover leaf design, the top petal garden for gray artemisias, the right hand petal for the creeping thymes, the left for low perennial herbs, a hedge of rue; borders of the walk of chives, hyssop, dwarf winter savory and thyme. Length, 75 feet. The rectangle is the nineteenth century "front garden" of spring flowers; the square is one half the "back" garden, symmetrical on both sides of the walk.

if one were absent-minded or preoccupied. But he agrees, as does every other gardener of Elizabethan times and long thereafter, that the "Square is the most perfect and pleasant form that you can lay your Garden into." But, he points out, you can divide it into lesser squares without being subject to reproach.

Meager washes his hands of the whole responsibility, other than to tell you to do your carting before you fence it in and then "cast it into what form you think fit, or as the bigness of your ground will handsomely bear," and he continues:

"I have for the ease and delight of those that do affect such things, presented to view divers forms or plots for Gardens, amongst which it is possible you may find some that may near the matter fit most ordinary grounds, either great or small; and shall leave the ingenious Practitioner to the consideration and use of that he most affects."

After all, what more can be said?

INDEX TO BOOKS AND AUTHORS

INDEX TO SUBJECT MATTER